THE ANCIENT WISDOM OF TAO

INCLUDING
THE TAO TE CHING BY LAO TZU,
THE BOOK OF CHUANG TZU,
THE BOOK OF LIEH-TZU,
AND MODERN TAOISM

JEFFREY PINE

ISBN: 979-8-9882629-1-6(hardcover)
ISBN: 979-8-9882629-0-9 (paperback)
ISBN: 979-8-9882629-2-3(ebook)
LCCN: 2023916106

All illustrations in this book other than the photo of galaxies are
adaptations by Yiduo Zhu of ancient Chinese artwork.

Explanation of artwork on cover:
The image of the three Vinegar Tasters is taken from a 16th century
Japanese painting. It represents the relationship of the three teachings of
Confucianism, Buddhism, and Taoism which together dominated Chinese
religion and philosophy for most of the past 2,000 years. The figure on
the left is meant to be Confucius, who tasted the vinegar (representing
life, itself) and experienced it as sour, needing to be closely regulated
to prevent it from degenerating, the figure in the middle represents
Buddha, who experienced the vinegar as bitter and dominated by pain
and suffering, and the figure on the right as Lao Tzu who smiled and
experienced the vinegar as being just right—the exact way that vinegar
(life) is meant to be.

This book is dedicated to all who come hereafter, with hope that their world will be a free, happy, fulfilling, moral, and prosperous one.

Contents

Section III
Modern Taoism
317

Preface

Like most Americans, I suppose, I had heard about Taoism now and again since I was a small child and as a result figured out long ago that many commonly heard truisms came from the ancient Chinese philosophy. That was about it. I didn't know anything more substantial about it than that until I was a young adult and became interested in the martial arts. Jim, one of my Tae Kwon Do instructors, was also a student of Tai Chi and various other forms of ancient Chinese wisdom, and his occasional references to Tao and Taoism eventually piqued my interest. I bought an English language translation of the *Tao Te Ching* and found myself struggling to understand whatever in the world it was trying to tell me. Only by means of frequent detours to the explanation pages did I eventually get through it with some confidence that I had understood the lessons it was trying to teach. Later I bought a different translation of the same book with a different style of explanation page, and with that I had a little better luck in comprehending its lessons. Later still, I heard about Chuang Tzu and bought and read a translation of his book. For some reason, I took a liking to Taoism and found that I enjoyed trying to understand and appreciate the simple wisdoms the philosophy expressed. The books were like puzzles to me, I guess. A year or two after that, I heard about and also read the Lieh-Tzu book.

Over the course of the next few years, I consumed multiple versions of each of the three Taoist classics, read several works written by modern Taoist authors, read *The Way of the Peaceful Warrior* by Dan Millman, slogged through a tome about Chinese history, read a couple of scholarly texts about Chinese philosophy in general, and finally found and studied a book called *The Tao of Physics* by Fritjof Capra—a book that changed my perspective on Taoism completely.

Until I read *The Tao of Physics*, Taoism represented to me an interesting and unique ancient philosophy that taught me a few valuable lessons throughout its pages about life and allowed me to see the world a little differently—but all of it always from the perspective of it being a very old Chinese philosophy! As I read *The Tao of Physics*, I came to realize that Taoism wasn't just a moth-eaten old philosophy at all. Its basis in physical reality, as was known at that time and as was depicted in several places in the three texts, although primitive and incomplete, was not significantly inaccurate at all, and that somehow made the philosophy just as relevant to me today as it was twenty-two or more centuries ago. Even more so, in fact, because modern understandings of physics not only did not dispute it but actually supported it.

Taoism, I realized, isn't just an ancient philosophy; it is a timeless understanding of the world around us and of humankind's relationship to it. The more we come to know about our world, the more accurate and better Taoism becomes. Learning its lessons and living one's life according to them allows followers to fit into the flow of their lives more comfortably, and because of that, each tends to be happier and more successful. And that is just as true today as it was back when Taoism was the common way to understand life for everyone in that part of the world. The gradual lessening of its importance in China since that time was probably not because it, by itself, came to seem antiquated and irrelevant but because it was first corrupted by Confucianism and later by Buddhism, and also because over the course of more than two thousand years, the classic texts became harder and harder to understand because they were repeatedly copied and recopied with little alteration in a world where everything else, including the language they were written in, was constantly changing.

And after even more thought, I realized that Taoism isn't just still relevant—its comprehension and spread might even be pivotal for helping create a happier future for everyone living in our own society, today. Our people are currently suffering from a lack of moral guidance. Faith in the ancient religions is waning. Families are breaking apart. Drug use is rampant. Our young, in many cases, are suffering from depression and lack of motivation. Many seem to be emotionally and morally lost, floundering in an ever more dangerous world. The crime rate is skyrocketing. Suicides are becoming almost commonplace among the youth. Perhaps a popularization of Taoism would help our populace fill its spiritual void. While not a religion, it certainly does provide moral guidance and an accurate understanding for the follower of his or her place in life, along with lessons on how best to live it.

After realizing that Taoism was not only still relevant but might even have real value for readers in modern America, I decided that my own purpose for this last part of my life should be to try to organize and present the philosophy in a form that the modern person can read, understand, enjoy, and benefit from a little more easily. It took a few false starts, but what you find in this book is my attempt to do that.

Most presentations of Taoism in this country today (other than brief truisms such as "Even the longest journey begins with the very first step") are translations of the work of one single ancient Taoist philosopher—usually Lao Tzu and his *Tao Te Ching*. What I decided we needed was a compilation of the works of all three written in an accurate but easy-to-understand fashion, along with a discussion of the origins and history behind the philosophy, information about the preservation of the books through the centuries, and then also, of course, my thoughts as to how Taoism might be applied to life in modern times.

In order to solidify my own understanding of the various aspects of Taoism, and also so that I might be able to present them to the reader in an organized and logical fashion, I took each passage from each author and classified them all in terms of the messages they told and the lessons they taught and organized them from that into a logical order. The results of that procedure are presented in the last section of this book, "Modern Taoism."

I've noticed in my many years of life that a small but well-timed and well-placed idea or action can sometimes move cultural mountains. Read and consider the value of the lessons of the ancient sages as presented herein. If they make sense to you, try to learn to follow them. I think doing so will help you in your life just as it has helped me in mine. And perhaps if enough of us do that, we can help America find and follow the Way of Tao.

SECTION I

The History

TIMELINE OF TAOISM

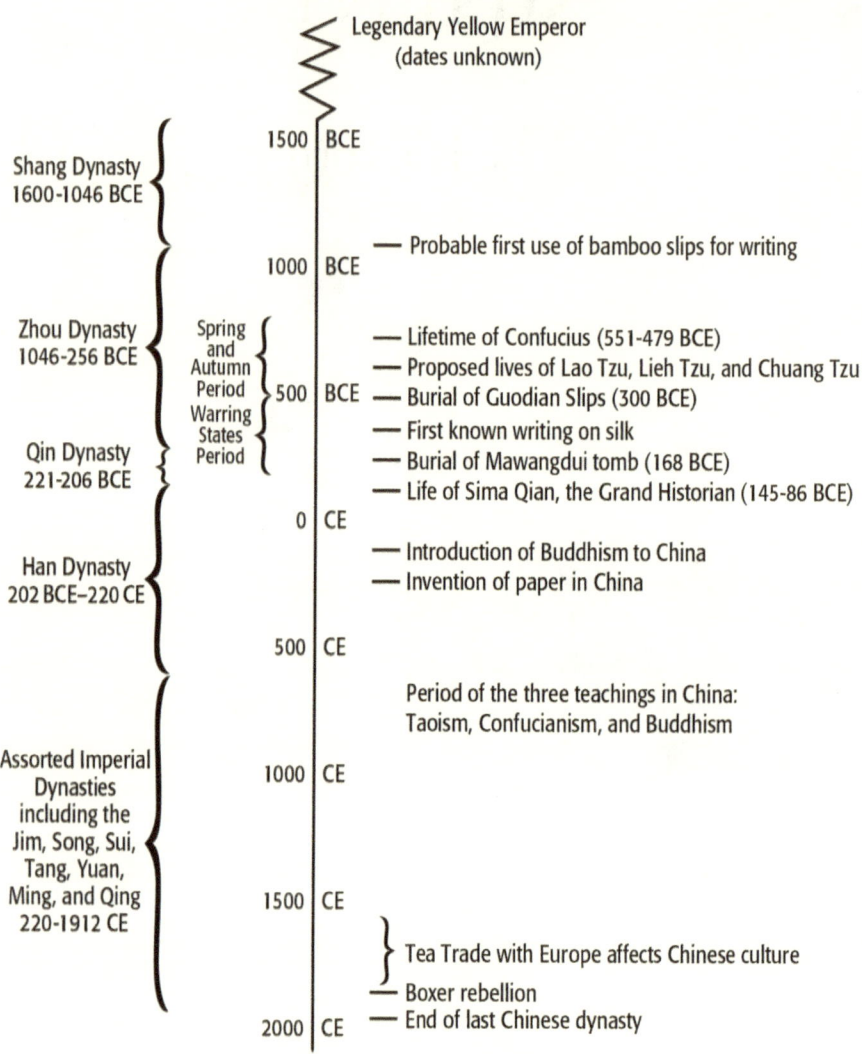

Legendary Yellow Emperor
(dates unknown)

1500 BCE

Shang Dynasty
1600-1046 BCE

— Probable first use of bamboo slips for writing

1000 BCE

Zhou Dynasty
1046-256 BCE

Spring and Autumn Period

Warring States Period

— Lifetime of Confucius (551-479 BCE)
— Proposed lives of Lao Tzu, Lieh Tzu, and Chuang Tzu
500 BCE — Burial of Guodian Slips (300 BCE)
— First known writing on silk
— Burial of Mawangdui tomb (168 BCE)
— Life of Sima Qian, the Grand Historian (145-86 BCE)

Qin Dynasty
221-206 BCE

0 CE

— Introduction of Buddhism to China
Han Dynasty
202 BCE–220 CE
— Invention of paper in China

500 CE

Period of the three teachings in China:
Taoism, Confucianism, and Buddhism

Assorted Imperial
Dynasties
including the
Jim, Song, Sui,
Tang, Yuan,
Ming, and Qing
220-1912 CE

1000 CE

1500 CE

Tea Trade with Europe affects Chinese culture
— Boxer rebellion
2000 CE — End of last Chinese dynasty

1

About Taoism

Historical Background

The historical background of the time in China that birthed the Lao Tzu, Chuang Tzu, and Lieh-Tzu classics is a tale of long dynasties initiated by good kings, a gradual descent through the following centuries for each dynasty into incompetence and immorality by that king's descendants, revolution, and then new dynasties founded by new good kings. It begins back in the mists of prehistory in the central plains of the Yellow River Valley of northern China with the mythical god-like Yellow Emperor and continues down through the ages to the last few weak and dysfunctional kings of the Zhou dynasty.

The Yellow Emperor was reputed in ancient Chinese legend to have been the original unifier of humankind in the world they knew—the bringer of civilization, of laws, of knowledge, and even of the first conceptions of Tao. According to legend, blending gradually through time into written history, several mythical kings immediately followed him, and then three long dynasties prior to the compiling and writing of our three Taoist classics—first the Xia Dynasty, then the Shang Dynasty, and finally the Zhou Dynasty. In each case, the initiator and first king was a virtuous and powerful man—a unifier! He was a man who had earned and been granted the "Mandate of Heaven" for himself and his descendants to rule the land. In each case, after that first "good king," the dynasty he initiated consisted of a succession of his descendants ruling the kingdom through the following centuries—some good, effective, and virtuous men themselves and some not—but in general becoming ever more dysfunctional as the generations passed. And in each case, ultimately, the dynasty lost the Mandate of Heaven to rule because a final descendent had become so unvirtuous and incompetent that the gods allowed him to be overthrown or his armies to be defeated in some final battle. Then there was a period of chaos and violence until a new, more virtuous leader gained control, won a new Mandate of Heaven, and started a brand-new dynasty.

The classical period of Taoist philosophy of interest to us here took place at the trailing end of the Zhou Dynasty. Various client states and provinces had broken off from the empire to become increasingly independent; manage their own affairs in their own ways; vie with each other over power, resources, and land; and pay only token heed to the dictates of those last few Zhou kings. It must have seemed clear to everyone that after eight hundred years of the relative peace and prosperity of the Zhou Dynasty, it had finally lost its Mandate of Heaven to rule—but nobody knew what would happen next or who would ultimately win that last final battle and therefore earn the new mandate to rule them. It was a chaotic and probably rather frightening time in history for the heartland of China.

Religion in Ancient China

Looking back again to the very distant past, before cities, before writing, before science, and even before agriculture, when the early people of China wandered across the land each day searching for their next meal, they tried to identify and understand the various features of nature they encountered that were unusually frightening, confusing, challenging, or beneficial to them in one way or another. Each of those unusual aspects of nature tended to then be personified, labeled, and associated with a unique personality that somehow characterized it. Those things gradually became what we now think of as local or minor gods to them, and the Chinese people in the Yellow River Valley in ancient times came to believe in many of them.

There were separate gods for particular mountains, rivers, and oceans. There was a dragon god that represented safety, success, righteousness, and heroism. There was a goddess of motherhood and a god of fatherhood. There was a monkey god that loved to stir up trouble and cause mischief, a god of thunder and a goddess of lightening, and many others. And presiding over them all for many centuries was Shangdi, the king of the gods, who was always much too busy keeping the lesser gods under control and occasionally considering the affairs of human royalty to ever involve himself directly with the concerns of lesser Chinese mortals.

Having so many gods in control of so many aspects of their lives created difficulties for the ancient Chinese. The gods were moody and capricious. They were also distant and, by nature, had little concern about the problems they so often unconcernedly inflicted on mere mortals. The gods needed nothing from humankind, really, but people and especially kings and other powerful people needed two things in particular from the gods—to know the likely outcomes of various decision-choices they were considering and to be able to create ways to improve likely outcomes for choices they desperately wanted to make but thought would likely result in undesirable consequences. They believed that the gods controlled future developments, and people, especially kings, needed to know how those future developments were likely to unfold, and they also wanted to be able to gain some leverage over the process for themselves and for the good of their realms. Luckily, as we will see, they thought they had found a way to arrange all that.

When people died, if they had lived a good life, if they had been buried with all the proper rituals and respect, and if they continued to be honored and their burial sites continued to be properly cared for by their descendants, it was believed that their spirits would be allowed to live an afterlife and interact with the gods almost as if they were gods themselves. And ancestors, unlike gods, did have a natural interest in the affairs of their living descendants.

Help from one's ancestors was far from automatic, though. The first problem involved establishing a means of communication with them. You certainly couldn't just sit down with a dead ancestor and have a conversation wherein you asked for help and he promised to talk with his god-friends to see what he could do to assist you. So, the ancient Chinese turned to divination, first with scapula bones and later with the lower part of turtle shells. They determined that if you wrote a question on one of those objects (using the very early Chinese script of the time) and asked about the future results of possible current actions, and then if you heated the object up in just the right way under exactly the right conditions, your ancestor would be able to understand your question, consult with the gods, and respond by causing cracking on its surface from the heat that could be read and interpreted by those practiced in that art, and from that process you could determine the correct answer to the question.

It was a complicated, time-consuming, and expensive way to communicate, especially when using the turtle shells since they had to be imported from a distant region, but the ancient Chinese were convinced that they could tell what the future would bring, what decisions would be likely to produce what results, and that they could sometimes alter and improve otherwise undesirable future outcomes with the help of the gods by that means.

The other problem with having your ancestors intermediate on your behalf with the gods was that, just like parents with children, ancestors might not approve of the choices you had been making in your life, on any particular day they might just be feeling difficult and cranky, they might not like your attitude, or perhaps they might not even like the way you framed your request for help. If you wanted the help of your ancestors when dealing with gods, you needed to have a good relationship with them, and that was not always easy to achieve.

Therefore, with almost unlimited means at their disposal, with an especially strong need for information and help from the gods, and of course, with their need to stay in good favor with their ancestors and the gods in order to maintain their "heavenly mandate," kings had the entire interaction between man, ancestor, and gods developed into a distinct field of study, and data regarding every aspect of each divination procedure was recorded, stored, and then studied for years afterward by the kings and their administrators of first the Shang Dynasty and then the Zhou Dynasty—for a period altogether of as long as perhaps a thousand years. How should the question on the scapula or turtle shell be worded? How should the baking of the object be performed? How should the cracking be interpreted? What rituals and sacrifices should be performed to most please the ancestors and gods? Are certain times for the procedure better than others? And of particular interest to us here, what personal behaviors and attitudes by the supplicant were most likely to encourage the best results from the ancestors and the gods? Each aspect of each divination procedure was analyzed and, based on the result, improved over time.

But nothing ever remains the same for long, and some aspects of the ancient religion of that region of China began to change during the Zhou Dynasty in the centuries leading up to the classical period of Taoism. Most significant for our interest, the concept of Shangdi, the king of gods, slowly changed from being a personified deity with a distant personality and inscrutable moods into becoming a more natural and systematic entity that was perhaps a little more predictable. It's helpful to point out that in Chinese tradition, unlike our own, the universe was not seen as being a creation of gods. It was seen as being present first, and gods, like people, were believed to have come after its creation. The gods were seen as only being capable of rearranging certain things to be the way they wanted them to be and then of helping direct the action of the universe a little way into the future. Evidence shows that during that period, the personified character of Shangdi gradually changed into being a more systematic natural character representative of the background composition of the universe seen to have existed before his fellow gods. Most likely, much of the reason for that change in perception of Shangdi's characteristics was due to the fact that he was associated with the Shang Dynasty, and when that was succeeded by the Zhou Dynasty, the anthropomorphic personality of Shangdi began to lose its significance. And as a result of the change, the concept of Shangdi slowly evolved and became the more realistic physical basis of the universe behind the philosophy of Taoism.

Although in practice it has other meanings to the Chinese, the word "Tao" translates into English to mean "the Way" and in the context of Taoist philosophy "the Way" refers to the way to do things most effectively and productively by doing them in accordance with the natural realities and rhythms of the universe. In reference to the divination studies of the Shang and Zhou dynasties, it means that when one did follow "the Way," one's ancestors and their god-friends would be most likely to listen and to be helpful. But unlike Judeo-Christian religions, the Chinese gods, even while demanding virtuous behavior, never pointed out specifically what they expected virtuous behavior to mean— what particular behaviors were expected from those who were asking for their information and assistance and what behaviors were not! The Chinese of that era had to figure those things out for themselves. They had to determine by themselves what "the Way" should actually be.

That desire to keep their ancestors and gods happy and helpful can now be seen as the impetus behind the entire philosophy of Taoism. Because of it, ancient Chinese scholars for centuries strove to understand and fulfill the expectations of the gods and ancestors with regard to virtue and proper behavior in their communications with them, and they dedicated themselves to trying to understand the unseeable and barely knowable foundational structure of the universe behind and beyond which they and the gods lived, including the physical manifestations and processes of Earth, life, and the interrelationships of all things in nature. Those activities through the ages came together to become the basis of the philosophy we know as Taoism, and therefore of the Lao Tzu, Chuang Tzu, and Lieh-Tzu classics through which we are now able to know it.

The Classical Period of Taoist Philosophy

As mentioned above, the classical period of Taoist philosophy took place during the last few waning centuries of the Zhou Dynasty as it gradually lost its control over the various semi-independent regions of the lower Yellow River Valley. The period is divided by historians into two roughly equal parts called the Spring and Autumn Period and the Warring States Period, and the two together lasted from 771 BCE, when the Zhou Dynasty's original capital city was overrun by barbarians and was therefore moved to a safer but more remote location, until 256 BCE when a king of Ch'in finally defeated all his remaining rivals and started a new, but short-lived, dynasty called the Ch'in Dynasty.

For our purposes, then, the classical period of Taoist philosophy can be seen as a roughly five-hundred-year gradual descent in that part of China from being a unified land of law and order and stability into a final long period of war-torn division, violent conflict, and continuous military restructuring. As the authority of the last few kings of the Zhou Dynasty diminished, the various dukes and other feudal lords began to vie ever more fiercely with each other in attempts to dominate their regions and absorb any weaker vulnerable neighbors they might detect around them. What began as squabbles and raids ultimately ended up being characterized by extended warfare with battles sometimes lasting weeks and involving conscripted standing armies numbering into the hundreds of thousands. In some battles toward the end of the period, records claim that one hundred thousand soldiers died in the fighting before one side was able to finally declare victory over the other.

The increasingly deadly military competition between the dozens of fledgling states at the beginning of the period made it ever more important for each to become as strong militarily, economically successful, efficient, and popular within its borders as was possible in order to avoid being conquered by another. Repeatedly fielding large armies required money as well as a sympathetic and willing citizenry—and remember that rulers at the time knew they had to be thought to deserve the Mandate of Heaven if they wanted to be successful for long and to continue to be victorious.

Those factors led to a demand within each still-surviving state for talented and qualified administrators. Each one needed good generals and military strategists; people who knew about trade, taxes, and business; educators; and philosophers. Having all the right people around a ruler advising him helped him also to advertise to his own people as well as to the citizens of other nearby states that he and his country were powerful and virtuous, and that they did certainly deserve the Mandate of Heaven to win more territory and perhaps eventually to start a new dynasty built around them to replace the current dying one that was still supposedly in charge.

At the same time those changes were taking place within and between states, demographic changes were taking place in the population of the region in general. In the beginning of the period, before military casualties began to take their toll, the population had begun to burgeon, and it was a population with a common heritage, culture, and language because of the ancient dynasties they had all so long been a part of. Despite the frequent hostilities between states, there was a sense of common identity among the people in the valley. They all considered themselves to be the "civilized people," whereas any from beyond its vast watershed were considered to be barbarians. For the most part there was also a free flow of trade, ideas, and individuals even across the borders of hostile states. An active, healthy market economy was a normal part of everyone's daily life.

Another relevant dynamic was taking place as well. Between the realities of a continuing breakup of the Zhou Dynasty, a growing population, and a strong demand within states for talented people, the importance of noble birth was rapidly diminishing at the same time the importance of education and personal talent was increasing. More and more people were becoming educated, coveting and accumulating professional expertise, and looking for gainful employment wherever they might be able to find it. Their worth no longer depended so much on who their parents were or on their relationship to the Zhou royalty but increasingly was based instead on their education, talents, and credentials.

As a result of all those factors, the central plains on the lower reaches of the Yellow River Valley at that time became a place of talented and educated military experts, merchants, craftsmen, teachers, and philosophers. Even amid increasingly violent battles and within war-torn societies, artistic creation, new medical developments, prosperous trade, invention, and political and philosophical speculation became part of the cultural norm!

The Philosophies of the Classical Period

As we've seen, the last few centuries of the waning Zhou Dynasty, known today as the Warring States Period, was a time of seemingly endless wars, constant change, and new intellectual developments. A whole new class of "intelligentsia" consisting of hundreds of educated, mostly upper-class men wandered from place to place seeking employment as "experts" in various fields of interest to the rulers and noblemen of the remaining states of the time, presenting their credentials and their ideas and hoping to impress those rich and powerful men with their wisdom, so that they might find a patron to hire and support them.

Some advocated a return to the proven virtues of the distant past, some were specialists in military matters, and some offered radical new theories related to government structure and finance. In each case, the ideas offered were presented as being the most natural and therefore the best way (the Tao) of doing what needed to be done to help the country survive, win victories, and help its ruler to deserve the Mandate of Heaven.

Out of the hundreds, and perhaps thousands, of such hopeful prospective government advisors, there is now knowledge of only a few, and of those few, there are even fewer whose teachings and beliefs we can still know today in any great detail. That is primarily because while writing had been developed centuries earlier for divination purposes, for recordkeeping, and to keep track of important events, those uses were mostly performed by and for governments and perhaps big mercantile companies. The processes and tools for writing were evolving rapidly but were still quite primitive, and writing for such things as storytelling, complex concepts like philosophy, and for personal reasons was still unusual. But historical facts that are only passed down orally from generation to generation through centuries become legends and fables. Details are lost or are embellished by the imaginations of the storytellers, and so we only really know things with any certainty about those philosophers whose beliefs were, for one reason or another, recorded and preserved.

Confucius (his actual name at the time was more like Kongzi) believed that the height of civilization and virtue had taken place in his ancient past and more specifically in the earliest days of the Zhou Dynasty. The rulers of his own time, including the last figurehead Zhou kings and most of the heads of the various smaller, almost independent states in his opinion were decadent, predatory, and self-indulgent, and in his mind that was the reason why his world was in the sad state of turmoil he saw around him. To Confucius it was clear that if all rulers were to learn and then follow the values and virtuous behaviors of the ancient kings, all the world would most likely revert back to the peaceful and prosperous conditions he believed it had seen in that more desirable past.

Confucius believed that it was possible for rulers and gentlemen (and for any person, for that matter) to study, learn, and emulate the morality and virtuous behavior of the ancients and that if they did, they would automatically attain the state of grace of the sage, and then all around them would follow their virtue and the entire world would become a more peaceful and happier place. Confucius once said that "the virtue of a gentleman is like the wind, and the virtue of a common person is like the grass. When the wind moves over the grass, the grass is sure to bend in the direction the wind is blowing!"

Confucius eventually became probably the best known of all the philosophers of that era in China but only after his death, because interestingly, he and his beliefs were not particularly successful during his lifetime. For thirteen years he apparently wandered through the various kingdoms of the time looking for a nobleman somewhere who would employ him but eventually ended up in the kingdom of his childhood working as a low-level clerk. But Confucius continued developing and presumably writing down his ideas and eventually established a small but dedicated cadre of followers, and not long after he died, his book *The Analects* became a common addition to most royal libraries of the time in that region.

One reason Confucius and his ideas are still so well-known today is because some who came after him studied his book and appreciated his teachings enough that they supplemented and improved on his ideas and then left a written legacy of their own related works. Between the writings of Confucius himself and those of such later advocates, Confucianism, like Taoism, is still a well-known and powerful philosophy today, some twenty-five hundred years after the philosopher's death.

Mohism gained popularity near the beginning of the Warring States Period, not long after Confucius's death, in part because Mozi, its founder, refuted certain aspects of Confucius's philosophy. He especially disapproved of the excessive and expensive funeral-related rituals Confucianism advocated and also of the favoritism Confucius encouraged followers to advance to their own families and friends. Mozi believed that all actions should be decided solely from the perspective of what is and what is not in the best interests of society and the world in general and that all people should be seen and treated in the same light regardless of one's relationship to them. In the eyes of Mohists, it was favoritism that caused most of the evils in the world. They believed that if everyone were to just treat all others as they would like to be treated themselves, there would be no crime or injustice anywhere, and that if everyone were to think of all other nations with the same regard as they thought of their own, there would be no wars.

Mohists are especially remembered for their early use of logical debate and thought experiments in the development of their tenets. One of the conclusions they reached by those means was that humankind inherently had no fixed nature and therefore all people were reliant upon government and its laws in order to coexist peacefully and for society to advance. People, they determined, were malleable to the rewards and punishments of government, and it was therefore essential for government to act according to what was beneficial to its citizenry and to the world in general. And in order for it all to work properly, it was important that all citizens be treated equally and that all benefits of society be awarded strictly on the basis of merit.

Sun Tzu's specialty was warfare, and he can be thought of as an early Chinese philosopher of military strategy. His thoughts are still known and studied today because of his book, *The Art of War*, which was influenced, like all the philosophies mentioned here, by Taoism. Sun Tzu taught that national unity was essential for victory in warfare and that it could only be attained by a government that was devoted to the welfare of its people. Additionally, he taught that the wisest conquerors won their wars prior to any actual battle by frustrating their enemies' strategies, breaking up their alliances, and spreading dissent and chaos within their governments and among their people. Only if a nation could not defeat its enemies in those ways should it then go on to fight them in actual battle. And, of course, he went on from there to explain how that warfare might best be fought whenever it did turn out to be necessary.

The Chinese philosophy of Legalism originated with a man named Sheng Yang, who was a minister of the state of Ch'in about halfway through the Warring States Period. In order to make his state more efficient and therefore more competitive with its hostile neighbors, he engaged in a radical restructuring of his nation. He divided it into districts for easier management, registered each citizen so he could maintain a record of who he ruled, raised taxes, instituted military conscription, and standardized all weights and measures. An elaborate system of rewards and punishments was instituted to encourage behaviors deemed desirable to the state and to discourage those deemed undesirable.

Sheng Yang described the philosophical underpinnings of Legalism in writings of his own, but few of them have survived and most of what we now know of the philosophy was written later by others. At its foundation, however, was the belief that every individual was primarily motivated by greed and self-interest and needed to be controlled by laws designed to ensure domestic stability and encourage behaviors that would benefit society in general (i.e., the state).

Each of these philosophies that we have just discussed was Taoist in that each was developed to describe to leaders and prospective patrons the preferred "Way" of doing something—the best and most-likely-to-succeed manner for the leader to, for example, administer his government or conduct his war in order to achieve the goals being addressed. That best "Way" was by definition aligned with and therefore in tune with the natural flow of reality. In no case was Tao or Taoism itself explained in any of those philosophies because there was no need for it to be. All people at that time in the central plain of Northern China knew what "Tao" was and lived their lives within their understanding of it, just as all Italians or Frenchmen in the Middle Ages knew what Christianity was and lived their lives within their understanding of that.

In fact, although Taoism was an integral part of everyone's life, it was also said to be impossible to learn with words. In order to try to become truly adept at Taoism (i.e., a sage), one had to study and spend long periods of time under the tutelage of a noted Taoist sage like Chuang Tzu or Lieh-Tzu, and even then the person would not learn it so much from his words as by emulating his behaviors and learning to understand his motivations. But eventually—perhaps because circumstances began to threaten traditional beliefs and it was feared that they might be lost if not written down, or perhaps just because reading and writing became more commonplace and made the event almost predictable—Taoism, itself, did eventually come to be described in writings, at least somewhat, and the three "books" that are the result, and the philosophy of Taoism that they describe, are the topic we discuss as best we can herein.

It's interesting to note that the book of Lao Tzu (the *Tao Te Ching*), the *Book of Chuang Tzu*, and the *Book of Lieh-Tzu* each has a very different story behind its creation, that the authors of each (if there even were specific authors) almost certainly never even met one another, and that each book is quite different in most respects from the others. It's also interesting to note that Taoism itself was not even considered to be a specific philosophical genre until several centuries later when some clerk or librarian somewhere decided to group some old manuscripts together because of their similar topics and to label them as "Taoist." But that turned out to be a fortunate decision for those of us today who try to understand the concepts of the philosophy because the three books together go a long way toward defining and explaining Taoism to one now who studies them and tries to understand their implications, and they do so in a quite complimentary fashion. A little further along, we will learn more about each of the three Taoist classics and about what is known of their authorship and history.

Tao and Taoism to the Ancient Chinese

But what actually was Taoism to the ancient authors of the Tao Te Ching, the Chuang Tzu, and the Lieh-Tzu books when they were written more than two thousand years ago, and how did it affect people's lives? To answer, let's start by noting again that the word "Tao" in Chinese translates to English to mean "the Way." Taoism was an understanding of life and an attitude about how best to live one's life based on "the Way." But "the Way" of what?

The origins of Taoism as mentioned above most likely go all the way back to that early time before agriculture when humankind in China lived in small hunter-gatherer groups interacting with and being a part of nature daily. Those people believed in many anthropomorphic gods of varying importance, and all those gods were able to affect them in negative or in positive ways. And as you will remember, those early people are also known to have believed that the basic order of the universe was even more fundamental than all the various gods. People and gods both had to live in accordance with the basic order of the universe. Those most basic realities of the universe in the background of everything and their effects on people's lives were the basis of "the Way!"

"The Way" teaches one to accept, work with, and enjoy the progression of events that occur in the natural universe behind any and all gods, but it also presupposes that humankind's language, culture, and intellectualism, though a part of human reality, automatically tend to take us away from those more fundamental natural things, and that we benefit by first noticing the ways in which it does so and then by trying to minimize and compensate for them. In that way, according to Taoism, humankind in general and each individual in specific will benefit by being happier, healthier, and more successful in achieving whatever goals they attempt to achieve.

Explaining more specifically what Taoism meant to the ancient Chinese is difficult. The three Taoist classics and a few other lesser-known sources not referenced herein can give the student some insights, but there are no in-depth explanations anywhere that were written at the time, and in many ways the philosophy of Taoism was originally meant to be orally taught and more intuitive than written and specific. The *Tao Te Ching* itself states that "the true Way can never be grasped from words. Even its name is just a sound!"

Therefore, for the most part, I will just let the writings of the sages explain as best they can their concepts of Taoism as you read section II of this book, but I do want to point out four basic tenets of Taoism first so that the reader will know what to look for as he or she reads the stories and passages of Lao Tzu, Chuang Tzu, and Lieh-Tzu that follow:

1. The foremost and most fundamental reality about Taoism is that the philosophy is based on the physical underpinnings of the universe and that to understand it, one must achieve at least a basic conception of what that physical basis of the universe is.

2. Human language and culture by their very nature tend to lead people away from "the Way," but language and culture are nevertheless realities of human life and must be accounted for, and so Taoists, being realists, live and act within and as a part of our culture as best they can while at the same time trying to avoid as many of the pitfalls as possible that doing so presents. The most insidious aspect of human life and culture leading people away from "the Way" that Taoists try to minimize and compensate for is the effects of their egos.

3. Achievement is a fundamental part of all life, even if it only entails what is required for continued survival. Most people, including most Taoists, seek to achieve many things beyond mere survival, but for Taoists, what they choose to achieve and how they choose to achieve it are quite import-

ant. They try to only do things that are in tune with the natural flow of Tao and to do them in ways that are also in tune with it.

4. A basic goal of the Taoist is to become a sage—a person who has learned to live his or her life in perfect harmony with "the Way" of Tao—selflessly and effectively accomplishing good things in a manner that benefits those around him, as well as himself. No person is ever perfect, though, and Taoists are always realists, so no true sage would ever declare himself or herself to be one, even though others might choose to see him or her as such.

This will all be explained in more detail in section III, wherein I will introduce you to my conception of what Taoism should be when modified to reflect the knowledge and understandings of life and the universe as we know them in the twenty-first century!

2

Taoism since the Classic Period

The Warring States Period of Chinese history ended with the fall of the Zhou Dynasty and victory for the kingdom of Ch'in in 221 BCE. And with that transition, came the end of the short era characterized by multitudes of curious, open-minded, and thoughtful Taoist philosophers and the beginning of an even shorter era of intolerance to all such thought. The kingdom of Ch'in had won its victory over its rivals because of its strategic and naturally fortified location, its well irrigated and naturally fertile farmland, its dedication to modern weaponry, its determined militarism, its strict efficiency, and the strict top-down, reward-or-punish hierarchy called for by the philosophy of Legalism, but it was not confident enough in its victory to allow any of the other alternative philosophies to continue to exist at all.

Legalism, you will remember, had been one of several competing theories of government during the Warring States Period. Its tenets were based on the opinion that humankind was inherently self-centered and therefore selfish and prone to immorality. Therefore, it was the job of a king and his government to harness those human tendencies for the good of the state through strict laws, rewards for actions that benefited the state and punishments for all those seen as detrimental to it, and to harshly eliminate any dissent or questioning of their authority. And with the victory of the Ch'in state over its rivals came the victory albeit temporary of Legalism over all the other rival philosophies.

That victory almost became complete starting a year or so after the last battle when the new emperor, Shi Huangdi of Ch'in and his ministers decided that philosophies contrary to Legalism were a waste of time and a danger to his fledgling empire and determined to eliminate them from his land completely. He ordered that all writings, documents, and books (other than those in his own royal libraries) not related to medicine, agriculture, divination, or the official records of Ch'in be destroyed and that anyone not complying be severely punished. Later, to press home the point, hundreds of scholars of alternate philosophies who had for some reason been labeled problematic or subversive were put to death. And to make the near-extinction of Taoism, Confucianism, and other various philosophies of the Warring States Period even more complete, when the Empire of Ch'in later fell to invading armies, the royal palace along with its royal library was apparently burned too, destroying even more of the ancient books.

The Ch'in Dynasty lasted only fifteen years before it was beset by succession chaos and destroyed by the armies of rebels. It was then replaced by the Han Dynasty, which did not apparently persecute those interested in the ancient philosophies, but neither did it encourage them, and by then the damage was already done. Most books were gone, along with the educated elite who could read them and had an interest in doing so, and so for the most part, interest in Taoism, Confucianism, and other philosophies of the Classic Period were left to the unwritten, evolving beliefs and interests of the common masses.

In fact, the ancient written understanding of Tao presented

by Lao Tzu, Chuang Tzu, and perhaps Lieh-Tzu (since there is some question as to when his book was written) might have been lost forever if not for the work of the first true ancient Chinese historians—a father (Sima Tan) and his son (Sima Qian) who lived roughly a century after the Ch'in book burnings and who dedicated their lives to recovering, gathering together, and recording all they could of China's pre-Ch'in past. It is only because of their dedication, labor, and sacrifices that we know most of what we do now know about the Warring States Period, the ancient philosophies, and many other events and cultural products of ancient China.

The gradual acceptance of and appreciation for Sima Qian's book, *The Records of the Grand Historian*, that took place over the next few centuries initiated a revival of interest in the by then already ancient philosophers. A few remaining copies of books that had somehow survived the Ch'in purge were located, copied, widely distributed, and studied. The writings of Lao Tzu and Confucius especially became so popular to the increasingly educated citizenry that they became deeply ingrained into Chinese culture. But while they were just two different perspectives on Taoist philosophy with different foci when originally written, when studied later separately and in isolation, they seemed to many people to be quite contradictory to each other. For some at least, the writings of Lao Tzu and Confucius came to seem almost like opposing scriptures, and Lao Tzu and Confucius themselves almost like opposing prophets. But then Buddhism was later introduced and added to the mix, and a natural balance between the three philosophies seems to have developed.

Buddhism originated from the teachings of a man called Siddhartha Gautama near the end of the fifth century BCE in what is now India. The first written indication that knowledge of it had reached China is from the first century AD, so it was already a rather old and established religion in southern and southeastern

Asia by the time it first began to spread in popularity in China. China in those days was somewhat isolated from the rest of the world by deserts in the north, the wilds of central Asia to the west, the Himalayan mountains to the south, and the Pacific Ocean to the east, but between coastal trading along the eastern seaboard of Asia and constant trade with India and the Mediterranean world by means of the Silk Road that wound its way around the western edge of the Himalayas, there was a constant trickle of communication, and that communication eventually brought Buddhism to China. By the end of the second century AD, worship in China of Buddhism is clearly attested to in major towns and provincial centers, and by the end of the third century, it had cast its long shadow securely across the land.

But Buddhism did not supplant Taoism or Confucianism entirely in the minds of very many Chinese people. In China at that time, it seems, no one doctrine was believed to have a monopoly on the truth, and so each person came to see his world, his faith, and his concepts of proper behavior through a blend of Buddhism, Taoism, and Confucianism in his own way according to the currents of the time and his own personal background. At certain times, in certain places, and with certain people, one of the three took precedence and at other times, in other locations, and with other people, another did. But together, they were usually seen as the three teachings—complimentary and harmonious in various blends as one!

Throughout the centuries, Taoism, though not always in the foreground of Chinese culture, during some periods indeed was. It has always, since the time of Sima Qian, influenced Chinese thought, and at times it has dominated it. In the middle of the fourth century, a so-called Taoist messiah overthrew one dynasty and founded another, and at roughly the same time, in another part of China, an emperor became so enamored of Taoism that his rule came to be considered a Taoist theocracy. In the eighth century, Taoism was acknowledged as the official religion of the Tang Dynasty.

But through the centuries, the popular idea of what Taoism was gradually morphed into something barely recognizable from the philosophy that Lao Tzu, Chuang Tzu, and Lieh-Tzu had written about so long before. Their original words were edited, reinterpreted, and reimagined. New Taoist schools of thought contributed their ideas to the mix. Anything enigmatic and not directly attributable to Buddhism or Confucianism gradually became associated with Taoism, and so shamans, miracle workers, fortune tellers, and magicians labeled themselves as Taoists. The philosophy-turned-religion became associated with psychic phenomena, sexual disciplines, and even immortality.

This phenomenon reached its apex during the Boxer Rebellion in 1900 when influential Chinese elites of the time who had grown tired of foreign intervention in their internal affairs, along with the backing of the government, encouraged a popular peasant Taoist society called the Yihequan, meaning the "righteous and harmonious fists" (hence the nickname Boxers) to take up arms to cast the foreigners out. As many as one hundred thousand people died as a result, many of them Boxers because they believed that the magic of their Taoist rituals would make them immune to the danger of Western bullets and therefore were slaughtered in large number by British guns.

But the problem had already, in reality, started much earlier than that. China, for many centuries arguably the most advanced society on Earth, had faltered. Between being a little too self-confident and secure nestled in the safety of its surrounding mountains, deserts, and ocean and being perhaps a little too self-absorbed trying to perfect its culture and religious ideology, China had failed to keep up with Western nations with regards to science, technology, and world events. The Western countries, driven primarily by almost constant warfare among themselves and a ubiquitous search for fortune and trade, had begun to explore the world and change quickly. Their understanding of science and technology, and especially military technology, had come to far exceed China's.

When the people of England, at that time in the midst of the nation's famous industrial revolution, took a strong liking to tea, available then only from China, and the waning Qing Dynasty of China arrogantly decided to accept only silver bullion in exchange for their tea, it led to a conflict that did not go well at all for China. The battle that resulted, in fact, illustrated all too vividly to the world just how weak China had become and initiated more than one hundred years of assorted wars and scrimmages between China and other nations of which China won almost none!

By the time of the Boxer Rebellion, China had already suffered deep humiliation from a whole series of losses. They had lost two "opium wars" with England and other European countries in the mid-nineteenth century and as a result been forced to lose the islands of Hong Kong. Then China lost a war with Japan and as a result was forced to cede part of its province of Manchuria and its island of Taiwan. Then, after the Boxer Rebellion, Japan invaded China again and annexed the rest of Manchuria, and then, finally, at the onset of WWII, Japan invaded China a final time and conquered the nation entirely, virtually enslaving its people until Japan's final defeat at the hands of the Americans and their allies in 1945. Given that sequence of demoralizing events, it's not surprising that by the end of the Second World War, the Chinese people had in large numbers become more than willing to cast aside their ancient dynastic form of government and much of the rest of their culture and fight a civil war to adopt communism, still a new and seemingly innovative concept at the time.

The communists in China did not like many of the ancient traditions of China at all and saw them, along with the ruling Qing Dynasty, to be the root cause of China's repeated recent humiliations. Their goal was to shed all the outmoded characteristics of the old empire and its culture completely and to remodel China to fit into the twentieth century. The three teachings of Taoism, Confucianism, and Buddhism were not only old fashioned to them, but they were also embarrassing!

The mystical version of Taoism popular at the time was particularly problematic to the communists because of its stress on individuality and resistance to state control, and so the new communist government condemned and tried to ban it all together, and what they were unable to abolish completely they tried to limit, control, and direct into a form more compatible with their agenda.

But, in truth, the Taoism of the nineteenth and early twentieth centuries was far removed from the Taoism of Lao Tzu, Chuang Tzu, and Lieh-Tzu anyway, and perhaps its loss to the world is not a great one. Luckily, thanks in large measure to Sima Qian and his father and to other great Chinese scholars through the centuries, the original writings of the ancients have survived and been passed down in close to their original form. The loss of the perverted, mystical, more recent version allows us to see and appreciate more easily the significance of the original!

Transmission into the Present of the Ancient Taoist Texts

At the time the three Taoist classics were first written, the art of writing in China had been known and used by priests and royal recordkeepers for one thousand years or so, but it was still fairly new and unusual for it to be used for such things as storytelling or the recording of philosophical beliefs. There were still relatively few people outside of the royal courts who could even read or write at that time.

As mentioned earlier, the very first known Chinese writing was done for divination purposes on baked scapula bones. At some point it was decided that baked turtle shells worked better for that purpose and that became the norm. Neither medium for writing was very practical for anything except the most cursory of information storage, though, and so when it was deemed important to record events and store larger amounts of tax and inventory information, a more practical form of writing was needed. Therefore, sometime before the fifth century BCE, the idea of writing on bamboo slips and slats of wood was invented to serve that purpose. Though bulky and heavy, it was far more practical than turtle shells, and therefore that was the writing medium that the original versions of the Lao Tzu, Chuang Tzu, and perhaps the Lieh-Tzu books were recorded on.

Such recordkeeping and early "books" of bamboo and wood consisted of numbers of slips (splits) of bamboo wood or slats of regular wood about three fourths of an inch wide and roughly nine inches long that were usually tied together sequentially with leather or silk cord near each end in a form similar to our modern venetian blinds so that they could be rolled up for storage or unrolled to be read. Text was written vertically from top to bottom of each slip or slat and from right to left with pens made of bamboo and ink usually of wet soot. For a long "book" made this way, the slips of each early chapter or group of chapters would be joined together as a separate rolled bundle until it became too heavy or bulky for more to be added, and then further chapters would likewise be separately joined into additional rolled bundles. Any "book" of considerable length, then, would have to consist of a significant number of such heavy and bulky rolls.

Sometime in the early Han Dynasty, silk also began to be used as a medium for writing. Though less heavy and bulky and therefore more practical from that perspective, silk was too expensive to be used in any quantity except by the very rich, and so for many decades, scribes were faced with the dilemma of either writing on bamboo, which was heavy and bulky, or on silk, which was very expensive.

Sometime before 100 AD, paper was first invented in China. It is believed that the first paper was created by the director of the imperial workshop from the lint and other detritus formed as a residue from the washing of the royal laundry. Over the centuries after that surprising origin, the quality of Chinese paper gradually became better and its use for writing slowly increased.

At first many different materials were mixed together with the hemp fibers used most commonly at the time for clothing to try to improve the quality and lower the cost of the paper, including such things as grass stems, bark, and even shredded old rags. For a long time rattan was considered an essential ingredient for making the best paper, but so much was used so quickly and the plant grew so slowly that supply eventually became a problem. Then, for a while, bamboo fibers were commonly used, and after that the boiled bark of the mulberry tree. As a result of trial and error, therefore, Chinese paper eventually became renowned for its quality and even became a valuable commodity traded far and wide, especially west and south along the Silk Road.

So, the Taoist classics have been passed down through the generations for more than twenty centuries, being copied over and over again, first on bamboo, then on silk cloth, and then on progressively better qualities of paper. Over those centuries, they survived Ch'in Dynasty's attempts to destroy all copies of them, the introduction and increasing popularity of Buddhism, the long period of populist and revisionist religious Taoism, and in the last century, communism. Throughout that time, Lao Tzu's *Tao Te Ching* in particular was analyzed, interpreted, reinterpreted, philosophized about, idolized, and even revered. In recent centuries it has even been translated into some seventy different languages and become a subject of interest to people all around the world.

One had to wonder, though, given all those centuries, given all the recopying, and all the outside influences, how close to the original writings of Lao Tzu, Chuang Tzu, and Lieh-Tzu were the versions of the texts available today? All versions available prior to only a few decades ago were "received" versions, meaning they had all been copied and recopied over the centuries, and so there was no way at all of knowing how altered they had become from the originals of so long before because of it.

With regard to the Chuang Tzu and the Lieh-Tzu books, that is still the case because no early versions have as yet ever been found in any ancient archeological sites, but with regard to the *Tao Te Ching*, the foundation of Taoist thought for more than a thousand years, that is not in question any longer. In 1973, in order to build an extension on a hospital at a place called Mawangdui in the southern province of Hunan, excavators found themselves having to allow archeologists to excavate three immense tombs that were in the way of their construction, dating back to the second century BCE—the period of the Han Empire, which succeeded the book-burning Ch'in Dynasty. What those archeologists found was an incredible cache of funerary goods including a large number of ancient texts in one of the tombs. Included were maps, histories, medical texts of all types, books on political philosophy, the earliest known version of the I Ching, and of particular interest to this discussion, two slightly different renderings of the *Tao Te Ching* written on silk.

We know from an inventory list found in the relevant tomb that its occupant and his belongings were buried April 4, 168 BCE, and therefore that the two versions of the *Tao Te Ching* in the tomb had to have been written prior to that date. There is additional evidence due to details of the writing style that indicates that the two texts were actually written within a decade or so of each other probably around the year 200 BCE. And it's important to note that despite the twenty-two hundred years of repeated recopying that could have altered the received versions we are familiar with today, it turned out that while there were some interesting differences, the current versions are remarkably faithful to the ancient versions written all those many centuries earlier.

But then, in 1993, another ancient tomb was excavated that also contained well-preserved versions of the *Tao Te Ching*, even older than the Mawangdui texts and written not on silk but on bamboo slips. Those earlier versions of the classic were dated prior to 300 BCE, perhaps not long after its various passages (commonly referred to today as chapters) were first written in any form at all. The tomb they were found in was in a cemetery near a town that is now called Guodian and served in ancient times as the capital of Chu, one of the warring states of the Warring States Period. Evidence in the tomb seems to indicate that its occupant and the owner of the texts found within it might have been a tutor to the crown prince of Chu at the time, who lived and died not long before the Ch'in conquest of Chu and the other rival states.

The Guodian bamboo slip *Tao Te Ching* literature, though similar to the Mawangdui and the received versions in much of the material they do contain are also quite different in a number of significant ways. First of all, rather than being presented in the form of a two-part book (the Tao and the Te) as the other versions are, they were found in the form of three different bundles, apparently from three different sources, since each of the bundles was formed and bound somewhat differently than the others and each appear to have been written by a different scribe. Each of the three bundles contain passages on the slips comprising it that are the same basic ones we are familiar with from other sources, but there are only thirty-six of them in total in the three bundles instead of the eighty-one in the received versions, and only sixteen are complete and in more or less the exact same form we see elsewhere. The other twenty are either missing segments that were apparently added later or consist of detached segments located in different places that were later put together to form the longer passages found in more recent versions.

The thirty-six passages that are present are also in a totally different sequence than we are used to. The passages in each of the three bundles are different than the ones in the other two bundles with one significant exception—a passage that is duplicated, interestingly, in somewhat different forms in two different bundles. And none of the bundles or the slips that comprise them are labeled or numbered in any way. As a result, there is no way of knowing whether or not the owner of the bundles, when alive, thought of them all as being parts of the one unified body of work we now call the *Tao Te Ching*, or even if they were all the work of one single author. Although there is no way to be certain, the various realities of the Guodian bamboo slip *Tao Te Ching* literature seems to indicate that those possibilities are unlikely.

It has long been traditional belief that one ancient scholar called Lao Tzu wrote the book called the *Tao Te Ching*. Sima Qian declared that to be the case in his "Records of the Grand Historian" several hundred years after the event. He even included a tale of exactly how the passages laying forth the tenets of Taoism first came to be written by Lao Tzu—but in truth few modern scholars of Taoism, especially outside of China, believe the tale to be the true story—or at least not to be the complete one. The bundles in the Guodian tomb and other evidence strongly suggest that the compilation and transfer into writing of the philosophy we now call Taoism in the form of the book known as the *Tao Te Ching* took place over the course of multiple decades and perhaps even a period of as long as a century. Several different authors probably wrote down the Taoist adages that they were familiar with in oral form from their own regions and those gradually accumulated in royal libraries and private collections until at some point they were united into the mostly consistent form now called the

Tao Te Ching. It could well be, though, that one of the scholars involved in that process was indeed known as Lao Tzu (which translates into English as "old master"). The findings at Guodian and Mawangdui seem to indicate that that process was still ongoing in 300 BCE but that the current form of the *Tao Te Ching* had become well established and standardized by the year 200 BCE.

We have discussed at length the origin and evolution of the *Tao Te Ching* traditionally accredited to the author Lao Tzu, but what of the other two Taoist classics—the *Book of Chuang Tzu* and the *Book of Lieh-Tzu*? The stated authors of both books are known to have been real people who almost certainly lived during the Warring States Period and were well-known sages of Tao at that time. Each was mentioned in several places by ancient sources—Chuang Tzu notably by Sima Qian and Lieh-Tzu notably in the Spring and Autumn Annals of Lu, but all known versions of their books are received versions. Unlike the *Tao Te Ching*, none have been found in recent times in any ancient tombs to compare received versions with, and so any discussion of the exact authenticity of the versions we know today must be mostly speculative. At the beginning of chapters 3, 4, and 5 herein, there will be further discussion of those traditionally accredited authors and what is known about the transmission of their books through time to the present.

At any rate, while the *Tao Te Ching* can be thought of today as the framework of classic Taoism, setting forth its basis and basic principles, the Chuang Tzu and Lieh-Tzu books can be thought of as the body of Taoist thought built upon that framework, illustrating how sages of old lived their lives and taught their students Taoism according to Taoist principles.

SECTION II

The Taoist Classics

Notes to the Reader

Definitions

Undoubtedly, the most common problem modern English-speaking readers have in understanding Taoism as presented in the translated versions of the three Taoist classics is the multiple and imprecise meanings of the word "Tao." In various contexts in the texts, the word is used to mean 1) the physical make-up of the universe that people live within and are a part of; 2) the changes through time that characterize and affect that universe; 3) the manner in which people should think and act to best coordinate their lives with the universe and its changes; and 4) the philosophy in general. To help the reader overcome the problem of confusion from those different definitions, I have specified the different meanings of the word (and several others) throughout this book in the following ways:

Tao: The basic framework of the universe and the interrelationships of its parts as now studied in the science of physics, along with other aspects of it that are studied by students of other sciences. Therefore, Tao is the physical universe we are each a tiny part of and that we are able to experience around us with our five senses in our day-to-day lives.

The Flow of Tao: That characteristic of Tao that results in the changes that take place to Tao through time. We experience the Flow of Tao as days, seasons, years, aging, births, deaths, weather, and all the other changes that take place from day to day throughout our lives. But, of course, the Flow of Tao has occurred everywhere constantly in the universe since the Big Bang and will continue to do so until the end of time.

The Way of Tao: sometimes referred to just as the Way: A life-style based on an understanding of Taoism and on being in tune with the Flow of Tao that allows the practitioner to be more successful at accomplishing what he or she has chosen to accomplish and to be happier and more at peace with himself or herself in their life as they do so. One who becomes quite adept at following the Way of Tao might be seen by others as a sage!

Taoism: The philosophy based on Tao and the Flow of Tao with which one studies the Way of Tao in hopes of learning to live a happy, harmonious, and fruitful life.

Achievement without friction: Called Wu Wei by the ancient Chinese. Learning through a variety of strategies how to accomplish one's objectives in the easiest and most effective ways by choosing one's goals carefully and by taking into consideration the Flow of Tao and using that flow to help to do so instead of fighting it or going against it.

Sage: One who has become adept at living according to the Way of Tao. Such a person may or may not be known or even notable to many other people. He or she might be rich or poor, of any race or culture, or be characterized by any type of personality, but those who do know such a person know him or her to be honest, open-minded, sincere, selfless, happy, and good-natured, and to be a person capable of great achievement when driven by his or her objectives. No true sage would ever identify himself or herself to be a sage, though, because that classification for the Taoist is only an unobtainable ideal.

These terms and other aspects of Taoism in modern life will be explained in more detail in section III of this book.

Tao vs. Dao

Chinese script is made up of symbols called logograms that represent syllables in the Chinese language instead of individual sounds, as letters represent in Romanesque languages like our own. There are thousands of such syllables in the Chinese spoken language and therefore thousands of logograms in their written language that represent them—usually in combinations to form Chinese words. Because of the two different types of script and the characteristic tonal qualities of the Chinese language, translating from written Chinese into written English is difficult and different techniques have been used through recent centuries to do so.

Because of those changing techniques, the ancient Chinese philosophy this book discusses has traditionally been spelled in English with a "T" (i.e., Tao, Taoism, and Taoist), while more recently it is often spelled with a "D" (i.e., Dao, Daoism, and Daoist). Either way, of course, it is the same philosophy. I don't know which representation most closely follows the pronunciation Chinese people use when referring to it in their own language, but in this book, because it is still the most common spelling here in the United States, because most commonly used Taoist related keywords use the "T" form, and because it is the way I have learned to think of it, I use the "T" form of the word.

3

Tao Te Ching

Lao Tzu

As to the historical origins of the Tao Te Ching, the Mawangdui and Guodian versions of the text give us hints, but there is nothing that can be known with any certainty about its authorship. Traditionally, there was said to have been only one author, a man known as Lao Tzu, but that name simply means "old master" in Chinese and that, in itself, doesn't tell us anything at all about who the actual person was.

The earliest historical references to Lao Tzu are in the *Re-*

cords of the Grand Historian, presumably collected and copied from earlier sources by Sima Qian in the first century BCE. There are three different such mentions in the manuscripts that provide three different personal names, cite two different possible time periods for his life, and detail three different stories about him and his career. Unless archeologists find a cache of ancient records somewhere with more information, it is unlikely that we will ever know anything more specific with any certainty about the individual(s) we now know of only as Lao Tzu.

According to one ancient legend, Lao Tzu's real name was Li Erh, and he was a scholar in charge of the royal library of King Wu (or perhaps at the imperial court of Zhou). According to the legend, he wearied of the moral decay he experienced in the court and also noticed a deterioration in the local political situation and therefore determined to leave the city and move to a safer and more peaceful location. By chance, though, as he was leaving the kingdom, a border guard recognized him and, after hearing his plans, asked if he would please remain at the border station for a while and record some of the knowledge he had learned as the kingdom's librarian. Lao Tzu agreed to do so and proceeded to briefly summarize the wisdom he had learned in writing—and from that summary, the Tao Te Ching was born. It is a compelling legend, but whether there is any truth to it at all is, of course, completely unknowable. For the sake of simplicity and precedent, we will just continue to refer to the author of the Tao Te Ching as Lao Tzu!

About the Tao Te Ching

Regardless of authorship, the Guodian bamboo slip texts seem to indicate that by around the year 300 BCE, the Tao Te Ching was still in the process of being compiled and standardized, while the two copies found at Mawangdui demonstrate that by 200 BCE, the book had become fairly formalized and seemingly well established. Few significant changes to it have occurred in the thousands of years since then.

The "received" versions of the *Tao Te Ching* are comprised of eighty-one passages or "chapters." Most had the structure in the Chinese language of a short poem using paradox, repetition, symmetry, analogy, ancient sayings, and rhythm to teach lessons about Tao and Taoism. Translated into English, of course, much of that is lost. In the first section of the received texts, simply labeled "Tao," the chapters supposedly focus more on the characteristics of Tao, while in the second section, chapters supposedly focus more on Te, the noble behavior expected of someone who has become a sage. In truth though, the organization of the chapters is quite haphazard, and many English renderings today, including this one, do not bother to distinguish between or even label the two different sections.

Because of the broad range of material specifically describing the tenets of Taoism that is presented in it; because of its concise, opaque, and almost mystical style; and also because it is the best known and probably the oldest of the three Taoist classics, the *Tao Te Ching* is usually considered to be the foundation of Taoist philosophy, while the books of Chuang Tzu and Lieh-Tzu are appreciated more for adding depth and context to that foundation. But that is not meant to imply in any way that the other two books are less significant or relevant. It is only by reading, considering, and appreciating all three that one can really hope to understand and learn about the ancient philosophy of Taoism.

My Approach to the *Tao Te Ching*

I am not a scholar of the ancient Chinese language, or even of modern Chinese, and my versions of the passages (chapters) of the *Tao Te Ching* that follow are not presented as being exact translations of the originals. There are many good translations available to choose from for readers wishing to engage with that challenge, but most such versions available in English today must include explanations next to each passage because the direct translations are difficult if not impossible for the average reader to understand without them. My objective in writing this book has been to present the material in a way that is easy to understand and to relate to for the modern reader without the need for explanations.

I have tried to present the material in a manner that is as understandable to the modern reader as possible without losing its mystical nature or the ancient Chinese context in which it was originally placed. More than anything, while doing that, I have tried to accurately present the lessons the original passages were intended to teach and to make the points they were originally intended to make in the same manner as the original author or authors intended.

To avoid confusion, I have presented my versions of the passages of the *Tao Te Ching* for the most part in the same order and with the same numerical designations as the received versions, even though that order does not seem to be meaningful in any particular way. Doing so created some difficulty in the number sequencing in several places, though, and therefore called for the following exceptions. Passage #42 appeared to be too long and also dealt with two different topics, so I divided it into a part "A" and a part "B" and passage #80 seemed to me to be a perfect conclusion to the *Tao Te Ching*, while passage #81 did not, so I took the liberty of switching them around and renumbering them. I apologize for any confusion those changes might create, but it seemed to me like the preferable way to treat the material.

Lao Tzu #1

The Tao can never fully be grasped with words.

Even its name is just a sound.

Beyond words, it is the basis for all that is,

While words only describe what is definable.

Immersed selflessly in Tao, one can start to sense its essence.

Otherwise, one only observes effects!

The describable and indescribable are both aspects of Tao,

Understanding them as one is the challenge!

Lao Tzu #2

When people labelled beauty as beauty, ugliness was created.

When they defined morality, so too came sin.

The concept of life created the concept of death.

Difficult created easy and long created short.

High created low and front created back.

Defining the universe with words affects our reality.

The real Tao is not so simple.

The sage, therefore, uses words sparingly,

And learns and teaches with them with care.

Events occur, but he does not casually label and describe them.

He senses and reacts but does not attempt to orchestrate.

He achieves his goals but does not brag nor talk them up.

And since he holds on to little, he has little to lose!

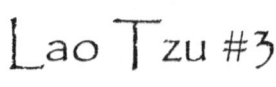

Lao Tzu #3

By not overvaluing status, you encourage others not to be overly competitive.

By not overvaluing beauty, you encourage others not to be vain.

By not overvaluing wealth, you encourage others not to covet possessions.

The sage avoids sowing the seeds of other people's destruction,

And focuses instead on helping them to satisfy their potential.

For those reasons, others tend to be sympathetic to his causes.

And so long as he always seems unstoppable to those he works with,

There is little he cannot achieve!

Lao Tzu #4

At its heart, the Tao is not a place of things, yet all we experience are things sprung from it.

Edges break and are sharp and then wear smooth.

Stars suddenly glare and then slowly grow dim.

Knots pulled tight someday all loosen,

Every dilemma ever faced will somehow be resolved.

And all that is young will someday grow old.

We know little more than the products and effects of Tao,

And yet its endless flow sets the tone, context, and rhythm of our lives!

Lao Tzu #5

In the resolute Flow of Tao, bad things sometimes happen.

The Tao is dispassionate and simply does what it must do.

The sage aspires to be dispassionate as well.

He accepts stoically what life brings him, for it just is what it turns out to be.

And while the Flow is like the workings of infinite numbers of bellows,

Constantly tightening and easing with constant interconnected challenges,

Words used to describe it all create an illusion of isolated events.

The sage avoids emotion and is cautious with words,

And looks for trends and interactions in the Flow behind it all!

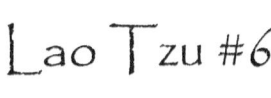

Lao Tzu #6

The infinite Tao is the origin of both Heaven and Earth

And can be thought of as the womb of the universe.

It is too complex and indistinct for us to ever fully know

And yet it will create all that will ever be until the end of time.

Lao Tzu #7

The Tao is the most eternal of all things! Why is that true?

Because the Tao is the most basic and selfless of things.

It is the foundation of the universe that allows all else to be.

And yet it never needs anything from outside itself to be so.

Sages learn from that and try to be just as selfless and self-reliant.

They think little about themselves and prioritize the needs of others.

And because of their selflessness, they achieve much and are fulfilled.

Lao Tzu #8

The best role model for anyone following the Way is water.

For water is humble and rarely rises above other things.

It is content with being essential and yet maintaining a lowly position.

To the sage:

The best home is unassuming.

The best mind is deep and thoughtful.

The best relationships are those of love and compassion.

The best words are those of honesty and sincerity.

The best management is fair and selfless, yet effective.

The best achievement is in tune with the Flow of Tao.

And because the sage does not do what he does to compete with others, others rarely try to compete with him!

Lao Tzu #9

Overfilling a glass will make it hard to bring to the lips without spilling.

Over-sharpening a blade will make it no sharper but will wear away the edge.

Overemphasizing the importance of wealth, power, or fame in your life

Will dull your empathy for others, lessen your joy of life, and waste your precious time!

Excess is counter productive. When the job is done, set it aside, enjoy life, and think of others.

Lao Tzu #10

In embracing Taoism and living according to the Way, can you resist temptation and backsliding?

In becoming strong and confident, can your heart and spirit remain gentle and non-assuming?

With exposure to worldly desires, can you maintain a simple life?

With the understanding of others and the ability to influence them, will you avoid manipulation?

With power and wealth and influence, will you retain compassion and thoughtfulness?

With knowledge, will you retain the benefit of insight and instinct?

Creating worthwhile things and nurturing them, gently guiding their development without dominating them, and happily allowing others to benefit from what you have created,

These are virtues of the sage!

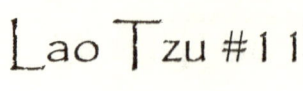

Lao Tzu #11

Thirty wooden spokes, a rim, and a hub are the parts of a chariot wheel, but it is the empty hole in the middle of the hub designed to receive the axle that allows it to function.

Clay pots can be made in a variety of shapes and sizes, but for each it is the empty space between the walls of the pot that allows it to be useful.

Houses can be large or small and made in many ways, but it is the empty spaces between the walls that make them homes where people can live, love, and raise families.

Therefore, while there can be value in what is solid and known of Tao, there is also value in what is not!

Lao Tzu #12

Bright lights and gaudy colors can desensitize one to more subtle scenes.

Loud noises and raucous music can numb one to quieter but more significant sounds.

Sweet or fiery flavors can inure one from the delicate tastes of more healthful foods.

A lust for impressive objects can bind one to them and make him forget more relevant objectives.

And a hyperactive life in general can lead one to shallow thoughts and poor judgment.

Sages usually focus on more basic things and the interactions between them and are cautious of all such excesses!

Lao Tzu #13

To those who cannot control their egos, both praise and criticism are things to fear.

Why is that?

Because criticism will cause them emotional pain and they will not like that and will do almost anything to avoid it.

And because praise will bring them great joy and they might do almost anything to experience it over and over again.

One who might be willing to compromise his good judgment to maintain the happiness of his ego cannot always be trusted.

And therefore, only those who love the world and others on it more than they love themselves should ever be entrusted with power!

Lao Tzu #14

We look but see only light reflecting off of things and into our eyes.

We listen but hear only the vibrations of atoms of air entering our ears.

We touch but feel only the molecules of something else pushing back against those of our skin.

The whole of Tao is more fundamental and extensive than we can ever fully know.

Our senses detect only manifestations of Tao – forms in something mostly formless.

The Tao is all things and yet it is also all one – a gigantic creation of swirling interacted knots of energy.

It began in the beginning and though ever-changing, will be here in some form until the end,

And although it is natural to think of it as something outside and separate from ourselves, it is not.

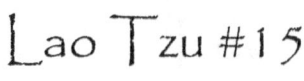

Lao Tzu #15

There is no way to ever know who first recognized the Tao as the basis for all that is in the universe, and then went on to study it and pass down its characteristics through the ages. They lived their lives and then died long ago! But they must have been very wise and, because of the wisdom they gained through their studies, they must have become:

Hesitant, like a traveler needing to cross a wintry stream.

Cautious, like one walking alone past strangers on a dark night.

Polite, like a guest for dinner in the home of a dignitary.

Loose and flexible like ice on a lake beginning to thaw.

Genuine and full of potential, like an uncarved block of the finest wood.

Confident and yet reserved, like a tigress protecting her cubs.

And deep and fertile of mind, like a broad river valley.

They must have seemed to others to somehow be serene and confident while at the same time being dynamic and effective.

There is no way I will ever know who those ancient sages were and yet I will try every day to be like them.

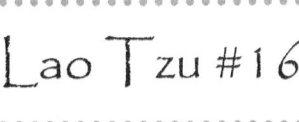

Lao Tzu #16

In quiet moments, observe the workings of the Tao.

New things rise in significance, become the norm, and then gradually decline.

Others start small, grow to a maximum, and then shrink away to nothingness.

Life is born, grows strong in adulthood, and then one day is gone.

Change is the only constant. Accept it. Work with it. Go with the Flow.

Find consistency within yourself. Follow the Way. Become the you you are proud of.

And as to that from outside of yourself, remain impartial and yield whenever your conscience and good sense allow it.

All that had a beginning will have an end. Resisting these realities destines one to a life that is out of touch.

Lao Tzu #17

With the best of leaders, followers hardly even know they are being led.

Leaders not quite so good are loved by their followers and praised.

Poor leaders are feared, and the worst are targets of jokes and scorn.

Great leaders trust and respect their followers and as a result are trusted and respected back.

They perform their duties carefully and calmly, and thoughtfully measure their words.

Such leaders quietly solve problems and accomplish objectives, and then when great victories come, everyone says excitedly, "Hooray, we did it"!

Lao Tzu #18

When a society loses its connection with the Way of Tao, the rule of law and concepts of goodness must rise to take its place.

When people must be concerned about the exact meanings of statutes, their world fills with deception in the midst of distrust.

When relationships are falling apart and families shattering, that's when people talk at length about compassion and social responsibility.

And when a country is in chaos and its economy is collapsing, that is when its leaders point out their virtues and love of country.

Lao Tzu #19

Eliminate pomposity and pretense, and the world will benefit in a thousand ways.

End self-righteous benevolence, and people will return to piety and real charity.

Eliminate greed and lusting for power, and honesty and sincerity can then prevail.

But how can we improve humankind in all those ways? By each of us doing it within ourselves. That is how!

Lao Tzu #20

If I were to stop overthinking things, my life would be easier!

"Acceptance" or "rejection", how do I decide and what difference will it make?

"Good" or "bad", isn't that just a choice in the mind of each person?

If others fear something, does that mean that I must fear it too?

Complicated and difficult to understand, the complexities of life often just seem endless.

Everyone else is happy and excited as if going to a festival, while I am unable to commit to anything.

I am like an infant, trying desperately to understand every little thing I'm capable of grasping.

Sometimes it exhausts me, as though I'm searching to find one single place where I can finally feel safe.

Everyone else always seems to have everything, while I forever hunt for what I need in darkness.

Others quickly make life-defining decisions, while I when I try, just seem to confuse myself.

Formless am I, like water in an ocean – shapeless, as if there's nothing inside of me with structure.

Mine often seems to be the mind of an idiot, forever confused and unable to decide.

But it is only my most fundamental desire that makes me different from all the rest,

For I always try to seek my guidance by following the Way of Tao!

Lao Tzu #21

The Way of Tao is the way of true virtue because it is based on the truths of the universe.

But it is so shapeless and hard to define! How can one even learn the Way of Tao?

While shapeless and hard to define, the Tao is the source of all we ever experience.

Things are like clumps of Tao, held together for awhile by the immutable forces of nature.

They are all real, but so is the Tao behind, below, and between the things.

It is ever moving and always changing, and all things made from it are, as well.

How do I know this all to be true?

Because sages have studied the Tao for thousands of years. That is how!

Lao Tzu #22

Be willing to yield things in order to gain things.

Be able to bend so that you will not need to break.

Be humble so that others won't work against you.

Be honest about what you know and don't know,

And about your strengths and weaknesses

So that you can make good decisions about what you should do.

Sages follow the Way of Tao and therefore become guides for their peers.

They do not posture and therefore can become prominent.

They avoid the spotlight and therefore shine brightly.

They do not brag and therefore can receive credit when it is due.

They do not assert leadership and therefore are often asked to lead.

They appreciate and respect others and therefore are appreciated and respected in return.

It is because sages do not compete socially with others,

That others usually choose not to compete against them.

These are lessons from the ancient sages.

Lao Tzu #23

The Tao only expresses itself aggressively occasionally and then only for a short while.

Howling gales only howl until temperatures and pressures equalize.

Thunderstorms only boom and pour rain until the storms pass or fade away.

Those are characteristics of the Flow of Tao and sages try to copy them.

They measure their words, only speak quiet words that are helpful,

And then say what needs to be said with authority.

Sages are thoughtful about their actions between words, as well.

For one adept at following the Way of Tao will become one with its Flow.

One who dedicates himself to virtue will eventually become one with virtue,

But one who wallows in uncertainty will eventually become one with uncertainty.

For the one who has become one with virtue, Tao will help him to succeed.

For the one who has become one with uncertainty, Tao will help him to fail!

Lao Tzu #24

Those who hold themselves above others will soon naturally fall.

Those who praise themselves display a lack of self-confidence.

Those who brag about victories create a friction against future wins.

Those who highlight themselves lessen their ability to naturally shine.

The sage recognizes such negative behaviors and tries to avoid them.

Lao Tzu #25

Somehow, in the beginning, the Tao was formed and from that came all else.

Itself silent, endless, and pure, the Tao is the most basic of things and lies behind and below the rest.

Ever moving and always changing, it is the foundation of all we know and see.

Inherently cyclical, its infinite aspects are all in some ways coming and in other ways going.

In some ways rising and in others falling, and in some ways growing and in others shrinking.

Having to identify it, I call it Tao. Having to describe it, I say it is the mother of all things.

To learn to be a sage, one must learn to follow the Way of Tao,

But the only rules the Tao need follow are the physical laws of the universe.

Lao Tzu #26

Careful consideration should override impulsiveness in any serious matter.

Well-justified confidence is the best barrier against unexpected disaster.

A wise traveler passing through dangerous places does not stray far from his luggage.

Only after reaching a safe destination will he relax and be carefree.

And, while a single person acting only in his own behalf can do whatever he wishes,

How can a leader with followers make whimsical decisions that might imperil them all?

Those with others who depend on them cannot neglect to think before acting!

Lao Tzu #27

The best travelers leave no traces of their journeys behind them.

The best speakers speak only words that help those who hear.

The best achievers only build and do things of beauty and value.

The best tiers of knots only tie knots that stay tied for years.

The best closers of doors close them quietly and peacefully.

During a sage's life, he is sometimes a student and sometimes a teacher.

When he is with someone who wants to learn what he knows,

He takes the role of the teacher and values the student.

And when he is with someone who knows something he would like to learn,

He takes the role of the student and values the teacher.

In either role, the sage only focuses on whatever seems worthwhile.

And he never rejects anyone or anything in which he sees something of value!

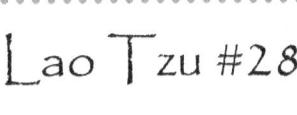

Lao Tzu #28

If you can be comfortably confident in the things you do and be dynamic and assertive when you feel strongly about something and the situation demands it,

Then people will be drawn to you as they are to a pleasant mountain stream on a hot summer day.

You will assume the natural focus and spontaneity of a newborn child!

If you can maintain a high level of personal integrity in the things you do while remaining humble and respectful toward those who might have faltered in that regard,

Then all will accept you and what you do and will have no cause to work against you.

Your horizons will become endless!

If you can accept public recognition for your accomplishments gracefully and remain humble and insist that credit be given to all who helped you,

Then others will seek you out to partner with in many of their projects.

You will become as fruitful as a fertile valley and as adaptable as an uncarved block of the finest wood!

And with the natural focus and spontaneity of a newborn child, with horizons that are endless, and with the adaptability of an uncarved block of the finest wood, imagine all that you, as a sage, will be able to accomplish!

Lao Tzu #29

Those driven to conquer and control societies could never succeed for long. People and their cultures are too complex to control completely. Attempts to do so would only destroy the societies as he knew them. And he would not even like the then damaged society that he got!

Some things lead while others follow.

Some things grow hot while others grow cold.

Some things rise while others fall.

Each is separate and yet all are one.

All just aspects of the greater Flow of Tao.

The sage just observes and pursues the Way,

And sometimes others will follow!

. . . .

Lao Tzu #30

. . . .

Those who follow the Way will rarely advocate for war.

For even with victory, disastrous effects usually ensue.

Where armies have fought, only thorns and thistles are likely to grow.

And afterward, people suffer for years from hunger and poverty.

Great leaders advance their nation's interests with strategy, strength, and tact,

While avoiding actual conflict whenever possible.

And from that, battles where soldiers must die rarely need be fought at all.

Such leaders respect their opponents and don't bully, brag, or threaten,

And with tactics short of force, they achieve their best results.

. . . .

Lao Tzu #31

. . . .

As for weapons of war, they are tools of misfortune and most people do not love them.

If a sage of Tao must fight with weapons, he will do so with determination but not with joy.

For they are not his preferred tools for solving problems.

When he can, the sage will honor peace, but if he must fight, then he will honor victory.

But no sage sees weapons as things of beauty, for one who does must therefore see beauty in death.

And if one puts that little value on the lives of others, he must also put little value on his own.

Therefore, when people are at peace, it is because nearby leaders all chose to honor peace,

And whenever they must mourn the deaths of warriors lost in battles they did not even want to fight,

It is because some leader not following the Way valued his own goals beyond the welfare of his people.

And so, even when sages are victorious in battles in which soldiers died, they do not celebrate the victory but instead treat it as they would a funeral!

. . . .

Lao Tzu #32

. . . .

The Tao and its flow are the eternal reality behind all things.

It burst into being many eons before humankind evolved,

And gave things names,

And it will endure for eons after humankind is gone

And the names are all forgotten.

Humankind is driven by our nature to organize and name things.

What we know and name are based on what we can sense of Tao,

But because of the limitations of our senses, that is not complete.

To follow the Way of Tao, one must try to know the essence of it

Behind and below the human words and simple understandings.

If all the leaders of all the lands were faithful followers of the Way,

Their people would faithfully follow them wherever they led,

And the Flow of Tao would usually favor us all with good fortune!

Lao Tzu #33

To understand others is to be smart. To also understand yourself is to be wise.

To conquer others is to be strong. To conquer yourself is to be mighty.

To be happy with who you are and what you have is to be contented.

To be successful doing what you enjoy doing is to be wealthy.

To know and accept your place in the Flow of Tao is to be satisfied.

To upgrade your role in the Flow of Tao over time is to be dynamic.

To not be concerned at all as to when you might die is to be long lived.

Lao Tzu #34

The Flow of Tao can be likened to a river passing through the land, always moving forward – over, under, or around all obstacles.

It leads where it leads, does what it does, and provides what it provides, and is usually taken for granted for doing so.

All in the universe are gifts of Tao, and yet it makes no demands upon anything in exchange for what it gives.

Eternally without needs or desires, it might be thought by some to be irrelevant, since there is nothing it asks for,

But since all things are products of Tao, it will be recognized by those more thoughtful to be almighty.

And because it does all that it does and yet does not claim greatness, it is all the more truly great!

Lao Tzu #35

For the Taoist who holds true, good things will happen.

All around him will feel safe in his presence,

And he will usually be held in high regard.

But it is good food and pleasant conversation that most people enjoy,

Not a discourse on the merits of the Way!

When looked for, the Way is invisible; when listened for, unheard.

But unlike food and beverage, the benefits of the Way never cease.

Remember that it is the example and not the words that matter most!

Lao Tzu #36

If you feel you should shrink it, it's often best first to stretch it.

If you feel you should weaken it, it's often best first to strengthen it.

If you feel you should abandon it, it's often best first to promote it.

And if you want something from it, it's often best first to give something to it.

With subtle strategy, the weak can often overcome the strong,

And the wise can achieve their goals.

Lao Tzu #37

The Flow of Tao pursues no selfish agendas and yet there is nothing it does not achieve.

Those who follow the Way subtly and without self-centered agendas do not impede the Flow's peaceful progress,

While those who don't and selfishly advance themselves alter it rudely for the worse.

When people follow the Way of Tao and are gentle with the Flow, it can proceed toward a natural future.

And with a natural future, our world remains a happier and more peaceful place for all.

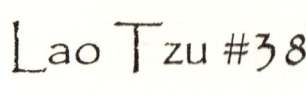
High virtue is spontaneous, done without forethought, and is therefore the truest virtue.

Low virtue is consciously decided upon, and therefore is not nearly so noble.

No real virtue involves engineered actions or is done in pursuit of an agenda.

Benevolence does involve engineered actions although they might not be done to pursue an agenda.

Righteousness involves engineered actions that are performed to achieve an agenda.

Etiquette involves engineered actions done for a purpose, and expects or demands a proper response.

Therefore, when the Way is being lost, society falls to virtue,

When virtue is being lost, society falls to benevolence,

When benevolence is being lost, society falls to righteousness,

When righteousness is being lost, society falls to etiquette,

And those who live in a world of etiquette endure a life wherein a thin shell of loyalty and sincerity hovers constantly over the brink of retribution.

Those who do good deeds only after thought and to satisfy a purpose are like flowers of Tao – showy, but of little substance.

The sage prefers to follow the Way and not to pursue the showy flowers of agenda and appearance.

Lao Tzu #39

It is only because of the natural characteristics of the Flow of Tao that:

Our planet revolves around our sun in a predictable way,

The features and traits of our planet can be trusted to support life,

Life does prosper here and interacts in ways that strengthen us all,

And some individuals have been blessed with the circumstances and abilities necessary to become successful in life.

Without the natural characteristics of the Flow of Tao:

There would be no sun, no Earth, and no stable solar system,

Our planet would not be a suitable place for the perpetuation of life,

And we would not live in a society that allowed some lucky and able citizens to attain success.

Therefore, no one should ever become arrogant simply because they have attained wealth, power, or fame.

We are all equal products of Tao and its Flow and should remain humble and strong like granite, rather than trying to impress and dazzle as if we were jade.

Lao Tzu #40

Whenever any part of the Flow of Tao becomes too excessive or extreme, that part will reverse itself.

Therefore, all of Tao is cyclical!

Every part of the Flow of Tao is constantly changing—whether we experience the change as being fast or slow.

Therefore, the Way of Tao calls for flexibility.

All that we can experience is only the tip of all that we cannot!

Lao Tzu #41

When a few people hear about Taoism, they study the Way and dedicate themselves to learning how to live it.

When most hear about it, they learn something about it and try when it's convenient to follow it.

And when others hear about Taoism, they scoff and continue on as they always have.

If some did not scoff, it would not be Taoism!

For when it comes to the Way of Tao:

The brightest Way often appears to be drab,

The Way that goes forward often appears to go backward,

The smoothest Way often appears too rugged to follow,

The highest virtue often appears to be lowly,

The firmest virtue often appears to be flimsy,

The purist white often appears to be soiled,

And the clearest reality often seems too nebulous to even detect.

The great square has no clear corners,

The great vessel has been known to leak,

And the great tone is sometimes too quiet to hear.

The Tao and its Flow might seem by some to be incomprehensible,

And yet the Way of Tao is the answer to every question.

Lao Tzu #42 Part A

The unity of Tao is the foundation of all that is in the universe,

but Tao is the result of balance between two equal opposing forces,

And the complex natural interactions through time and space between them.

So the one that is all can be said to be the product of the three.

Lao Tzu #42 Part B

It is disharmony and imbalance in the world they live in that people detest more than all else.

And they experience those most often in the form of isolation, personal loss, and unfulfilled needs.

And those are often caused by the demands of leaders in order to fulfill their own selfish agendas.

Satisfying their demands requires sacrifice from the very people the leaders are meant to serve.

And requiring too many such sacrifices is what causes the disharmony and imbalance.

But I will teach what I have found to be true, and that is that bullies and tyrants never live joyous lives nor die peaceful deaths.

That is one of the most basic lessons I have learned from my lifetime of experiences.

Lao Tzu #43

I have found that the soft, subtle, and intuitive can often win over the hard and strong, but more obtuse,

And that the clever and flexible can often pass through the solid and intransigent.

They do so by following the Way and moving wisely and without friction within Tao's Flow.

The benefits of following the Way of Tao are incomparable.

Lao Tzu #44

Which is more important to you – freedom or fame?

Freedom or wealth – which is most dear?

If your need to attain wealth, power, or fame is strongest,

It might be wise to rethink your priorities!

For the more of each you happen to attain,

The more freedom you will find you have lost.

And, too, the higher you climb,

The further you may someday find you must fall.

Happiness comes from being content with what you have.

It is what you do, not what you attain, that is important!

Lao Tzu #45

Great completion might seem unfinished,

But nothing more need be done.

Great fullness might seem half empty,

But nothing need be added.

Great straightness might seem somewhat crooked,

But is the shortest route to the goal.

Great skill might sometimes seem clumsy,

But the job could not be better done.

Great eloquence might sound provincial,

But words could not be better said.

Action creates heat, while tranquility cools.

Accept what is and go forth confidently to achieve!

. . . .

Lao Tzu #46

. . . .

When the world follows the Way, beautiful horses pull bright carts through city streets by day,

And graze peacefully in green meadows by evening.

When it doesn't, those same horses might be used to pull chariots bearing warriors across bloody fields

While stepping over and around the dead and wounded.

Of crimes, none is greater than having too many selfish desires.

Of disasters, the worst is not knowing when one has already demanded enough.

Of defects, none is worse than one feeling the need to take something that belongs to another.

So, as you can see, satisfaction with what one already has is a very desirable trait!

Lao Tzu #47

The Tao can be found any place one decides to look.

It can be found anywhere inside of yourself.

It can be found in the hearts and minds of others.

It can be found in the beauty of a moonlit sky.

And it can be found in the hustle and bustle of a city street.

But it's easy to get lost if you stray too far from yourself.

From somewhere close to that, do what you can to come to know it.

Lao Tzu #48

Pursue knowledge and you will fill your mind with information.

Pursue wisdom and you will purge your mind of untruths and irrelevancies.

Concerns of self, self-image, and ambition waste time and clutter the brain.

With a mind empty of such trivia, there can be focus,

And then, by moving with the Flow, there is little you cannot achieve.

Go forth and master your world!

Lao Tzu #49

The sage participates in his community and keeps his mind open.

Those commonly seen as good, he sees as good, as well.

Those not commonly seen as good, he sees as good, regardless.

In that way, he attains goodness.

Those his community commonly trusts, he trusts as well.

Those his community doesn't commonly trust, he gives a chance.

In that way, he earns the trust of everyone.

The sage is one with his world and opens his heart and mind to it.

Those who know him, respect him, and he sees them all as friends.

Lao Tzu #50

We naturally emerge into life being fearless, open, warm, and soft,

And then we sink into death being fearful, and then rigid and cold.

Yet many assume those traits of death while still in the prime of their lives.

Why would anyone choose to live their life that way?

Because such people value their lives too much!

Surely you have heard of people who have a talent for holding onto life.

When walking through the wilderness, they don't worry about tigers or wolves,

And when going into battle, they don't bother with shields or armor.

And yet, the tigers and wolves never seem to find them, and the weapons never seem to cut them.

Why is that? Because such people don't concern themselves with life or death at all!

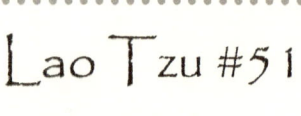

Lao Tzu #51

The Flow of Tao gave birth to life here millions of years ago and Tao's inherent integrity continues to nurture that life today.

Interacting with the Flow's many aspects shapes that life and by continuously surviving what it experiences, the life becomes ever stronger.

The Flow of Tao, then, births life, nourishes it, teaches it, strengthens it, reproduces it, and thereby perpetuates it.

And, despite doing all that for the benefit of life on Earth, Tao never expects anything in exchange from any living thing.

It is only with its unwavering determination to continue to exist that each living thing honors Tao for the life it was given.

That is the profound natural integrity of Tao and its Flow, and it provides a role model for sages.

Lao Tzu #52

The Tao and its Flow are the source of all people and things.

Knowing the source, one can understand the people and things.

And knowing the people and things without losing track of the source,

One can understand himself or herself and determine their purpose.

Be thoughtful of the consequences of what you say and do.

While small careless words and actions can have negative consequences,

Small tactful ones will help you move forward.

Focus intently on what you experience and all its implications,

have empathy for the weak and vulnerable,

Don't distract yourself with irrelevancies and unproductive entanglements.

and you will find it easier to follow the Way of Tao.

. . . .

Lao Tzu #53

. . . .

In following the Way of Tao, the greatest danger is that of being led astray.

For, although the Way is usually clearcut, it is often not the most alluring path.

Government buildings are monumental and are often made of the finest marble.

And those who work in them dress in fine clothing and eat and drink the finest fare.

And keep guards by their sides to protect them and their belongings from the common man.

While out in the streets, many have no jobs or homes and must beg for food each day.

But who is it that pays for the buildings, fine clothing, guards, and food and drink?

The commoners begging in the streets! And to me this is thievery, and thievery is not a part of the Way of Tao!

Lao Tzu #54

That which is firmly held will not easily be lost.

That which is strongly built will not easily be broken.

A widespread following of the Way today will benefit many generations to come.

Cultivate the Way in yourself and virtue will emanate outward from you.

Cultivate it in your family and your children's virtue will be passed down to their children.

Cultivate it in your community and its virtue will be noticed and followed by others.

Cultivate it in your country and its virtue will be seen and noted for its joy and prosperity.

Cultivate it in the world and peace, harmony, and prosperity will be boundless for all.

How can that be accomplished?

See others as a part of yourself,

See other families as a part of your family,

See other communities as a part of your community,

And see other countries as a part of one large world family.

That is how!

. . . .

Lao Tzu #55

. . . .

One who follows the Way of Tao can be compared with a new-born child.

No verbal barb can sting him, nor any insult offend him.

He is soft and flexible but still has a firm and sure grip.

He is enthusiastic and quick to learn because his energy is boundless and his focus is clear.

He can stay alert and active all day, nap quickly when tired, and rarely become overly upset or weary.

And it's all because there is little he fears, and because his mind and body are naturally in tune with Tao's Flow.

Those who do not follow the Way of Tao must work too hard to accomplish the things they do.

And are more likely to worry and suffer from stress that might tend to quickly tire and age them.

. . . .

Lao Tzu #56

. . . .

Those who speak, often do not know. Those who know, often do not speak.

The sage is cautious about what he allows into his body,

And thoughtful about what he allows out in the form of words and actions.

He is not arrogant nor selfish, helps others when he can,

And does not knowingly cause needless problems.

He is good-natured, does not have a bitter tongue, and avoids dangerous relationships.

His attitude about all such things could be described as being casually circumspect.

There is no way to become overly intimate with him, but there is no way to shun him.

There is no way to corrupt him, but there is no way to threaten him.

There is no way to exalt him, but there is no way to debase him.

Because of his moral steadfastness, he is valued by those who know him

As a pillar of his community.

Lao Tzu #57

Leaders should devise unexpected and clever strategies against their enemies during conflict,

But they should always be honest, straightforward, and fair with those they lead.

And they should always remain uninvolved in the personal lives of everybody!

How do I know this to be true?

Because the tighter the supervision of a ruler is, the more resentful his people are likely to be.

The more repressed his people feel they are, the more rebellious they are likely to behave.

The more deceitful they must be to do what they want to do, the more deceptive they will be in whatever that is.

And the more numerous the laws are that they must obey, the less respect they are likely to have for any law.

Therefore, the sage ruler says:

I lead subtly and therefore my people are happy!

I am honest and therefore my people are upright.

I don't micromanage and therefore my people are creative.

And I am generous and kind to those I lead,

And therefore, my people are honest and loyal to me!

Lao Tzu #58

When leadership is casual and gentle, those being led tend to concern themselves with their own affairs.

And when it is demanding and strict, those being led will tend to become sneaky and defiant.

But bad fortune is defined by comparison with good fortune.

And good fortune is thought good by comparison to bad.

There are few certain outcomes, and one cannot be sure of anything.

That now thought right often later becomes thought wrong.

And that now thought good often later becomes thought bad.

Such judgements change over time by those who consider them.

Sages therefore just follow the Way at each moment and try to be:

Righteous without being self-righteous,

Honest without being judgmental,

Straightforward without being cruel,

And confident without being arrogant!

Lao Tzu #59

To best interact with the Flow of Tao and achieve one's goals,

A sage must be able to follow the Way of Tao comfortably and efficiently,

And for that to happen best, it is desirable for the sage to learn it at an early age.

For that is when one can most easily learn not to be driven by ego and unvirtuous desires.

And when one is not driven by ego and unvirtuous desires,

He can learn to follow the Way most naturally and achieve oneness with the Tao.

Such a person is quite likely someday to achieve and be entrusted with power,

Because his connection with the Flow has deep roots and a firm foundation.

. . . .

Lao Tzu #60

. . . .

Managing difficult people is like frying small fish – both should be accomplished with quick and careful confidence.

And managing one's personal demons and foolish fears are also much like the fish and difficult people, in that regard.

The sage accepts their presence but pays them little heed when they try to dominate his attention and control his actions.

He knows that his demons and fears by themselves can harm no one and that he, himself, would never do so, either.

And therefore, the demons and fears lose any power they might have once had to make him hesitate or do foolish things.

Sages accept their presence and are polite to them, just as they are to the difficult people, but otherwise give them no credence,

Because then the sage's own personal wisdom, strength, and integrity can always prevail.

. . . .

Lao Tzu #61

. . . .

Powerful people are in some ways like beautiful women.

Both just naturally attract opportunities and interest others.

And both, nonetheless, benefit by remaining humble and pleasant to be with.

All people, whether powerful or beautiful or not, just want to survive, be happy, and achieve their goals.

In the case of the powerful or beautiful, the goals desired are likely to be expansive.

In the case of the not-so-powerful or beautiful, they are likely to be more modest.

In any case, those that are humble and pleasant will be the ones most likely to succeed.

It is just more difficult to remain so for the powerful and the beautiful!

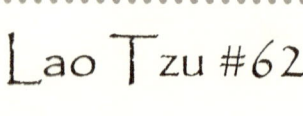

Lao Tzu #62

For its fairness and impartiality, the Tao should be appreciated by all.

Except for its social aspects, it never rewards nor punishes anyone.

The good do not necessarily succeed and the wicked do not necessarily fail.

The benefits of Taoism come from knowing and following it.

The accolades of society are a great reward for talent, effort, and achievement,

And society's punishments can give guidance to those it decides need correction,

But the natural blindness of the rest of Tao to success, failure, and guilt is even more significant.

Through the Way of Tao, both the noble and the less-than-noble can always learn to find peace and redemption.

Lao Tzu #63

Achieve with little effort by sensing and following the Flow of Tao.

Notice the small, detect the few, and do all that you do with virtue.

Achieve difficult things through a series of easier things.

Achieve large things through a series of smaller things.

Because, by not being thwarted by what is large and difficult,

The sage can achieve greatly.

But those who assume tasks will be easy, often face problems that are difficult,

And those who promise things they cannot achieve will rarely thereafter be trusted!

Lao Tzu #64

The mightiest oak began with an acorn.
Every new building starts with a foundation
And the longest journey begins with the very first step.

It is easy to guide what is already going in the proper direction.
It is easy to organize what has not yet become confused.
It is easy to break up that which has not yet coalesced.
And it is easy to quash that which is still small.
Anticipate problems and act before they become entrenched.
Neutralize dissent appropriately before the rebellion begins.

Sages act with the Flow of Tao and therefore never need fight
against it.
They don't try to micro-manage and therefore rarely see their
projects fail.
They see their own visions, choose their own interests, and follow
their own paths.
And once they commit to a project, they follow it
through to its end.

Lao Tzu #65

The Way of Tao is not meant to make one cleverer or to create a more complicated way of thought.

Instead, it is meant to help one live a life of straightforwardness and honest simplicity.

Life becomes unhappy and complex when a continuous need to conceal truth forces one into frequent lies and duplicity.

And such needs for concealed truths and duplicity arise because of past lies, guilt, secret thoughts, and other effects of ego.

A life of honesty and straightforwardness avoids all such fears that new words might not jibe with old words,

Or that a foolish slip of the tongue might reveal awkward truths and create embarrassing moments.

And a life of straightforwardness and simplicity comes as a result of living your life forever following the tenets of Taoist virtue!

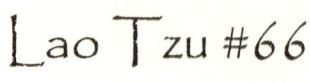

Lao Tzu #66

Because of natural forces, almost everything that is now on land will eventually be eroded from it and into a river, and thereafter someday into a sea.

Like the Tao that it is a part of, water is humble and usually assumes a lowly position at the feet of other things,

And yet, because it inevitably carries everything else away, it can be said that water is the shaper of the land.

The sage notes that it is only because water is usually flexible and humble that it can perform that natural function, and he learns from that.

He learns that if he wants those around him to respect him and his objectives, he must also respect them and their objectives.

And if he wants them to listen to and consider his opinions, he must also listen to them and consider their opinions.

And because he does, people do respect him but do not feel that they must, and do consider his opinions, but know he will also hear theirs.

Therefore, those he is with enjoy his presence and do not tire of him, and because he does not contend with them, they do not contend with him.

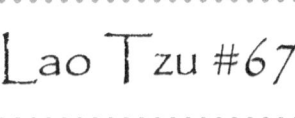

Lao Tzu #67

Some people believe that my understanding of the Tao is too expansive because it includes all that is in the universe,

But it is only because it does include all in the universe that I know it to be the basis of all things and non-things - the Tao!

There are 3 wisdoms inherent to the Way of Tao that the sage knows and values above all others.

The first is compassion, the second is frugality, and the third is humility.

Compassion, because true bravery comes from one valuing the lives and happiness of those he cares about more than he values his own.

Frugality, because true generosity requires that gifts given to others have value to the one who is giving them, and

Humility, because only those who are humble are likely to value and respect the knowledge and opinions of others.

And if you value your own life and happiness more than you value that of others and try to be brave; if you try to be generous when you don't even value the gifts you are giving; and if you try to achieve worthwhile things without accepting the knowledge and opinions of others,

Then you are likely to fail at them all!

With compassion, frugality, and humility, you will be more likely to win when asserting and to stand firm when defending!

. . . .

Lao Tzu #68

. . . .

Experienced fighters always remain calm and bold.

Confident fighters feel no need to bully or brag.

Clever fighters try tact and diplomacy to solve problems before resorting to battle.

The cleverest fighters will find a way to succeed without any need for battle, at all.

And profoundly clever fighters will remain humble and magnanimous even upon victory.

For there should be strategy even in victory and it is always helpful to heal wounds and defuse anger.

Lao Tzu #69

Military strategists agree that it is better to be known as the innocent victim than as the initial aggressor,

And, as the one negotiating reasonably rather than the one making outrageous demands.

For, having those be true is like winning the first battle without having to fight a first battle at all.

So, work for peace, encourage coordination rather than confrontation, and cause no neighbor to feel threatened.

But also, don't underestimate a rival or allow one to overpower you, because that is the fastest route to disaster and to the loss of your freedom.

And then, should battle nevertheless need be fought, you, as the innocent, honorable, but well prepared victim, will have the advantage.

Lao Tzu #70

Taoism is based on ancient knowledge long known to be true.

Its teachings are easy to learn and not too difficult to follow,

But Taoism requires self-discipline because the Tao does not automatically reward nor punish,

And the Way of Tao is not always the most alluring path to follow.

Believers are sometimes ridiculed by the ignorant and feel no need to proselytize.

So, sages assume the demeanor of everyman and hold the jewel of their beliefs firmly within their hearts!

Lao Tzu #71

It is best to recognize and admit when there is something you do not know.

To not know but think or claim you know is a personal failing.

And only when one recognizes his personal failings can he overcome them.

Sages dedicate themselves to seeing and overcoming such personal failings.

And, because they do, despite the failings, they become almost flawless!

What more could anyone do?

Lao Tzu #72

When citizens lose patience with those in power, disaster can result for everyone.

Leave people alone in their private lives!

Allow them to work, earn a living, and improve themselves!

If you do not oppress your people, they will be happy, and will remain loyal to you!

When sages attain positions of authority:

They follow the Way of Tao, but do not try to force Taoism on those below them,

They practice compassion, frugality, and humility, and therefore can be confident in the things they do,

And they avoid micro-management by only hiring people they can trust, and then by trusting those people to do what they were hired to do!

Lao Tzu #73

The bold but prepared will usually succeed at whatever they do.

The bold and reckless will usually struggle just to stay alive.

The first usually spread benefit, while the second usually spread disaster.

The recklessly bold seem almost an offense to Tao because of their foolishness.

The Flow of Tao, itself:

Never contends and yet always succeeds at winning.

Rarely speaks and yet always provides the proper response.

Is always wherever it needs to be without having to be summoned.

And never hurries but always does what needs to be done at the perfect moment.

The heavenly net is vast and loosely woven, and yet nothing ever slips through it!

In a society where the fear of death is only one of many dire concerns for most people,

Execution will not be an effective deterrent!

While in a society where most people love and enjoy their lives and therefore wish to live,

It will be!

But in all societies, the most desirable executioner is the natural Flow of Tao,

Because any person assuming that role would be like a small child using an axe to fell a tree.

It is most likely that he would damage himself at least as much as his target.

Lao Tzu #75

One reason many citizens must struggle to feed themselves and their families is because of the high taxes their governments require them to pay.

Because of those taxes, those citizens are forever poor and unruly!

One reason many citizens find it hard to get ahead and make better lives for themselves is because of the many onerous rules their governments have imposed upon them.

Because of all those rules, those citizens are oppressed!

Many citizens, because of taxes and oppression, have little chance to enjoy life or create better futures for themselves.

While those who govern them, on the other hand, spend their time enjoying the wealth and power they have usurped.

But those who must remain so focused on daily survival that they have little time to enjoy life or consider their futures,

Are superior in many ways to those who sit back enjoying their power and luxuries, and valuing themselves and their futures too highly!

Lao Tzu #76

Most living things are yielding and flexible when young and become hard and brittle near death.

Thus, being yielding and flexible is usually more desirable than being hard and brittle.

For example, the hard and brittle old tree is more likely to break from the wind of a storm than is the yielding and flexible sapling,

And the large, staid, and entrenched army is quite likely to lose to the bold, flexible, smaller one.

Therefore, when accomplishing his objectives, the sage always tries to avoid being hard and rigid and instead aspires to be bold, yielding, and flexible!

Lao Tzu #77

The natural balance inherent to the Flow of Tao is like an archer engaged in stringing his bow:

That which is too tall is brought down lower and that which is too short is stretched out longer.

With the Tao in general:

That which is excessive will, at some point, be reduced.

That which is deficient will, at some point, be added to.

And should something disappear completely, another somewhat similar is likely to rise to take its place.

The way of many people is quite different.

It is common for the rich and powerful to take from the poor and weak.

And for people to buy when things are popular and expensive,

And then sell when things are old and have lost their value.

But the sage tries to emulate the Tao and looks for and encourages balance.

He supplements deficiencies, fights injustice with justice, and avoids contributing to excess,

He donates his extra money to the poor and needy, and his extra time to fight the power of oppressors.

. . . .

Lao Tzu #78

. . . .

There is nothing that is softer or more yielding than water,

And yet for moving and shaping the Earth, there is nothing that is more effective.

So, we know that the weak can overcome the strong, and the flexible overcome the rigid.

"It is often only a matter of time, patience, and perseverance—and for people, of thought.

But how can one put those realities into practice in his own life?

The sage says:

He who is known to have endured unfair humiliation by the state, can by those means master the state,

And he who is known to have endured unfair persecution by the state, can by those means conquer the world.

The Way of Tao can sometimes seem counter-intuitive!

. . . .

Lao Tzu #79

. . . .

When negotiations between rivals grow bitter, resentment is likely to persist even after an agreement is reached, and that is undesirable.

Therefore, the sage prefers to position himself as the negotiator with only reasonable expectations of his opponent.

Because those who are being reasonable are those in charge of the negotiations, while those who aren't are only in charge of demands.

And, while the Flow of Tao never automatically favors one individual over another, it does usually seem to somehow favor the fair and virtuous over the selfish and unreasonable!

(#80 and #81 have purposely been misordered)

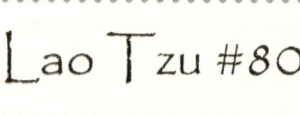

Lao Tzu #80

Sincerity does not necessarily come in the form of eloquence, and eloquence does not necessarily denote sincerity.

Experience does not come from reading books, and words in books cannot give one experience.

The best of people do not amass wealth just to possess it, and one who amasses wealth just to possess it is not among the best of people.

The sage does not amass wealth just for the purpose of possessing it.

After doing much of what he has done for the benefit of others, he finds that he is the one who has benefitted the most.

And after giving all that he doesn't need to those who need it more, he finds that he has all that he could ever desire.

The Way of Tao is to create benefit for all without causing harm to any and to encourage everyone to be the best they can be by being a role model to all.

(#80 and #81 have purposely been misordered)

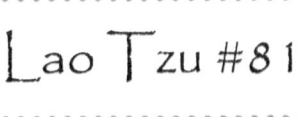

Lao Tzu #81

May the world someday be covered with intimate little countries that are not overcrowded.

I would have every citizen of every country be armed if they wished and know how to use their weapons, although I would hope that none ever felt the need to do so.

And I would have the citizens of every country be happy in their lives and with their families and have them be proud of themselves and their communities.

I would want all to have the freedom and ability to travel and explore but would never want any to feel the need to escape to somewhere safer or more prosperous.

I would want everyone to be able to work in a pleasantly challenging but stress-free job and to have it be relatively easy to feed one's family and to fulfill their basic needs and goals.

And finally, I would want everyone to be able to live in a secure and comfortable home situated in a safe and friendly community located on a healthy and thriving planet.

And may all these ideal countries I dream of communicate and trade peacefully with each other without ever coveting or trying to steal each other's resources.

I would expect each country, like it's citizens, to be able to defend itself so that no other would ever presume to dominate or subjugate it.

And if all my dreams were ever to come true, every person everywhere would be able to live a long, healthy, and happy life without ever needing to engage in violence with any other!

Words of Wisdom Attributed to Lao Tzu

Knowing and improving yourself:
- Understanding others is smart; also understanding yourself is wise.
- He who conquers others is strong; he who conquers himself is mighty.
- Dedicate yourself to your misfortunes and you will eventually become one with misfortune; dedicate yourself to virtue and you will eventually become one with virtue.
- Well justified confidence is the best barrier against unexpected disaster.
- No sage sees weapons as things of beauty, for one who does must therefore see beauty in death.
- It is what you achieve, not what you attain, that is important.

Life as a part of Tao:
- Change is the only constant. Accept it. Work with it. Go with its Flow!
- Even a journey of a thousand miles begins with the very first step.
- Action creates heat while inaction cools. Accept what is and go forth to achieve!
- The Way of Tao is usually clearcut but is not always the most alluring path.
- If you want something from it, first you must often give something to it.
- Yield things in order to gain things; bend so that you will not need to break.

- The best travelers leave no ugly traces of their journey behind them.
- It is the example and not the words that matter most.
- The Way of Tao is the answer to every question.
- That which is firmly held will not easily be lost; that which is strongly built will not easily be broken.
- Achieve difficult things through a series of easier things; Achieve big things through a series of smaller things.
- The Flow of Tao is never in any hurry but always does what needs to be done at the perfect moment.

Interactions with others:
- Anyone willing to compromise his values to please his ego cannot be trusted.
- When the best leader's work is done, the people all stand back and yell, "Hooray, we did it!"
- Those who speak, often do not know; those who know, often do not speak.
- Only those who love the world and others in it more than they love themselves should ever be entrusted with power.
- Bullies and tyrants never live joyous lives nor die peaceful deaths.
- Whenever he can, the sage honors peace, but when he must fight, then he must honor victory.
- With the best of leaders, followers hardly even know they are being led.
- Measure your words, say only that which is helpful, and then say what needs to be said with authority.
- Those who hold themselves above others will soon naturally fall.
- If all the leaders of all the lands were faithful followers of the Way, their people would comfortably follow them any-

where they led, and the Flow of Tao would usually favor us all with good fortune.

- Of crimes, none is potentially greater than powerful leaders pursuing selfish ambitions.
- Those who promise things they cannot achieve will rarely thereafter be trusted,
- Sincerity does not come in the form of flowery words, and flowery words do not denote sincerity.
- I would have every citizen be armed if they wished and know how to use their weapons, but I would hope that none ever felt the need to do so.

4

The Book of Chuang Tzu

Chuang Tzu

Of the three Taoist classic authors, Chuang Tzu has the highest likelihood of having actually existed as a specific historical individual and of having also been responsible for at least most of the writings passed down in the book we now associate with him. In *Records of the Great Historian*, Sima Qian noted that Chuang Tzu's birth name was Chuang Chou and that he was born in the town of Meng, believed to have been in what is now Anhui Province. The references of Sima Qian also provide us with associations that have allowed experts to determine that Chuang Tzu probably lived from about 369 to 286 BCE.

That period, you will remember, was the Warring States Era in China when Taoist-based philosophies of many kinds were being formalized and popularized. Most of the teachers of those philosophies were sponsored by rulers of the various states in China, and their teachings were centered around different forms and styles of government that might interest those rulers. Chuang Tzu was definitely not one of those writers. According to Sima Qian, Chuang worked during part of his life as a minor official in the state of Song, but his philosophical teachings were not developed and spread for the sake of a salary. Instead, being a well-known Taoist sage, it was done as a work of personal interest.

Chuang Tzu had no desire to work for rulers at all, as pointed out frequently in his book. He was, it's evident, a bit of a hermit and a rebel. He saw rulers not as patrons but more as one of the serious problems in life. He was, in fact, antagonistic toward bureaucrats, petty officials, and the mechanisms of government in general. Chuang believed in the right of individuals to find their own place in the natural order, and he generally disliked anything that directed or controlled the human spirit or separated it from that natural order. In fact, he was opposed to anything that sought to pervert the natural flow of any aspect of Tao.

And even though Chuang Tzu wasn't sponsored by the ruler of any kingdom, his writings and philosophy were widely read and dispersed. Sima Qian comments that Chuang Tzu's teachings spread over the region like a tidal wave that could not be stopped. Its popularity might have been despite the fact that it was so revolutionary, controversial, and subversive, or it might well have been because it did have those characteristics. There is no way today to know.

Another factor in his success, not just during his lifetime but through the subsequent centuries, has been his compelling writing style. Chuang Tzu refused to take the aggressiveness, ambition, and self-importance normally needed to compete successfully in society very seriously, and he drove that message home through his use of clever, humorous, and enigmatic tales, stories, and amusing discussions told in ironic ways, often using birds, fish, frogs, and other strange characters with funny names as important characters in his stories. His techniques resulted in a sparkling, dashing style that has always made his book entertaining and easy to read.

And though he was a social critic, his criticism never comes across as being bitter or harsh. Irony and parable are his chief tools, and the mood set by the stories in his book is one of tolerant impartiality that avoids preaching or being dogmatic. He never sets himself apart from his readers. He may be the person telling the tales, but other than that he comes across as just another guy!

The philosophy of Chuang Tzu not only had a strong impact on philosophical thought during his lifetime, but it has also continued to do so all the way through to the present. When the Buddhist religion became established in China in the first few centuries CE, for example, it transformed Chinese culture and philosophy, but Taoism, including Chuang Tzu's perspective on it, transformed Buddhism right back. The blended combination of the two very different views of the universe evolved into what is now called Zen Buddhism.

Chuang Tzu has simply turned out to be one of the greatest innovators of human thought of all time. Anyone who comes to understand his philosophy and then considers it in the light of modern society will realize that it is at least as relevant and compelling today as it was when he originally developed it more than twenty-three hundred years ago. Perhaps even more so.

The Book of Chuang Tzu, as commonly passed down to us today, consists of thirty-three chapters that have long been grouped into three sections, but there is no rational explanation for the three sections that bears any scrutiny, and the thirty-three chapters do not define parts of any progressive story that leads the reader to any specific logical conclusion. Each is simply a collection of stories, tales, and dialogues teaching Taoist principles and beliefs, loosely tied together with somewhat rambling tidbits of ancient Chinese legend, discussions of historical figures from long ago and their genealogies, and understandings of the world that people held at the time. *The Book of Chuang Tzu* is definitely a collection of concepts, not a developing argument.

And as with the other two Taoist classics, there is also some controversy as to who actually wrote various parts of the *Book of Chuang Tzu*. In general, it's agreed that Chuang Tzu, himself, probably wrote most of it, but it's also generally accepted that his students probably wrote some of it as well—perhaps after his death in order to reflect additional experiences they had with him. Indeed, some of the tales in Chuang Tzu's book are about him rather than being written from his perspective. There is little doubt that as the book was rewritten repeatedly through the centuries, there have been many modest (and perhaps sometimes not so modest) modifications made to it.

One likely source of such modification is thought to have occurred in the fourth century CE by a man named Kuo Hsiang. It's believed that Kuo reduced the book from its original fifty or so chapters to its present thirty-three, and that he then grouped those chapters into the three sections that the book is commonly divided into today. It's believed that he probably made various other editing changes as well.

And since there is nothing compelling about preserving the exact structure of "*The Chuang Tzu*" including the three sections and thirty-three chapters, or in preserving the rambling non-Taoist tidbits between relevant stories, lessons, and beliefs, and since my focus throughout this book is always that of presenting the ancient Taoist philosophy in a manner most instructive to the modern reader, I have taken the liberty of separating out and presenting only 48 stories and passages from the book that I think my readers will most benefit from in their quest to understand Taoism, while eliminating all that is not relevant to that goal and that I think would only bore them. In doing so I have been careful to present Chuang Tzu's most compelling Taoist material as accurately and faithfully as possible and of changing little else other than to make the writing style a little more modern and comfortable to absorb for the modern reader!

Chuang Tzu #1

The understanding of those that are small is different than the understanding of those that are big, and the understanding of the short-lived is different than that of the long-lived.

How do I know this is true?

Because no ant can ever know the countryside that the camel sees on its journeys and the flea only knows a small part of the dog it lives on.

The morning mushroom can never know about the waxing and waning of the moon, and no cicada ever experiences three of the four seasons in a year.

How much, then, can even the oldest and wisest sage ever come to truly know of the infinite Tao?

Chuang Tzu #2

Hui Tzu was talking with Chuang Tzu and said, "I received some seeds from a friend of mine for an unusual sort of gourd, and the plant grew to an enormous size in my garden. Much of the fruit was big enough to hold ten or twenty gallons after being hollowed out. I was going to use the gourds to hold water, but they turned out to be too heavy when full to even pick up, so I tried cutting them up and using the pieces for various other things, but nothing really seemed to work very well, so I ended up just throwing them all away."

Chuang Tzu listened to his friend's story and then responded by telling Hui of a family he had once known in another region. The family had made their living by bleaching silk for many generations. Doing so was very hard on the skin of the hands, so one of their ancestors had created a special hand cream that was very effective at moisturizing the skin and protecting it from the bleach they used. The family had made and used that hand cream for many generations in their work.

One day, a local merchant who had heard about the hand cream came to visit and offered the family a hundred pieces of gold for the formula used to make it. That was far more money than the family had ever earned by bleaching silk, so they readily agreed.

At that time it was winter, and the king of Wu was at war with the country of Yueh. The cold, wet weather was causing the soldiers of both armies to have hands so badly chapped and cracked that they could barely wield their weapons in battle, so the merchant went to the king and offered to make enough of his marvelous new hand cream for the army of Wu to use for the rest of the winter at a very reasonable price. Partially, perhaps, as a result of its use, the army of Wu ended up winning the war soon afterward, and the merchant was rewarded for his help with the gift of a vast estate in the newly conquered territory.

The hand cream had done nothing more than prevent hands from being chapped for both the family of silk bleachers and for the merchant, but in the one case it resulted in nothing more than personal comfort for the family and in the other it resulted in the gain of an invaluable estate.

"So, sir," concluded Chuang Tzu to Hui Tzu, "perhaps the problem with the gigantic gourds you grew was not so much a deficiency of the gourds themselves as it was a deficiency of your imagination in determining how they might best be used!"

Chuang Tzu #3

Hui Tzu was talking to Chuang Tzu and said, "I have a big tree on my property that is totally useless. Its trunk is so knotted and its branches so twisted that, even though it's not far from the road, no carpenter will ever even bother to look at it. Your teachings are much like my tree—too big and of no real use, and therefore everyone just ignores them."

Chuang Tzu responded, "Have you ever watched a fox? Foxes are agile and quick. When catching prey, they crouch and then leap this way and that, high and low, and then just like your teachings, they usually just end up falling into a trap.

"On the other hand, have you ever seen a yak? As vast as a thundercloud Yaks stand, solid in all their might. Sure, yaks are useless for catching mice, but who with any sense would ever expect a yak to catch mice anyway?

"And, as for your tree, does no one ever stroll idly by it marveling at its age and durability? Does no one ever rest comfortably in its shade on a hot summer afternoon? It's good that no one has any desire to chop it down and cut it up. It will probably continue to stand there for a long, long time!"

Chuang Tzu #4

Contentment and anger,

Sadness and joy,

Hope and disappointment,

Doubt and certainty,

Force and submission,

Eagerness and fear!

Each word just sounds like wind rushing across the mouth of an empty jar.

Or more, perhaps, like mushrooms popping up in damp soil.

The Earth turns and we have night and day.

Why? Why? Enough! Enough!

We have what we call night and what we call day!

Who needs to know more than that?

I can't know the reason for everything!

Chuang Tzu #5

When we are born into this world, we each have one life to live from that beginning until our life's inevitable end.

Sometimes conflicting with others and sometimes in harmony, our one life seems to gallop past like a runaway horse.

We each struggle to survive and raise our family and yet earn little rest or relaxation in return along the way.

We try to achieve worthwhile things and do what is right, but things often go awry, and we rarely receive much joy or appreciation for all that we do.

Oh sure, we may look up occasionally and think with joy to ourselves, "I'm alive, I'm alive!" but so what? What does it matter?

And then, in the end, when our bodies wear out and die, so too do our minds, memories, and all the hard-won lessons we have learned.

It really seems quite tragic, and when I stop and think about it, rather ridiculous! Or is it only me being ridiculous, and that is just the Flow of Tao?

Chuang Tzu #6

There is nothing that is not "this" when it is near to me and "that" when it is far away.

Therefore "that" arises from the concept of "this," and "this" arises from the concept of "that."

Each means nothing at all except in its relationship to the other.

Compare "life" with "death" and "death" with "life," or "possible" with "impossible" and "impossible" with "possible."

Only because there is a "there is" can there be a "there isn't" and only because there is a "there isn't" can there be a "there is."

The sage tries to recognize the entire range of such concepts together as a whole. "This" becomes a part of "that" and "that" becomes a part of "this."

The pivot point is at the center, and the range extends in either direction from there.

When "this" and "that" no longer stand against each other, the light of the Way shines just a little brighter.

Chuang Tzu #7

A monkey trainer was reviewing his accounts one evening and decided that he was spending too much money on food for his monkeys. And since he had noticed that they were becoming too pudgy anyway, he decided to cut back on the number of treats he was giving each one with its meals. So, early the next morning, he mentioned the situation to his monkeys and announced that from then on he would give each one three acorns in the mornings and four in the evenings along with their meals instead of the eight per day they had been getting.

As he had known they would, the monkeys became very upset. They wailed and chattered and banged on the sides of their cages, and so after a while the trainer pretended to relent. He sighed loudly and said, "All right, all right. I don't want you to be unhappy, so instead of giving each of you three acorns in the morning, I'll give you four, and then in the evenings, I'll give each of you another three. The monkeys were delighted by this "concession!" They happily ate their four morning acorns and were soon playing and frolicking just as they always had.

The two different meal plans were essentially the same, but by means of his clever strategy, the trainer achieved a solution that fulfilled his needs with minimal turmoil and unhappiness for the monkeys. His strategy is called "walking two roads to reach a destination," and it is a strategy a sage might consider whenever he must do something unpopular to achieve a worthwhile goal.

Chuang Tzu #8

One night I, Chuang Tzu, dreamed I was a butterfly flitting around in a beautiful garden, traveling back and forth from flower to flower, and thoroughly enjoying myself. I had no idea at the time that I was Chuang Tzu. Then I woke up in the morning, and I was Chuang Tzu again. But it occurred to me then that I had no way of knowing for sure which way it really was. Was I Chuang Tzu remembering a dream in the night of being a butterfly, or was I actually still a butterfly now dreaming that I was Chuang Tzu?

Chuang Tzu #9

Cook Ting was butchering an ox for Lord Wen Hui. Every movement of his hand, every shrug of his shoulder, every step of his feet, every thrust of his knee, every sound of the sundering flesh, and every swoosh of the descending knife were in perfect harmony, like the Mulberry Grove Dance or the rhythm of the Ching-Shan.

"Ah, how excellent," said Lord Wen Hui, watching him work. "How did you ever develop such superb skill?"

Cook Ting put down his knife and said, "What I, your servant, love best is the Way, which is better than any specific skill. When

I started cutting up oxen, what I saw at first was just the ox in front of me. After three years, I learned not to see the ox as one whole thing but instead as the parts it would soon become. Now I practice with my mind, not with my eyes. I ignore my senses and follow my spirit. I see the natural lines and my knife slides through the hollows, follows the cavities, using what is there to my advantage. Thus, I miss tough sinews and even more important, the hard bones.

"An ordinary cook must change his knife every month because he hacks through the meat. A good cook changes his knife annually, because he slices. The knife I now have, I have been using for nineteen years. It has cut up thousands of oxen, but its blade is as sharp now as it was when it was still brand new.

"Between the joints there are tiny spaces, but the blade of the knife has no real thickness at all, and if you put what has no thickness in those tiny spaces, there is plenty of room, certainly enough for the blade to work through. But when I do come to a difficult part and can tell that it will be difficult, I take care and pay due regard. I look carefully, and I move with caution. Then, very gently, I move the knife until there is a parting, and the flesh falls apart like a layer of snow sliding off a warming roof. Then I feel a moment of pride in my accomplishment, wash and dry my knife, and put it away until the next time I need it."

"Splendid!" said Lord Wen Hui. "I have heard Cook Ting explain his art, and from his words I have also learned how to live my life better."

Chuang Tzu #10

Soon after Lao Tzu's death, Chin Shih visited his home to pay his respects. He walked through the door, looked around the room, grunted three times, and then turned around and walked right back out again. A student of Lao Tzu who was in the room with other mourners and who had seen him come in, rushed out after him and asked, "Wasn't Lao Tzu a friend of yours?"

"Of course he was," Chin Shih responded.

"Then why didn't you stay and mourn with us?" the student asked.

"When I walked into the room, there were old folks weeping as if they had lost a child and there were young people wailing as if they had lost a parent. Everyone was talking even though Lao Tzu would not have wanted them to talk and weeping even though Lao Tzu would not have wanted them to weep. Engaging in such behaviors is disrespecting the natural Flow of Tao and disregarding the wonder of the life that was given to him.

"When the master was born, it was because it was his time to be born, and when he died, it was because it was his time to die. His life came and went just as it was meant to do. When people just accept what is meant to be, then sorrow like that being displayed in Lao Tzu's house right now need never even touch them!"

Chuang Tzu #11

Duke Ai of Lu said to Confucius, "In Wei there was a man with a horrible appearance by the name of Hi Taito. Despite his ugliness, all who knew him thought the world of him and even the most beautiful women who knew him loved to be in his company. He knew little about the world beyond the edges of his town and was never known to take the lead in anything, but he was always in accord with others, and they all seemed to flock to him.

"It was clear that he was different from other people, so even though he was ugly enough to frighten the entire world, I asked him to come and visit. He had only been there for about a month when I began to really appreciate him. After a year, I had come to trust him completely. I came to have such high regard for him that I even let him help me run the government.

"But eventually he chose to leave, and now I've heard that he has moved back to Wei, where he came from. Frankly, his departure saddened me, and I took it as a great loss. I no longer had anyone to share the cares of the state with. What a strange kind of man he is!"

Confucius listened and then replied, "The outer body is just a shell, and as with a nut, its appearance of no great importance. It is what's inside the shell that one will come to love or not after he or she has gotten to know it."

Chuang Tzu #12

Nan Po Tzu and Nu Chu were discussing former students, and Nu Chu said, "And then there was Pu Liang Yi, who had the genius of a sage but had never studied the Tao before, at all. I taught him for the first several days to ignore all worldly matters. Having dispensed with all worldly matters, it took him another week or so to be able to ignore all other external things. Having disposed of all other external things, it took him yet another week to recognize the irrelevance of his own self. Having finally discerned the irrelevance of his own self, he was able to see with true clarity. Being able to see with true clarity, he could cancel out all he had ever believed about his own place in both the past and the future and having canceled out all he had ever believed about his place in both the past and the future, he was able to enter the state where his own birth and eventual death were also both completely irrelevant. He could then follow anything without emotional attachment, and he could observe anything without emotional judgement. For him all in the world was comfortably being destroyed second by second at the same time it was also comfortably being rebuilt. That is known as 'tranquility in change,' and 'tranquility in change' is the perfect starting point for learning the Way!"

Chuang Tzu #13

Two students of Tao met each other for the first time and discussed the challenges they had encountered in following the Way. They agreed that to be successful one needed to forget any emotional associations he or she had formed from events in their past and also needed to avoid allowing emotional associations to influence plans they might make for the future. They agreed that one needed to eliminate his or her ego as much as possible and all emotions associated with it, and that he or she needed to recognize that life and death along with being and nonbeing were all really the same. The two students also agreed that if they could keep their minds empty of all those things, if they could allow themselves to be guided in life by their instincts more than by their intellect, and if they could also live happily from day to day without worrying about what the future might bring, they could be successful at following the Way. And by virtue of their mutual understanding of Taoism, they became close friends.

Many years later, one of the two became sick with a horribly debilitating disease and the other dropped by to visit him. "How interesting the Flow of Tao is!" the sick one said to the other. "My back is now the back of a hunchback, my internal organs are now almost as high as my head, and my chin is at the same level as my navel. My shoulders look down on the back of my neck, and my topknot now points directly up toward the sky." And with that he limped over to a nearby garden pond and looked at his reflection. "The Flow of Tao has made me completely deformed!" he exclaimed with awe.

"Does that upset you?" his friend asked.

"Not really" was the reply. "Perhaps my left arm will soon become a rooster and I will be able to warn everyone of the dawn. Perhaps my right arm will become a crossbow and I will be able to shoot birds out of the sky to feed my family and friends. Perhaps my buttocks will become wheels and my arms a horse so that I can be a chariot and drive myself around town.

"I was born because the time was right for me to be born and I will die when the time is right for me to die. In the meanwhile, I am what I am. Those who are content with whatever the Flow of Tao happens to bring them can avoid both joy and sorrow and accept whatever occurs. Nothing can change fate, so why should I allow the realities I face from day to day to upset me?"

Chuang Tzu #14

Do not do what you do for fortune, power, or fame, and do not make intricate plans for distant futures.

Do what you do because you enjoy it and find it valuable, and then do it as well as you possibly can.

When you want to accomplish big things, break them down into little things and then accomplish those little things one at a time.

Do not try to know everything about everything and don't assume to know things that you don't for sure know.

Focus on doing what you are doing in the here and now and assign whatever that is the highest possible priority.

Consider and use the Flow of Tao as best you can to accomplish what you do, but never assume that it will go where you expect it to go.

And empty your mind of all considerations of self and of all the emotions that considerations of self bring with them.

The sage's heart is like a mirror reflecting the world in front of it exactly.

It does not look for things.

It does not assume things to be there that might not be.

And it does not react emotionally to that it sees.

The sage's heart just observes what is there and responds appropriately to it.

And as a result, the sage can handle everything and be little harmed by anything.

Chuang Tzu #15

The emperor of the North Sea was known as Dramatic, and the emperor of the South Sea was known as Change. The land between the two was called Chaos, and it was ruled by a king called Justice. Dramatic and Change were very good friends and they liked to meet and enjoy each other's company, and so they often got together in the land of Chaos to do so.

In those days, Chaos was a pleasant country and was well run by its king, and Justice always treated them well whenever they were visiting, and so Dramatic and Change decided to give him a valuable gift of appreciation. They had noticed that everyone else had seven orifices in order to eat, hear, breathe, eliminate wastes, and such, but that Justice had none at all. "Let us bore some holes in him so he can have orifices, too!" they decided. And so, the very next time they visited Chaos, they proceeded to drill one hole in Justice each day, but on the seventh day Justice died, and because of that, Chaos came to be the way it is today!

Chuang Tzu #16

One who is following the Way of Tao should not try to change his or her personal nature.

Each person has strengths, each has weaknesses, and each has a unique personality.

Enjoy the personality you have, maximize your strengths, and minimize your weaknesses.

But always accept and appreciate yourself for exactly who you are!

That which is ideal within you is fine and that which is not ideal within you is fine as well.

That which is short is not too short, and that which is long is not too long.

A duck's legs are certainly short, but it would not benefit a duck to lengthen them.

A heron's legs are quite long, but to shorten them would only cause the bird pain.

That which the Flow of Tao has made unique within us is a gift; using it to one's benefit is the Way!

Chuang Tzu #17

Wild horses living on open prairies are marvelous creatures to watch. They buck and prance and chase each other here and there with a joy that is hard to even imagine. They fight and frolic and mate with whoever they choose.

At one time, all horses were wild like that, and all were able to live lives in accordance with their innate natures. Then the population of people burgeoned, and humankind spread over most of those open prairies. They fenced and farmed the land, and they took control over most of the horses.

One day, a man named Po Lo went to the emperor and said to him, "I have learned how to train horses, and when they are trained, they can be useful to us," and so the emperor gave him control over all the horses. Po Lo shaped the horse's hooves with files and trimmed their manes and tails. He branded them, put halters on their heads, bridled them, hobbled them, shut them up in stables, and trained the horses to do all sorts of work so that people would not have to do it. Some of the horses died because they couldn't live under such conditions, but others finally adapted to their new lives.

Then, as part of their training, Po Lo began to control how much the horses ate and drank. He chose which mare could breed with which stallion. He raced the horses and paraded them. He taught them from the front to fear the bit and from the rear to fear the whip. Even more horses died, but the rest eventually submitted to the training.

In the very early days, when there were fewer people in the land, when the ground was still covered by thick forests and fertile fields, and when horses were still wild and untrained, there was no emperor over all the people, no kings, governors, armies, police, or tax collectors. People lived in tribes or small communities and leaders were chosen by the people to lead because of their wisdom, practical knowledge, and social skills. No leader would ever even try to control or manipulate those he led, especially not by using force, because if he did, he would simply be replaced by someone who was less of a problem. In those early days, people, like horses, were still able to live joyful lives in accordance with their natural instincts!

. . . .

Chuang Tzu #18

. . . .

Confucius came to visit Robber Chih one day to try to convince him to stop ravaging nearby villages and farms with his gang of thieves and to give up his life of crime. But Chih had become very rich and powerful by terrorizing the region and had no interest at all in changing. He was also in a horrible mood on that particular day and was not at all impressed by Confucius or his ideas. Soon the conversation came around to the topic of the Tao.

"I know something of your Tao," Chih said, with steel in his voice. "As a thief, before each raid I must determine what's worth stealing and how to do it without being caught by the king's soldiers.

That shows great intelligence. My courage is demonstrated by my willingness to take the risks I must take each day to do what I do. My benevolence is shown by the way in which I divide up the spoils of our raids fairly among my men, and my righteousness by the fact that I always make a point to be the last one to leave the place at the end of each raid. Without those four attributes, no one in the world could become as great a thief as I am, and therefore I am a sage of the Tao of thieves!"

"It is true that there is only one Tao and that we all live within its vast flow," Confucius responded, "and it is also true that you are very clever in your understanding and use of that part of the flow related to your thievery. And each person must find his or her own path to follow, so you may certainly say that you are a master of the Tao of thieves, but the Way of Tao of sages is far more demanding than that! Our goal is always to emulate the Tao itself. The Tao provides all that is ever needed and asks for nothing in return. It always does what it does because that is the next best thing to do based on all that has gone before.

"A sage of the Way of Tao emulates its Flow and melds with it. He works within it to earn what he needs in order to support himself and his family and to accomplish all his worthwhile goals. Like the Flow of Tao itself, he does not do what he does for the sake of wealth, power, or fame, as you do. But if those things should come to him as a result of what he does, they simply become tools for him to do additional worthwhile things.

"We each alter the Flow of Tao somewhat just because of our very existence, but the sage of Tao does what he does whenever he can gently and with care as to its consequences on others. You, on the other hand, slash and burn and destroy lives with no consideration of anything other than your own desires. And because of the harsh way with which you treat the Flow of Tao, your own life is not likely to last long, either. You may be a master of the Tao of thieves, but you are not a sage of the Way of Tao!"

And with that, Confucius bowed twice and turned and left, wondering as he did so if he would make it away before Robber Chih decided to have him killed and his liver added to the pile of fresh human livers Chih had said was to be cooked for that evening's meal.

Chuang Tzu #19

Long ago in the state of Chi, many small towns and villages were so close together that the dogs and roosters could call out to each other from one town to another. Fishermen cast their nets in the rivers and farmers plowed their fields. Throughout the thousands of square miles within Chi's borders, ancestral temples had been built and were being well maintained, and there were many shrines scattered here and there to honor the land and crops. The state itself and the town and villages within it were all well governed and prosperous, and happiness and wisdom seemed to prevail throughout the land.

Then one day Lord Tien Cheng and a few of his allies in the army took over the country. They killed the king, all of his sons, and anyone else who resisted them. They banished other members of the royal family. They took ownership of the king's palace and all his other possessions. They took control of the kingdom's treasury and all the country's tax collectors. And they took control of all the people of the nation because they had control of its laws and its army.

All the world knew that Lord Tien Cheng was a thief, murderer, and usurper, but what could anyone do? The citizens could do nothing because he controlled the laws and the army, and neighboring states could do nothing because Chi was still powerful and because it was not really any of their business, anyway.

For twelve generations, Lord Tien Cheng's descendants ruled the state of Chi. They formed alliances with some neighboring states and fought wars with others. Famous sages visited the palace to discuss the Tao and to teach virtue to the royal children. Benevolence and righteousness were professed at the palace gates, and each generation of rulers judiciously enforced the kingdom's laws so that any criminal who was caught or convicted of committing any serious crime could be put in prison or executed. And the Tao flowed on.

Chuang Tzu #20

To guard against thieves when one travels, a person should make sure that his or her luggage is always securely locked. Everyone knows that to be wise, but if a clever thief has the opportunity, he can simply grab the bags and run off with them, and then figure out how to open them somewhere else afterward. His greatest concern is likely to be that the straps and locks on the bags might break before he can get away from the scene of the crime! No matter how hard we try to prevent it, it seems, some people with an inclination to thievery will always figure out a way to steal!

Create a system of standard weights and measures to gauge things by, and some people will steal by cheating with the weights and measures. Require accurate scales for merchants to measure their product with, and some merchants will cheat by controlling the readings of their scales. Require formal written documents to record legal business agreements and some people will steal by altering the documents recording the agreements. Create a system of laws and regulations to prevent some from taking advantage of others, and a few will somehow pervert those laws so they can take advantage of the others anyway. Those with an inclination to thievery always seem to be able to find a way to do it.

Often, it seems, the harder we try to make it difficult for thieves to steal, the more the changes we make turn out to be to the advantage of the cleverest thieves anyway. A common thief who breaks into a house to steal a bauble or trinket, for example, is likely to be hanged if he gets caught, but a merchant with his finger on the scale is not. The trader who alters a contract is less likely to be executed for his crime than the robber holding up travelers along a highway and is also likely to realize a greater profit for his efforts than the highway robber.

And so, clever thieves often benefit from government's attempts to create laws making thievery more difficult. Like a good puzzle, the new laws just make it more challenging to determine how to succeed without getting caught and often seem to increase the prize while also decreasing the risk of punishment. In fact, the cleverest and most ambitious of all thieves seem to be attracted to work in the governments that create such laws. The spoils can be substantial and the risks relatively small, and if one is truly successful, he might even be able to steal an entire country!

Chuang Tzu #21

The action of achieving with little friction is the action of the Way.

Words of sensitive honesty are words of virtue.

To love all life and be willing to assist in bringing it success is benevolence.

To repair what was good and was somehow made broken is greatness.

To be undaunted by boundaries and barriers is to be limitless.

To have worthwhile interests and the ability to pursue them is to be wealthy.

To have and hold virtue is to have guidance throughout one's life.

To grow in the maturity of that virtue is to always be stable.

To be aligned with the Way of Tao is to be complete.

To be unwavering in that alignment is to be sage-like.

Chuang Tzu #22

The sage Confucius was talking with one of his followers and said, "Those who come to know the Tao are endowed with its virtue. Being virtuous, they are content in their bodies. Being content in their bodies, they are complete in spirit. And being complete in spirit, they naturally become aligned with the Way of the sages.

"They live in the world side by side with other people, traveling through life without concern as to where it will take them. Their simplicity may sometimes seem strange to others. They consider status, personal gain, and all fads and fashions to be unimportant.

"People like this do not go where they do not want to go, nor do what their hearts tell them not to do. Even if the whole world were to sing their praises, it would not faze them. And if the whole world were to accuse them of something they had not done, they would remain calm and unperturbed. Neither praise nor blame gives them either gain or loss. Such a one as this is a person of complete virtue. In contrast, I am just a windblown wave!"

Chuang Tzu #23

Duke Huan was sitting on a balcony at his palace reading a book, and the wheelwright Pien was down below him in the courtyard making a wheel. Pien looked up from his work and said to Duke Huan, "May I ask you, sir, what you are reading?"

Duke Huan replied, "The words of the sages."

"Are those sages still alive?"

"No, they are long dead," answered the duke.

"Then, sir," the wheelwright commented thoughtfully, "what you are reading probably has little more value than the bones at the bottom of those dead sages' graves!"

"How dare you, a wheelwright, criticize what I read," Duke Huan declared impatiently. "Unless you can explain your rudeness, I think I shall have to have you punished!"

"I'm very sorry I offended you, my lord. I was just looking at it from the perspective of my own work. I have been making wheels for seventy years now, and I have become very adept at it. To make wheels that are perfectly round and will last a long time, and to be able to do so quickly, is a complex skill. Much of what I know that makes me a good wheelwright is hard to describe in words. Some things must be done gently, and other things must be done with just the right amount of force. Some things I feel with my hands, other things I feel in my heart.

"I tried to teach the skill to my son, but even though he could watch me work and ask me questions, most of what he learned he had to learn himself from the experience of actually making wheels. And as hard as it is to learn a complex skill by watching and asking questions, it must be even harder to learn from words in a book. The book could contribute little more than a frame-work upon which understanding gained from experience could be attached—like the bones supporting a body. That is why I said that what you are reading probably has little more value than the bones at the bottom of the dead sages' graves!"

Although Duke Huan was annoyed by the distraction, he had to concede Pien's point, and so he allowed him to get back to work on his wheel.

Chuang Tzu #24

Rigid and arrogant, above the current generation and distant from its ways, talking about important traditions and critical and dismissive of recent events. That is the Tao of one who dwells above the rest—one who is not of this age and who is beginning to cast himself into the darkness!

Preaching about the importance of kindness, morality, fairness, and equality; confident in his beliefs—outgoing, involved, and active. Those are indications of a lack of sensitivity toward others, and of the Tao of one who wishes to reform the current generation by teaching them about the important causes of the day—whether they wish to hear it or not!

Expecting to accomplish great things and to become known for what one has done, involved in the relationships and actions between various groups and hierarchies—that is the Tao of one who values laws and politics, who wants to know and influence his leaders, one who loves his country, who does what he can, who seeks the power to make important changes!

Finding highest value in the peace and quiet of solitude, and therefore spending much of his time alone with nature or submerged in books or games doing whatever seems like it should be done next—that is the Tao of one who retreats from others to escape the distractions and challenges of society—of one who is not in any hurry to do things with his life!

Huffing and puffing, grunting and groaning, inhaling the new air and exhaling the old, challenging his body over and over in order to preserve himself and his soul. A long and strong life is his primary concern. That is the Tao of one who infuses himself with all the important elements of life, carefully feeding his body essential vitamins and minerals and hoping to live as long as Peng Tzu!

Achieving loftiness without bias and without looking down on those with different values, improving oneself as well as others around them naturally and thoughtfully, and doing so without concern for recognition or reward, being able to remain calm and confident under all circumstances because of one's own virtue and self-confidence, not being concerned about one's own life and death but remaining healthy and vigorous because of natural activity and attitude, needing little and knowing that he or she has all that is important, and drifting calmly, confidently, and effortlessly through life with good things happening around him—that is the Way of the Tao of the sages!

Chuang Tzu #25

The season of the autumn flood had come, and a hundred tributaries were pouring their water into the Yellow River. Its water was churning fiercely, and the river was so wide that looking from one side to the other, it was impossible to even tell an ox from a horse on the opposite bank. The god of the Yellow River was quite pleased with himself, thinking that the most impressive thing in the entire world was his. He was so proud of its might that he followed it east until he came at last to the great Northern Sea and gazed upon that for the very first time. There was no end to it all! He sighed and shook his head, and then, suddenly, he beheld Jo, the god of oceans.

"I thought my river was the greatest thing in all the world, but now that I have seen your endless vastness, I realize that I have been deceiving myself," he said.

"A frog in a well can't even know about a river like yours because of the isolation of his well," replied Jo. "A butterfly could never describe the snows of winter, because it only knows its own season. Now that you have come out of the banks of your river and seen an ocean, you will have a better understanding of your relationship with the rest of the world.

"Here on Earth, it is true that there are no greater waters than my oceans," Jo went on. "Ten thousand rivers like yours flow into them constantly and yet all that water never causes them to overflow. Yet on the other hand, when there is a drought and the water from the rivers lessens, my oceans never go dry either. They pay no attention to the floods or droughts of rivers at all. There is so much more to them all than the waters from rivers like yours that it's difficult to even compare the two!

"But I don't usually think too much about all that," Jo continued. "If I should ever begin to feel too proud of myself because of the significance of my oceans, I just look at the vastness of the sky with its sun, stars, moon, and planets. Compared with that my oceans are as inconsequential as a pebble on the side of a mountain. And beyond even that, there is the entire infinite Tao!"

Chuang Tzu #26

After meeting each other for the first time, the god of the Yellow River and Jo, the god of oceans, talked for a long time about many things. "Each creature has its own perspective on the things it experiences in its life," Jo commented. "Most basically, each naturally believes that those things that help it to survive are good things and those that threaten its existence are bad and, as one might suspect, such perspectives often tend to conflict with each other. When a fox hunts a rabbit for its dinner, for example, its success would be a good thing for the fox, but not such a good thing for the rabbit.

"But perspectives don't have to only be related to survival. To a flea on the back of a dog, that dog must seem quite large, but to a camel looking down on it, the dog would seem rather small.

"Because of their intelligence and language, people have many more individual perspectives on a wide variety of different topics than other creatures, and those perspectives are much more complex. People concern themselves with such things as "high" versus "low," with "beautiful" versus "ugly," with "valuable" versus "worthless," with "right" versus "wrong," and a wide variety of other such concepts. Each choice made in each instance within each range of opposing concepts varies from individual to individual and also often between people from different towns and regions.

"But Tao encompasses all things, including each of those individual people and each of those other types of creatures, and within its totality, which is the basis of all things, nothing is "high" and nothing is "low," nothing is "beautiful" and nothing is "ugly," and nothing is more "valuable" or more "right" than any other thing. To Tao, all things and all perspectives are just equal parts of itself. To Tao, only the next appropriate movement of its perpetual Flow is really relevant!

"One who is trying to be in tune with the Way of Tao might conclude from that reality that all perspectives are inappropriate in Taoism and should be eliminated altogether, since Taoists following the Way try to emulate Tao as much as possible, but such a conclusion would not only be unrealistic, it would also be foolish. The Flow of Tao created life, and for life to continue to exist at all, each creature must have its own perspectives. And for humans to have intelligence and language, and to be able to advance human society, they must have complex perspectives. Different views on things must exist, they cannot be denied, and they must be accounted for.

"How could a person have a concept of "right" without having a concept of "wrong"? "Order" without "disorder"? "Friendly" without "unfriendly," and all the rest? Only by considering each opposing perspective in the range can one possibly know the other. To refuse one is to refuse both. But no Taoist sage would ever cling to one end of a range of perspectives without at least recognizing the other, as well as all the possibilities in between. The closest to Tao there is for the Taoist trying to follow the Way is to recognize, for each topic, the full range of possible perspectives that other creatures and people might choose for themselves, consider why they might have made that choice, and then choose perspectives for himself or herself that are considerate of the others, but that are the most reasonable choice in his or her opinion."

Chuang Tzu #27

Jo, god of oceans, was discussing his thoughts on how to follow the Way of Tao with the god of the Yellow River, and the god of the Yellow River became confused, and asked, "If I'm not to follow what everyone else agrees is moral and just behavior when deciding what to do, and if the accepted concepts of "right" and "wrong" don't have any firm meaning, then how am I to know how I should behave?"

"I'm not suggesting that you cast aside all preconceived notions of morality and justice completely," Jo answered. "They are certainly important to use for guidance, but you must also be able to think for yourself. Our lives pass as parts of the Flow of Tao, and that is complex and difficult to predict beyond all understanding. Social standards for behavior, on the other hand, tend to be firmly set and inflexible for long periods of time, and therein lies the problem!

"Living within the Flow of Tao, you are subject to the events occurring in each of its many aspects and all their cycles that might happen to affect you. You are impacted by the people around you and what they do. You are impacted by your age, health, and any limitations of your body, your important physical and emotional needs, political events, vagaries of nature, your own ideas of morality resulting from your past experiences, and innumerable other things. All those are factors you might want to consider when deciding how best to react to different situations."

"You must also consider the likely consequences of the actions you might take. There are possible consequences for breaking laws, there will be consequences to others who will be affected by your decisions, and there might be many different personal consequences to yourself, your self-image, and your future situation that could result from whatever you decide to do as well.

"So, given all that, don't try to always be any one type of person; instead, be ever-changing in the light of each situation you face. And don't cling tightly to preconceived social concepts of behavior. They are useful much of the time, but they are also inflexible, and flexibility is important considering the perpetual and unpredictable Flow of Tao. There should be nothing fixed about yourself at all. During your life, there will be periods when you will be quiet, peaceful, and studious; times when you might be bored and lonely; and other times when your life will run along at a gallop, changing with every passing second. There will be times for noble and generous behavior and other times when it is more appropriate to be aggressive. It's all just a sort of balance between the circumstances of the moment, the likely consequences of your actions, what you are trying to accomplish, and what you personally believe in your head and heart to be the 'right' thing to do. In the decisions you must make at each point along the way, just recognize as many factors in the Flow of Tao as you can and choose your actions according to those factors!

"Looked at in that way, it might all seem rather complex, and events will often roll by you at such a rapid rate that you won't have the time or desire to sit and analyze everything, and that is when the accepted guidelines of socially acceptable behavior are helpful. They are a standard from which you can decide to deviate if you feel you must according to each unique situation. From that standard, you will usually be able to sense rather than consciously decide how best to act, and therefore you will be able to do the most appropriate thing while also maintaining the pace of action called for at that specific moment."

Chuang Tzu #28

To travel seas in a small vessel, far from the safety of land, and not be panicked by the possibility of encountering storms or dragons—that is the courage of fishermen!

To travel the countryside daily, far from any city or town, and not tremble upon meeting rhinoceroses or tigers—that is the courage of hunters!

To invest time and money planting seed in the springtime, not knowing whether drought or pestilence will ever even allow a harvest—that is the courage of farmers!

To clash swords with able opponents in battle and calmly accept your own death as a possible outcome of the encounter—that is the courage of soldiers!

To deny yourself thoughts, words, actions, emotions, and physical pleasures that are based on selfish interest and ego concerns; to assume the burden of always considering the past and present movements of the Flow of Tao before making significant plans and decisions, as well as considering any likely future effects that might result from them; and to be willing to suffer any social and lifestyle detriments that might occur as a result of your philosophical choices, all in order to best follow the Way of Tao—those are examples of the courage of Taoists!

Chuang Tzu #29

The king of Chu needed someone to administer his royal forests and parks and had heard of the wisdom of Chuang Tzu, and so he sent two senior officials to ask him if he would accept the position. Chuang Tzu was fishing along the banks of the Pu River when they arrived, and as he listened to the king's proposal, he didn't even bother to set down his fishing pole.

After they had finished, he said to them, "I have heard that here is a sacred tortoise shell that is three thousand years old in the palace of Chu and that it is used by the king's oracles to help determine the will of the gods and to foretell the future. It is polished and encrusted with jewels and is wrapped up in silk and kept in a beautiful ivory box whenever it is not being used. Tell me," Chuang Tzu continued, "if that tortoise could be brought back to life for a few minutes and asked if it would prefer to continue to exist as it does today on a shelf in the king's palace or instead to live a normal life again crawling about in the mud, which do you suppose it would choose?"

The two officials glanced at each other and then both replied, "Crawling about in the mud!"

So Chuang Tzu told them, "Then please go back to the king and thank him for his generous offer, but let him know that I have decided instead to stay here and continue to crawl about in the mud!"

Chuang Tzu #30

Chuang Tzu's wife had recently died, and his friend Hui Tzu came by to visit and console him, but when he arrived, Chuang Tzu was sitting cross-legged on the floor, beating on a battered old drum and merrily singing a happy song. Hui Tzu was surprised and asked him, "Why are you so cheerful? You and your wife have been together since you were both young and always seemed to get along well with each other. She bore and raised your children. You should be sad that she has passed!"

"Oh, I certainly was at first," Chuang Tzu replied, "but then I thought back beyond the time of our marriage to her childhood, her birth, and even back to the love her parents must have felt for each other long ago when she was conceived. And then I imagined her developing in her mother's womb. I pictured her birth and first breath. I remembered stories she told me over the years of her childhood. I remembered our courtship and the fun and excitement of our wedding day, and I thought of all the happy times we had together over the years while our children were growing up. And then I remembered when our children finally went off to marry and raise their own families.

"Each of those times wrought a transformation in her life—she was conceived, she developed a body, she was born, she grew up, she created a life for herself, she loved people and they loved her, she bore and raised another generation, she grew old, and now she has died. Her life was like the four seasons of a year in the way that spring, summer, autumn, and winter each naturally follow the other. She had a full and complete life and now she is in her chamber.

"If I were to continue to sob and cry now that I have thought of all those things, it would be as though I didn't accept the natural Flow of Tao. So instead, I have stopped, and now I'm celebrating the fact that I was once a part of the good life she was fortunate enough to have had!"

Chuang Tzu #31

Once upon a time in the capital of Lu, a townsman caught a beautiful and very unusual bird, and since no one had ever seen such a bird before and since it was so beautiful, the man decided to present it to the Earl of Lu as a gift.

The earl was quite impressed with the unusual bird. He carried it in its cage in a procession through the streets of the city to the ancestral shrine where he had music played for it and where it was offered special meat from a special sacrifice. But the bird, instead of being honored as expected, only looked confused and frightened. It would not eat the food nor even drink the wine he offered it. For a while the earl continued to treat the bird like royalty, but after just a few days, it died.

The Earl of Lu did not realize that if one wants to honor a creature and have it live a long and happy life, he will not expect it to necessarily do and want the same things that he, himself, does.

The sage allows others he cares about to live natural lives of their own choosing instead of trying to direct their lives for them. A forest bird must be allowed to fly amid the trees of its forest and to float on the forest's rivers and lakes. It must be allowed to eat what it is naturally supposed to eat and spend its time enjoying the company of other members of its flock. Anything else is not a kindness.

Chuang Tzu #32

"Have you ever noticed that some people just seem to lead charmed lives?" Lieh-Tzu asked gatekeeper Yu. "Everything always seems to work out perfectly for such people. They're happy and healthy, everyone loves them, they're successful at whatever they try to do, and they fear nothing, but nothing ever seems to harm them. While most people need to struggle just to get by, it's almost as if all the creatures on the planet, all the people, and even nature itself all go out of their way to help such people accomplish whatever they try to do. I have never been able to understand it!"

"Sit down and relax for a few minutes and perhaps I can explain," Yu replied.

"Everything and everyone that we sense around us has a face, a shape, and a personality—characteristics that we can recognize and associate with that specific person or specific type of thing. People and animals additionally are able to think, have emotions, and purposely accomplish things, and those are also traits we use to distinguish between individuals. It's essential for our survival to be able to do that for a wide variety of important reasons. But what most people have trouble understanding is that those differences we use to differentiate between individual things and people are actually quite superficial!"

Each one of those individual things, animals, or people is just a tiny cluster of the various particles of Tao that happen to be gathered together in one place for a short while, and although we are able to see them as definable and unique, they are destined to exist as separate things for only a relatively short time. And in truth, as parts of Tao, they never actually lose their connection with the rest of Tao or their interconnection with each other at all. The shapes, faces, and characteristics we recognize are just short-term manifestations of that tiny part of Tao! The actual reality is the perpetually changing Tao underlying each of the seemingly separate parts!

Anyone who has an accurate and intimate sense of that inherent interconnection between himself and all the other manifestations of Tao around him, as well as of their common connection in time within the Flow of Tao, has a natural advantage in life. For a few people, that sense of connection is intuitive and may come naturally without even any scholarly understanding of Taoism, but for most it must be learned, and the Way of Tao is meant to help people to learn it. For one who becomes adept, there is a unity between himself and all around him—his way becomes every way, his limits become limitless, and his understanding of what he experiences considers factors from the very beginning of time through to the very end! He might even be said to be living a charmed life!

"One part of following the Way is to maintain a healthy balance within yourself between the various aspects of your personality," Kai Chih commented.

"What does that mean?" Duke Wei asked.

"Well, as an example, a man named Shan Po used to live in the country of Lu, and he was very dedicated to his own personal mental development. He lived in a cave and only drank water. He spent most of his time meditating, and when he wasn't doing that, he would wander through the forest looking for plants to nibble on or trapping small animals to cook.

"He had no interest in family or friends, earning money, or any of the other things that most people care about. He became so gruff and unpleasant that soon everyone began to avoid him altogether. But one day a relative dropped by his cave to visit and found that he had been killed and eaten by a tiger.

"On the other hand, I knew a man named Chang Yi who was very sociable. He was never at his own home because he always wanted to be with other people. He was very good at telling stories and at making people laugh and he had many friends, and yet those who knew him well could sense that there was something somewhat sad about him. Eventually he caught a fever, became sick, and died when he was still quite young!

"You'll notice that Shan Po, who was so concerned about developing his internal self, died by having his body killed and eaten by a tiger—a threat from outside of him—while Chang Yi who was focused entirely on the external social aspects of his life died from a disease that killed him from within. Neither man had ever made any attempt to keep his flock of personality aspects in any sort of balance at all, and in each case, the aspect that was being ignored the most eventually ended up destroying him!"

Chuang Tzu #34

Chi Hsing Tzu was very talented at training fighting cocks, and therefore he was commissioned by the king to train one that seemed to have extraordinary potential. The king was very anxious to have the bird fight as soon as possible, so ten days after the training began, the king inquired if it was ready to fight yet.

"Not yet," was Chi's reply. "The rooster comes across as too arrogant. He struts back and forth and threatens. But it's all just false bravado. He still has much to learn!"

After ten more days had passed, the king had still heard nothing from Chi, and so he inquired about the bird again.

"Your rooster is still not ready," Chi answered. "When I introduce another bird into the pen for him to fight, I can detect a moment of panic in him. He needs to grow more confident!"

After ten more days had passed, the king asked yet again.

"He's getting close, but he still needs a few more days. Now he's glaring at his opponents. He still needs to be a little more sure of himself!" Chi answered.

Several days after that, the king received a message from Chi Hsing Tzu. "I believe the rooster is ready to fight now," it said. "When other roosters crow, he doesn't even seem to notice, and when he is in the pen and I introduce an opponent, he just stands there as steady and nonchalant as a rock, while at the same time his opponent is struggling desperately to stay out of the pen. I'm pretty sure he is now as good a fighter as any cock could ever be!"

Chuang Tzu #35

Confucius had become very well known in the region and had spent several years going from palace to palace as the special guest of various kings and other rich and powerful men in order to teach and spread his philosophy. But being in the constant company of so many people with big egos created a certain risk, and on this occasion, Confucius had definitely bruised the ego of a ruler with a particularly sensitive and vindictive one. As a result, he had found it expedient to beat a hasty and unexpected retreat at a particularly awkward time.

He was, as a result, in a small town at the edge of a battlefield between two warring armies. The roads were too dangerous to

THE ANCIENT WISDOM OF TAO

travel, the town was running out of food, and he had nothing better to do than sit around with his friend, Duke Jen, discussing their mutual dilemma.

"In your case," Duke Jen said, "much of the problem just seems to be the inherent characteristics of your profession. To do what you do, you must display your knowledge in order to astonish and impress the unlearned, and by building yourself up that way, you cast a light on their relative crudeness. And I have noticed that powerful men do not usually like to be shown up as being crude!

"In your knowledge and wisdom, you shine," he continued, "absolutely glow—as if you carried the sun and the moon along with you—but remember that the tallest and straightest tree is always the first to be cut down and the well with the sweetest water is the one that is used again and again until it finally runs dry. Perhaps that is why you keep finding yourself beset by so many disasters.

"You know," the duke said, with an apparent insight, "there is much to say for living a more modest and inconspicuous lifestyle than you do. Fame, even when it is achieved as a result of worthy deeds, is not the boon that many people believe it to be. It soon fades away, and then the celebrity who enjoyed it must mourn its slow loss as he sinks once again into the obscurity of being an ordinary person.

"It is, of course, the Tao that moves all people and things, and it often does that through those who follow the Way, but sages do not usually choose on purpose to stand in its light so that they will be noticed by everyone around them. The average sage is usually content to be seen as somewhat plain and ordinary. He usually has no interest in wealth, power, or fame at all, and he doesn't usually anger anyone enough to cause them to cast him out of their home, whether it be hut or palace. Which leads us to ponder the current situation of you, Confucius, our most famous sage."

Confucius took Duke Jen's comments very much to heart, and when they eventually escaped their unpleasant situation and found their way back to their homes, Confucius soon said farewell to those he knew and retired into a great swamp to enjoy a short period of introspection. There he put on animal skins and rough cloth and lived for several weeks on acorns and chestnuts among the birds and other wetland creatures.

Chuang Tzu #36

Chuang Tzu had been invited to a royal banquet so that the king of Wei and his friends and ministers could learn more about Taoist philosophy over a grand meal, but Chuang Tzu was a poor man and did not have any clothing appropriate for such an event. He considered borrowing something nicer from a friend but eventually just washed what he had, bathed himself in the river, trimmed his hair and beard, and went looking more or less as he usually did.

When he entered the palace, he was wearing a worn, patched gown made of coarse cloth and shoes held together with string, while the king and most of the other guests had on brightly colored silks with beautiful designs trimmed with fur and shiny gemstones. The king approached him and said, "Why are you in such a state, Master Chuang? Couldn't you have found something more appropriate to wear?"

"I am a poor man, Your Majesty, and these are the clothes I always wear," Chuang Tzu answered. "I considered borrowing others that were nicer but decided not to. May I explain why?"

The king nodded, so Chuang Tzu went on to explain. "Have you ever watched monkeys climbing around in the trees, Your Highness? When they are among the plane trees, oaks, and camphor, they leap from branch to branch and hide behind the leaves with such ease that not even the best archers can spot them, much less shoot them down with their arrows.

"But when they happen to be among the prickly mulberries, thorny date trees, or spiky bushes, they move much more cautiously, looking from side to side, shaking with fear. It is not because their sinews and bones have gone stiff or are unable to bend. It is because the monkeys are not in the environment where they are most comfortable, and so they are unable to use their usual skills in the usual ways. They become distressed!

"Earlier today, I knew I would be dining with the king of my country and many other polished and important people. I did not want to feel distressed. I wanted to be relaxed and comfortable so that I could discuss my philosophy most effectively with all of you. Therefore, I decided that with my Tao and my usual clothing, I would be able to feel much more like a monkey would in the plain trees, oaks, and camphor even though I was actually among the mulberries, dates, and spiky bushes!"

Chuang Tzu #37

Chuang Tzu and one of his students were passing through the royal park at Tiao Ling on their way to an archery contest at a nearby town when they decided to rest at the edge of a pleasant meadow. They soon noticed a cicada making its way slowly down the branch of a tree a few feet away from them. The insect was completely unaware of a praying mantis that was standing a little in front of it on an intersecting twig.

As the cicada inched forward, the praying mantis just stood there as still as a statue and perfectly camouflaged, waiting for its prey to come within striking distance. When it finally did, as quick as a flash, the praying mantis struck and then stood there triumphantly with the cicada grasped firmly in the crooks of its front legs. But before it could even take a bite out of its newly acquired meal, a large jackdaw swooped down, barely missing Chuang Tzu and his student, and snatched the praying mantis, cicada still in hand, and then rose back into the sky again to fly away. Reflexes alert, Chuang Tzu leaped up, grabbed an arrow, drew his bow, and tried to aim at the bird, but as quick as he had been, the jackdaw was a little too far away and flying a little too fast to target, so Chuang Tzu released the tension on his bow and put the arrow back in its quiver.

"What an amazing series of events," he noted to his student. "The cicada was so intent on reaching its destination that it did not notice the praying mantis right in front of it, the praying mantis was so focused on the approaching cicada that it did not see the jackdaw who must have been flying along nearby, and the jackdaw seemed to be totally unaware of us just a few feet away with our bows and arrows. There is an important lesson in this for us to learn: as important as it is to concentrate on whatever you are doing, it can be dangerous to lose sight of the big picture context within which it is all taking place."

And then, at just that moment, a forest ranger ran up, out of breath and obviously upset. "I was walking along the path on the other side of the meadow and saw you raise your bow and almost shoot that bird," he said with passion. "It's a good thing you didn't, because if you had released the arrow, I would have had to take you to the minister of parks, and you would have had to pay a big fine. As you surely must know, it's illegal to hunt here in the king's park!"

Chuang Tzu #38

Yang Tzu was traveling to Sung with a couple of his students, and they stopped one night along the way at an inn. The innkeeper had two young female employees working for him—one who was unusually beautiful and one who was not so beautiful. Yang Tzu noticed that the one who was not so beautiful was being treated exceptionally well by those she worked with and seemed to be favored by all the local customers as well, while the one who was unusually beautiful was being assigned all the most difficult tasks and was also not being treated nearly as kindly by the locals.

Yang Tzu commented on his observation to those at his table and wondered aloud why that might be the case, and a young boy from the staff who had overheard him responded, "The beautiful one knows she is beautiful and that makes her seem less attractive to those who know her, and so we don't think of her as being all that pretty, while the less beautiful girl does not act as though she thinks she is pretty at all, which makes her seem much more attractive to us."

Yang Tzu listened to the boy and then turned to his students. "Learn this lesson well!" he said. "If you can learn to lose awareness of yourself and also always treat those around you with friendliness and respect, they will be more likely to like you and to want to help you, and that will make everything you ever want to do that much easier!"

Chuang Tzu #39

"Where can one find this Tao that you are always speaking of?" Master Tung Kuo asked Chuang Tzu.

"There is nowhere it cannot be found," answered Chuang Tzu.

"Just give me an example," Tung Kuo demanded.

"It's in this ant," Chuang Tzu finally said offhandedly, pointing to a bug crawling along on the floor.

"Is it also in some lesser thing?"

"It's in that weed," Chuang Tzu said, pointing again.

"How about in something even less significant than that?" Tung Kuo inquired again.

"It is in this little piece of roof tile," Chuang Tzu said, picking one up.

"Is that it, then?"

"It was also in the turd that you left in your chamber pot this morning!" Chuang Tzu retorted impatiently. "Look, sir, your questions are missing the point entirely! Recognizing Tao is not like a government inspector judging the quality of a pig by poking it in its skinniest places. There is no more Tao in important things than there is in unimportant things. All things are made from Tao in equal measure. The Tao is everywhere, and it is the source of all things whether good or bad and whether important or trivial."

The king of Wu was sailing down the Yangtze River on his royal yacht one day, and he decided to stop for a few hours at the base of a mountain known for its many monkeys so that he and his guests could watch the monkeys play in the trees as they ate their lunch. But when the king and his procession got off the boat and walked to the edge of the forest, all the monkeys but one fled in terror and hid in the trees.

The one monkey that did not flee acted as if it was not afraid of the people watching it at all. In fact, it acted quite hostile about their presence. It swung about in the trees above them chattering threateningly and even throwing dead branches and fruit at the people below. The king finally raised his bow and shot an arrow at the belligerent monkey, but it simply caught the arrow as it went by and then threw it back at the king. The king of Wu was not used to being treated so disrespectfully, so he ordered all the soldiers with him to kill the rude creature, and it soon died in a barrage of arrows.

After the royal yacht returned to the capital city of Wu, news of what had happened spread rapidly throughout the kingdom. Chuang Tzu was with Yen Pu when he heard about it, and he turned to his friend and said, "It was certainly unfortunate for the monkey, but the monkey was just being a monkey and the king was just being the king, and when they found themselves together on that day, what happened was quite predictable. But there is certainly a lesson in it for us humans who have a little more control over our behavior than monkeys do, and probably a little more ability to learn from the mistakes of others.

"The monkey's death resulted from its rudeness at the wrong time and to the wrong person. It was acting arrogant and invincible, and that behavior irritated the king, who is arrogant himself, and who therefore decided to punish the monkey for its behavior. In general, treating anyone rudely and arrogantly can be dangerous. Most people feel the need to defend their egos, and one can never know what abilities someone with a sensitive ego might have for avenging rudeness if you subject them to it. But if, on the other hand, you always treat people respectfully, you can avoid most such vengeful attacks and as a result find that many of the things you try to do will succeed just a little more easily!"

Yen Pu listened to Chuang Tzu's words carefully and recalled them off and on for the next few days. He realized when thinking about it that he, himself, sometimes acted arrogantly toward others, and he could also recall times when it had seemed that those around him were purposely making it harder for him to achieve his objectives. And as a result, Yen Pu pointedly began to change his attitude about himself and about the people around him. He slowly began to realize that he was not really any better than anyone else. He was just another person—an equal part of Tao—and that the only things that set him apart were the worthwhile things he was able to accomplish. And as his attitude and his treatment of others improved, their attitude and treatment of him improved as well, and he soon realized that his life and his activities had both become a little more pleasant and a little more successful!

Chuang Tzu #41

The sage recognizes the Flow of Tao both within himself and outside of himself and eliminates the boundary between the two. And because of the understanding he has attained of his part in the whole of Tao and the philosophy of Taoism, his benign influence tends to benefit himself and all that is around him. But no true sage would ever even agree that he is a sage!

The sage only does what he does because he recognizes that it is the next most appropriate thing to do in order to fulfill his objectives, which he in turn sees as the next most appropriate things that need to be done. He does not do them for individual praise or acknowledgement. In fact, he avoids accepting any personal praise or acknowledgement altogether because he knows that whatever transpires is always an accomplishment of the Flow of Tao of which he has played only a small part. And any such recognition, in addition to not being appropriate, would also usually only impede his plans for future accomplishments!

No one who thinks he is great or claims to be great should ever be counted as such, nor should he ever be seen as being virtuous. Each one of us is only one small part of the whole of Tao, hopefully doing our part to improve ourselves and our world within Tao's Flow. No one who knows what greatness truly is would ever even decide to chase after it, and no one who knows what greatness is would ever alter his opinions or actions to try to achieve it. The very act of seeking greatness denies its achievement. The sage, being great, does not even see greatness within himself; he only sees the tiny flaws left, common to all, that he needs to improve so that he can do more and do it better!

Chuang Tzu #42

Many people these days devote their lives to the pursuit of material gain. Often, they do so automatically because that's what everyone else is doing, without ever even considering the possibility that there might be more worthwhile goals they could aspire to. Isn't that sad? The sage doesn't spend large amounts of his valuable time without considering deeply the real value of whatever it is he or she is hoping to accomplish.

Material gain can be a pleasant added benefit of successfully achieving other more significant goals, and it might be accumulated as a tool in order to achieve worthy purposes one aspires to for the future, but living one's life for the sole purpose of pursuing material gain is like using the pearl of the marquis of Sui as a slingshot projectile to try to strike down a bird in the sky.

If one were known to have done such a silly thing, the whole world would laugh at him. Why? Because he had thrown away something considered to be of great value to try to obtain something considered to be of much less value. Now surely one's life is worth even more than the pearl of the marquis of Sui!

Chuang Tzu #43

Yuan Hsian lived in Lu in a house that was only a few steps wide and had a leaky thatched roof. Its broken door was made from brushwood and the door posts were mulberry. Several earthenware jugs with their bottoms removed had been built into the mud walls to serve as windows and that day they had been stuffed with rags to keep out the cold wind. Although the floor was somewhat damp, Yuan Hsian was sitting on a bamboo mat laid over it, making music and singing when Confucius came to visit.

Confucius had heard that Yuan Hsian was a notable student of Taoism in the region and so had decided to come to talk about their mutual interest in the philosophy. He arrived in a beautiful carriage pulled by two stately horses, and he was wearing an inner robe of purple silk and an outer one of white.

Hearing the sounds outside, Yuan Hsian came out to investigate with a hat on his head made of bark and slippers that were worn through almost to the heels of his feet. Confucius took one look at him and his house and said, "Good grief, sir. You must be in terrible distress!"

Yuan Hsian just laughed and answered, "I have heard it said that to have no money is to be poor and to have studied Taoism but have no way to use it is to be distressed. In that case I am definitely poor, but I am not at all distressed!"

Chuang Tzu #44

It had been a chaotic year in China. States had turned against states, and the rulers of the Middle Kingdom all seemed to be trying to steal each other's territory. Confucius knew many of those rulers since, for years now, he had been going from patron to patron teaching them the Way of Tao—a few months in one capital city and then a few months in another. Recently, his reputation for wisdom, his impartiality, and his familiarity with so many important people had also made him an ideal envoy, and so he now found himself going from country to country helping rulers by delivering messages to each, discussing terms, negotiating, and helping them out in various other ways.

Unfortunately, passions were high and his newfound diplomatic duties, along with his preference for peaceful solutions, had turned several angry rulers, more inclined toward war than peace, against him. He had twice now been chased out of Lu, he had had to flee from Wei, he had been banned from Sheng and Chou, and now he, along with several of his followers, happened to be trapped between Chen and Tsai, which were at war with each other.

For seven days the group had had nothing to eat but a thin vegetable soup cooked without meat or rice, and their faces were becoming drawn and gaunt. Nevertheless, one day when Yen Hui came back from hunting for native vegetables to make their daily soup from and worrying about how little he had found, he found

Confucius once again sitting contentedly on the floor singing and playing his lute as if he didn't have a care in the world.

"How can you make music and sing so merrily when our situation is so dire?" he asked Confucius exasperatedly.

"What sort of talk is that?" Confucius answered, beaming a smile. "As you know, a person who follows the Way is supposed to focus on understanding the Flow of Tao, including where it has come from, where it seems to be going, and why it's doing what it's doing. He is supposed to recognize and accept his own position within the flow, and then he's supposed to act in accordance with all that to try to fulfill his goals without disturbing the Flow any more than necessary. We've done that as well as we could considering the unstable situation we've been facing. We've been open-minded and impartial, and we have tried to encourage peace between the nations. It certainly hasn't worked out like we had hoped it would, but we tried, and maybe we did sow the seeds of peace within our militant friend's head somewhat. So now we can only wait to see what happens next in the Flow.

"Just relax and don't worry, I'm sure we will eventually free ourselves from this dilemma and return to our homes and families." And with that, Confucius picked up his lute again and started to play and sing, and after a quick glance at each other, his followers began to sing and dance happily right along with him!

Chuang Tzu #45

"At one time," said Tzu Chang, "Both Chieh and Chou enjoyed the honor of living like sons of heaven. They each seemed to have all the wealth and power in the world and lesser noblemen all prostrated themselves before them. But each one was an evil and barbaric man, and today if you were to tell even an outlaw lurking on the side of a country road that he was behaving like Chieh or Chou, he would be insulted and shamed, for even the lowest person now despises them!"

"Confucius and Mozi, on the other hand, were both born and spent most of their lives as poor and common men. It was not until they were becoming elderly that each became widely known and respected. Today, if you were to say even to a duke or prime minister that he was as wise as Confucius or Mozi, he would become embarrassed and proclaim that he was not worthy of such a compliment, because each man is now revered by everyone.

"So, to be as rich and powerful as the son of heaven today does not mean that you will always be so honored, and to be poor and common today does not mean that you will always be seen as poor and common. Lives can be changed, and reputations change along with them. The difference between being honored and being despised will eventually be determined by the worth or worthlessness of your actions!"

Chuang Tzu #46

Confucius had endured a couple of difficult months. He had been banished from one kingdom twice, had been forced to flee another, and then had barely survived being stuck between the warring armies of two more. It seemed as if nothing at all had worked out properly for him for a long time, and he was currently lamenting his situation with a wise, white-haired fisherman he had met along his journey.

"I have no idea what I've done to create so much misfortune and to be so misunderstood," he told the fisherman. "Why does everything seem to be going wrong for me lately?"

The old fisherman put one hand on his left knee and rested his white-bearded chin in the palm of his other and considered what had been asked of him. Then he responded with a story.

"There was once a young man who was frightened of his own shadow and was also afraid of his own footprints," the fisherman said, "so he tried to escape them by running away. But each time he lifted his foot and brought it back down, he made another footprint, and no matter how fast he ran, his shadow was never lost. Thinking perhaps that he was just running too slow, he ran faster, never ceasing until he finally exhausted himself completely and then collapsed and died. It never even crossed his mind that by sitting in the shade he would have lost his shadow, and that by resting quietly he would have stopped making footprints. Perhaps you, sir, should find a shady spot to sit down for a while and contemplate why it is that you have been making so many frightening footprints!"

Chuang Tzu #47

Confucius once said that "the human heart is more dangerous than the untamed mountain or the raging river and yet is the most difficult part of Tao to ever know." Many people have a well-regulated exterior that they show to the world, while keeping their true nature closely guarded and hidden within themselves. So, one person can have a kind and generous demeanor but actually be quite self-centered. Another can come across at first as being wise and talented but turn out later to be a fool. Yet another can seem quite often to be addled and confused but then prove himself to be the cleverest person in the room. And yet another can come across as being firm and decisive, but when a crisis occurs, suddenly be unable to think and even less able to act!

The wise manager of people must test and observe those who work for him so that he will know whether he can trust each one to do the job properly and represent him well. I have found that there are eight traits of particular importance to test for and consider:

Loyalty can be determined by watching the employee from a distance to determine his or her attitude toward you and the business you both work for. Respect can be determined by observing the employee up close and noticing how he or she treats you and other managers. Skill level can be determined by confronting the employee with difficult tasks and finding out whether or not he or she can accomplish them. Requisite knowledge for the job can be determined by asking difficult questions at unexpected moments and determining how often the employee has the right answers. Reliability can be determined by noticing whether or not the employee always fulfills his or her obligations and does what they say they will do. Determination can be checked by challenging the employee to difficult tasks and noticing if they meet the challenges consistently. Self-control can be judged by placing the employee in festive situations to find out if he or she can remain sober and retain good judgement. And open-mindedness can be determined by putting the employee in a wide variety of situations and noticing how he or she reacts to each.

By faithfully testing each employee in all of those ways, the employer will be able to see through the well-regulated exterior of those they need to trust and determine with each whether or not the trust would be well founded!

Chuang Tzu #48

Chuang Tzu had become an old man and was obviously approaching the end of his days, and so his followers were planning a glorious funeral for him. But that was not what Chuang Tzu had in mind for himself at all.

"After I'm gone," he told them, "I would like you to find a nice meadow deep in the woods and just leave me there. That way I will have heaven and Earth as my shroud and coffin, the sun and moon as my symbols of jade, the stars and planets for my pearls and jewels, and all the wildlife that lives in the forest as my mourners. That way I will have everything anyone could ever ask for. Nothing will be missing. What more could I want?"

His followers were all aghast at his strange request and looked back and forth at each other with concern, and then one of them said, "We are worried that the crows and wolves and other creatures will just eat you, Master."

"Above ground I will be eaten by crows and wolves," Chuang Tzu answered, "and below ground by ants and worms. Aren't you being a little partisan with your willingness to feed the one group and not the other?" And so, when Chuang Tzu did eventually die, they did exactly as he had requested.

Words of Wisdom Attributed to Chuang Tzu

- A frog that has lived its life in a well cannot intelligently discuss the ocean.
- The outer body is just a shell, and as with a nut, of little importance.
- Do what you do because you enjoy it and believe it valuable, and then do it as well as you can.
- Books can only provide a framework upon which wisdom from experience can be added.
- No one who thinks he is great or claims to be should ever be counted as such.
- How you will be appreciated in the future will be determined by the value of your actions, not by the thickness of your wallet.
- Treat all you encounter with friendliness and respect, and they will help make everything you do a little easier.
- Am I Chuang Tzu remembering a dream about being a butterfly, or am I a butterfly now dreaming that I am Chuang Tzu?
- Once you learn to accept what is meant to be, sorrow will never hurt you again so harshly.
- I was born because the time was right to be born and I will die when the time is right to die. In the meanwhile, I will just appreciate being what I am.
- Enjoy the personality you have but minimize your weaknesses and maximize your strengths. What the Flow of Tao has made unique within you is a gift.
- We have done all we could do as well as we could do it. Now we sit back and wait to see what happens!

- The sage's heart is like a mirror reflecting the world in front of it exactly. It only sees what is truly there so that the sage can respond appropriately.
- To be aligned with the Flow of Tao is to be following the Way. To be unwavering in that alignment is to be sage-like.

5

The Book of Lieh-Tzu

Lieh-Tzu

There is little doubt that an individual named Lie Yukou once lived in the Yellow River Valley of China around 400 BCE—probably after Lao Tzu and Confucius but before Chuang Tzu—and who later became known as Lieh-Tzu. It is believed that he was born in Cheng but later moved to Wei. He apparently studied under other known Taoist philosophers of the era, was wary of politics, never held any government office, and other than having a group of faithful students and followers, was somewhat of a hermit.

Although he was not mentioned along with Lao Tzu and Chuang Tzu in Sima Qian's "Historical Records," he was mentioned in the *Spring and Autumn Annals* of Lu, is mentioned several times in the *Book of Chuang Tzu*, and was also referenced in several other more obscure sources. Little else is known about Lieh-Tzu as an individual except that he apparently had a deep and thoughtful understanding of the Tao, he became a well-known and respected sage of Taoism during his lifetime, and his name is now associated with the third Taoist classic, which is called the *Book of Lieh-Tzu*.

But, while the ancient existence of Lieh-Tzu as a person is generally accepted, there is considerably more doubt as to how much, if any, the book that now bears his name is associated with the man it is named after. The first known reference to such a book came some three hundred years after the time period when Lieh-Tzu is believed to have lived in the form of a reference by a scholar named Liu Xiang, wherein he comments that he had edited and collated material from a variety of sources related to Lieh-Tzu and reduced that material down to eight chapters by eliminating duplications. After that, another three hundred years passed with no references anywhere related to such a book, and then around the year 370 CE, an eight-chapter edition of the *Book of Lieh-Tzu* surfaced in the hands of a man named Zhang Zhan, who stated that it had been passed down to him by his grandfather. He then edited the book, wrote a commentary about it, and released it to the public. All currently existing copies of the book are derived from that one copy that was released more than six hundred years after Lieh-Tzu's death.

Because of that late arrival into the public arena and for several other reasons, some Chinese scholars have questioned the authenticity of Zhang Zhan's "*Book of Lieh-Tzu*". They say the text shows the influence of Chuang Tzu's work, even though Lieh-Tzu's life predated Chuang Tzu's, and they say that the book shows the influence of Buddhism, Confucianism, and several other philosophies that didn't even exist until centuries after Lieh-Tzu's death.

But despite those problems, the *Book of Lieh-Tzu* has been embraced by most Taoist scholars as one of the three Taoist classics. As noted earlier, there are numerous questions about the authorship of the other two Taoist classics as well. All three books came to us from many centuries ago when recordkeeping was sporadic to start with, and many of the records that did once exist have disappeared long since. Regardless of its original source and date, the *Book of Lieh-Tzu* seems to be a compilation of legitimate material that (for the most part) represents the same philosophical tradition as the other two books, and it contains much previously unknown and relevant thought written with enough sophistication to be valuable. It certainly complements and supplements the wisdom of the *Tao Te Ching* and the *Book of Chuang Tzu* in providing an understanding the Taoist philosophy.

Another reason that the *Book of Lieh-Tzu* has been accepted is that most of the book is written in one recognizable voice, and it is a pleasant and amiable one. It comes across as the voice of a real person even though it was written many centuries ago. Lieh-Tzu doesn't talk down to the reader; he writes with the voice of an equal talking about interesting things with friends. And he tells amusing stories with enough depth and profundity to entertain and enlighten adults and with enough imaginative imagery and simple lessons to also be attractive to children, as well.

While there are still those who dismiss the *Book of Lieh-Tzu* because of its cloudy origins, Eva Wong, who grew up in a bilingual family in Hong Kong and who is the author of *A Taoist's Guide to Practical Living*, points out that almost all Chinese books for small children include stories from Lieh-Tzu but that she has yet to ever find any such stories in children's books based on Lao Tzu's or Chuang Tzu's works!

Like the *Book of Chuang Tzu*, the *Book of Lieh-Tzu* was originally written in the form of a rambling text. There is a significant amount of material in it of little interest to most modern readers. There are stories that simply do not advance our mission of teaching Taoism; one section seems to have been written by another hand and that espouses a sort of selfish hedonism; and some stories are close duplicates of stories in the Chuang Tzu book. I have eliminated all of those, resulting in fifty-six passages or stories that I feel will best advance the reader's understanding of the ancient philosophy. I hope that you, the reader, will enjoy them.

Lieh-Tzu #1

Times were hard in Cheng, and it seemed likely that Lieh Tzu's prospects as a teacher of Tao would be more favorable in Wei, so he decided that he needed to move there to teach. But none of his few students in Cheng were able to move with him and they were all quite disappointed about his decision, and so they requested that before he leave, he give them some final words of wisdom that they might ponder and learn from in his absence.

Lieh Tzu thought about their request for most of a day and then finally said to them, "Nature is a wonderful teacher for those who want to understand themselves and their world better, because we are each, ourselves, parts of nature and therefore most of the behaviors and changes you see happening with the creatures around you, you will also see over time in yourself and in other people."

"All things, you will notice, have a time and a place to be, fulfilling their function just by being what they are and doing what they do. We each play our part in creating things, nourishing things, transforming things, destroying things, and then finally in being destroyed, ourselves. The creation of one thing leads to the destruction of something else, and the destruction of something leads to the creation of yet another. That is just a characteristic of the Flow of Tao and because of it, life continues on in the world forever. At every moment there is birth and death and coming and going. The process never ends!"

"At birth each of us, man and creature, takes on a shape and exhibits a personality and other personal characteristics; in growth we all undergo development and slowly grow into maturity; at some point our bodies, intelligence, and wisdom reach their zenith and then slowly begin to fade; and when the time for each of us to exist finally ends, we dissolve and return to more or less what we were before we were ever originally conceived. That is true for all creatures of nature, including ourselves. Our individual births, lives, and deaths are all just events in the natural Flow of Tao, and the personal shape, thoughts, and feelings that characterize each of us will all, unfortunately, then necessarily be lost."

"It's always sad to consider the need for ourselves and others we know to have to die, but we must always remember that only our deaths can open the way for a fresh generation of lives to have their time to exist, and for each new individual to have its own shape and personality and feelings until sometime in the distant future when their time to be also finally ends."

Lieh-Tzu #2

Lieh-Tzu went on to explain that "the very foundation of all we see, sense, and experience lies in the nebulous and unknowable realm where all is formless and undifferentiated—the infinite Tao. At that most basic level, the Tao has nothing we would recognize as structure at all. It consists of tiny bits of energy interacting with each other in a limited number of predictable ways. But the interactions of all those tiny bits of energy bring them together to form ever more complex relationships that sometimes 'clump together' to form a denseness that we experience as objects, or it spreads them further apart to form what we think of as air or empty space. This process gives rise to all that we recognize and interact with in the physical reality we all mutually know.

"That which is clumped together includes the natural things that we give names to, as well as those things that we, ourselves, have made with our hands and tools and also give names to. All 'clumped together' objects have characteristics that our bodies have evolved to be able to identify by means of our five senses. But although we experience each of those clumps of energy as being separate and distinguishable, it's important to try to remember that they are all just manifestations of Tao and are all still intrinsically parts of it and, through Tao, are all inherently connected to each other.

"It's even more essential for understanding Taoism to realize that we, ourselves, are also just clumps of energy bits, little different than any other except in complexity, and as such we too are each inherently a part of Tao and all its manifestations, including the plants, animals, other people, rocks on the hills, the hills themselves, and even the entire planet."

· · · · · · · · · · · · · · · · · · ·

Lieh-Tzu #3

· · · · · · · · · · · · · · · · · · ·

When you watch babies grow up, make babies of their own and then eventually grow old; when you see the sun rise in the morning and then set in the evening; when you see rain fall, collect into streams and rivers, and then flow out to the sea; and when you see the first snowflake at the end of a long hot summer, you are experiencing examples of the natural Flow of Tao. But people do things on their own in addition to such natural things, and so when someone creates a garden for growing their vegetables, when a king levies a new tax, when the kingdom of Wei declares war on the kingdom of Cheng, or when a potter teaches his child how to make pots, such actions are also parts of the Flow of Tao but are examples of its man-made manifestations. Even though they are not the result of actions of nature directly, such man-made manifestations do affect other aspects of the Flow of Tao, and humankind like all else is a part of it, so the things we do must be included as examples of its Flow.

In fact, all that changes through time in Tao is a part of its Flow, and since the Tao is all encompassing and always changing, all things are a part of it. But we, as individuals, can only each experience a minuscule part of its entirety. Our direct experience of the Flow of Tao is limited to what we can see, feel, hear, smell, and taste. And for the most part, that limits our knowledge of it to what is nearby, but fortunately, because of our language and intellect, we can extend that knowledge with what we learn from others, what we read, with what we can postulate logically, and with what we come to believe intuitively—so our individual extended understanding of the Flow of Tao can become significantly greater.

The way sages understand and interact with the Flow of Tao is what we call the Way of Tao, and the first and most important aspect of following the Way is to come to know that Flow by those means as well as one can possibly come to know it. That knowing for a sage must gradually become a knowing beyond consciousness; to be most effective, it must become an intuitive sensing of the Flow. But since the Tao is everywhere and encompasses all things, and since it is impossible to know all aspects of it in all places, the sage must learn to find specific areas of expertise near and dear to him within the greater Flow that he can become comfortable focusing on while also trying not to lose too much sense of the greater movement.

Sages try to emulate Tao as much as they can, but while Tao always creates and changes all things in the most appropriate ways without thought or effort, that aspiration can rarely be satisfied for sages in that regard. Being human, they generally have goals and dreams of what they hope to accomplish for the future, as most people do. The best they can do, then, is to choose goals and dreams that are in line with the current path of the Flow of Tao as they perceive it and then pursue little goals and dreams that are along that same path and that will lead eventually toward the fulfillment of their larger ones.

The sage uses his sense of the Flow of Tao to detect the most effective and least disruptive moments for applying strategic nudges in ongoing events in order to help him attain his worthwhile goals. He never fights or goes against the current of Tao's flow, instead always moving along with it to accomplish his ends. The more powerful and influential the sage happens to be, the more boldly he will be able to be in affecting its flow in that way to his advantage, while the less powerful and influential he happens to be, the more subtle he will need to be when doing so. But powerful or not, the goals and dreams of the sage will always be aimed at the betterment of society as he sees it, not toward self-gratification, and he will always consider the consequences of his actions and avoid what would negatively affect others.

Lieh-Tzu #4

Lieh-Tzu and his student Pai Feng were walking through the countryside on their way to Wei one day when they decided to stop to rest and eat their lunch. As they were sitting in a meadow near the road, Lieh-Tzu noticed an ancient human skull half buried underneath a nearby bush and pointed it out to Pai Feng with a stick, and asked, "Do you think he is unfortunate to be dead now and that we're lucky to still be alive, or do you think the truth might actually be the other way around? How can we possibly know for sure?"

"We do know that he was born long ago into the Flow of Tao as it was in his time. The cluster of energy bits that formed him worked together to maintain his life for a while, and they interacted with other energy clusters around him to help maintain the world as it was back then. We know that for a while he had a body with a shape and characteristics that others could identify. He had a personality, knowledge, memories, and an intellect that could understand and react, at least to some extent, to the world around him.

"Perhaps he married and had children of his own; maybe he didn't. Perhaps he was a happy person when he was alive; maybe he wasn't. Perhaps he died young in battle or from some illness; maybe he just died of old age. Perhaps he was rich and powerful, or maybe he lived his whole life as a peasant struggling to survive. We can never know any of those things, and it really doesn't matter now. His time in the Flow of Tao is long past and it is now our time to be a part of it. At some point and for some reason, the cluster of energy bits that physically formed him ceased to work together to keep him alive, and then he died. Now, the shape and form that people used to be able to distinguish is disassembling and reverting back to formlessness. Everything that has a shape and a form that we can distinguish will eventually disassemble and revert back to having no form!

"And what of the Earth itself? It has a shape and form, and it too is a part of Tao. Will the entire planet eventually disassemble and revert back to formlessness? I assume some day it must!

"But then, getting back to our unfortunate, or perhaps fortunate, friend over there," Lieh-Tzu continued, poking the skull again with his stick, "all I've just talked about refers to his physical existence. Did he—do we each—have a soul? What of it? How can anyone ever know for sure? Our bones belong to the Earth, and below even that, to Tao. If we each have a soul, who or what does that belong to? The Yellow Emperor is said to have once wondered, 'When my spirit departs my body and my bones return to the Earth, what then will become of me?' After all these many centuries, we still do not know!"

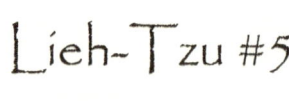

Lieh-Tzu #5

When Confucius and some of his students were walking along a county road near the foot of Mount Tai one day, they came upon an old man wearing ragged peasant clothing with a length of old frayed rope wrapped around his waist for a belt. The old man was quite noticeable because he was playing a lute and singing merrily to himself as he walked. Curious, Confucius politely asked him why he was feeling so happy.

Surprised at the question, the old man thought for a moment before finally explaining, "I have a lot of reasons to be happy. First, I'm a human being and human beings are the most intelligent and successful of the species. Second, there are two genders, and of the two I happened to have been born a male, and I have always been happy being a man. Third, many people die at a very young age. I didn't, and now I'm ninety and I feel very fortunate to have been able to live such a long and full life. And finally, even though I've never had a lot of anything and was certainly never rich, I've always had all I really needed and was never any poorer than any of my friends. So, yes, I do enjoy my life and hope to continue to do so until one day it ends. So, why wouldn't I be happy?"

"Excellent," Confucius said later to his students when they were discussing the conversation. "The man has learned to always be happy!"

Some months later, Confucius and his students were traveling along the road to Wei when they noticed an ancient-looking hermit in ragged clothing and a heavy old fur coat hunting in a harvested field for random grains of millet that had escaped the harvesters' baskets. He, like the old man at the foot of Mount Tai, was singing merrily as he stooped down to pick up the tiny bits of grain. Confucius watched and listened to him for a few moments and then asked Tzu Kung to walk out to the man in the field to ask him what he had to say about himself.

But while walking across the field, Tzu Kung began to feel pity for him. He appeared to be so old, poor, and alone! So, when he finally reached him, Tzu Kung commented, "I am so sorry your life has become so difficult for you at your advanced age, but would you please talk with me for a few minutes about what you've learned in all your years of life?" But the old man just ignored Tzu Kung as if he weren't even there and continued foraging for millet grains and singing.

Realizing that he might have accidentally been offensive, Tzu Kung followed behind apologizing and asking forgiveness, and finally the old hermit stopped, turned to the student, and with an amused grin, asked, "Why do you assume my life requires your sympathy? I am, perhaps, the happiest man in the entire kingdom!"

"How can that be?" Tzu Kung asked. "You've become quite old, you are obviously very poor, and it seems clear that you don't have anyone to help you take care of yourself!"

"I'm happy because I've lived a long life doing exactly what I wanted to do and being exactly who I wanted to be," the old man answered. "I never did anything just because I was told to, and I never wasted my time competing with others to be popular or successful. It is because I chose not to marry and have children that I've lived to be so old, and it is because I am so old and am approaching the end of my life that I am happy!"

"But nobody wants to die!" Tzu Kung insisted. "Why would you want to die?"

"No one who is alive knows what death will actually be like," the old man explained. "Maybe death is better than life. Maybe I'll be reborn as something or someone different that I will like even better than I like myself now. Maybe people are just being deluded when they fear death. I don't know the answers to any of those questions any more than you do, so I will just enjoy what is left of this life for now, and when death is ready for me, I will be ready for it as well!"

When Tzu Kung went back and explained to Confucius and his fellow students what the old hermit had said, Confucius chuckled and responded, "I knew he looked like someone who would be worth talking to. He seems to have a fairly clear understanding about life and death. But I think there are still some aspects of it that he has not yet fully grasped!"

Not long afterward, Tzu Kung became frustrated and weary of his studies of Tao. He went to Confucius to announce that he had decided that he needed to take some time off to go rest and recuperate, and that he expected to be back in a few months.

"There is no rest for the living," Confucius responded tersely.

"What! Am I never to get a chance to take a break and get some rest, then?" Tzu Kung asked impatiently.

"Of course you will," Confucius answered calmly. "Take a walk through a cemetery and know that that is the place where you will finally be able to take a break and get some rest!"

After a moment of puzzled thought, Tzu Kung finally said, brightly, "Now I think I understand! Death is a rest for the weary, it is peace for the troubled and for those in pain, and it is a release from guilt for those who have lived a life of bad decisions! Most of those who have lived a long and full life will probably not even fear it but instead will come to welcome it!"

"Exactly!" Confucius exclaimed. "Life is a journey, and every single part of it, all the way up to and including death itself, has advantages and disadvantages. All of it—the disadvantages as well as the advantages—should be experienced fully for one to get the most out of life. But like all journeys, whether you do or don't enjoy yourself along the way, it's always good to go home to rest and recuperate when the journey finally comes to an end!"

· · · · · · · · · · · · · · · · · · ·

Lieh-Tzu #6

· · · · · · · · · · · · · · · · · · ·

One of Lieh-Tzu's students approached him one day and asked respectfully, "Why do you tell us so frequently to avoid unnecessary opinions? Aren't opinions important? Without them, one can have no values! Doesn't a sage want to have values that he can hold firmly onto?"

"Thank you for asking that question," Lieh-Tzu responded. "It's an important thing to understand!

"I'm not suggesting that you should have no opinions at all or that you should treat the opinions you do hold lightly. It's important for you to develop firmly held moral opinions and also form opinions regarding your profession and other subjects of real importance to you. I'm simply saying that you should not form opinions casually or form them regarding matters you know little about.

I also say that you should be thoughtful about how you express your opinions, and to whom. Opinions, if ill-considered or too inflexibly held, can create real problems for you. Spouting out opinions as to topics you know little about is more likely to turn you into a fool than a sage!

"Opinions tend to attach themselves to the ego of the person who holds them and then to become a part of his self-identity so that his emotions get involved and he sometimes feels the need to defend those opinions passionately. And that can certainly create unnecessary problems, especially when the opinion was naïve or ill-conceived in the first place!

"And even if opinions were well thought out and were appropriate when they were first formed, nothing in life ever remains the same for long. Our daily experiences are all creations of the flow of Tao, including the society we live in, and everything within the Flow of Tao changes constantly through time. When one thing is shrinking over there, something else will be growing over here; when something is maturing on the right, something else will be decaying on the left; and when something changes in one way over here, something else will be changing in a different way over there.

"And, since the world and everything in it is constantly changing and everyone lives their lives immersed in that change, each person needs to have enough flexibility within himself for his understandings of the world to be able to change along with it. Opinions make that more difficult because they are like anchors trying to hold those who have them in one place in a world that is moving quickly around them.

"It's natural for people to become invested in their opinions and to feel the need to defend them, but when the basis in reality behind the opinions' original formulations inevitably changes, the holder of the opinion is in danger of becoming 'wrong!' And if he tries to defend his opinions as they begin to go 'wrong,' he is likely to find himself playing with verbal distinctions in order to try to make them seem to be 'right' again, and then it becomes ever harder for him to find his way back to honesty."

"But it's also not easy to just abandon old opinions and form new ones that are more valid. First, since opinions are emotionally attached and emotions are difficult to control, even if one were to consciously decide to change his opinion about something, his emotions regarding it might not be so easy to change. And, also, if one has opinions and changes them too often, people, including himself, might begin to see him as a flip-flopper.

"So, if you have opinions that have become outdated and you don't change them to fit new circumstances, you might be seen by yourself and others as being inflexible, but if you do change them and do so too often, you might be seen by yourself and others as a flip-flopper. Reality in our world is just far more diverse and ever-changing than a casually formed opinion can ever be.

"That's why I tell my students that it's best to just avoid forming unnecessary opinions in the first place. Being devoid of unnecessary opinions and the emotions attached to them provides a safe haven for a sage to dwell in. Whenever he forms opinions about topics he doesn't even need to have opinions about, that safe haven disappears!"

Lieh-Tzu #7

There was once a man in the country of Ch'i who became obsessed with fear that the sky, along with the sun, moon, and stars, would suddenly fall and crash into the Earth and destroy it, and that if it were to happen, he and his body would have no place to dwell. His fear of that possibility became so severe that he was unable to sleep, or even to eat because of it.

A friend of his was worried about the extent of the man's panic and about his threatened health, and so he came over to reassure him. "The sky is just the upper part of the air we breathe and exist in," he told his friend. "It sits on the Earth and moves around when the wind blows. It can't possibly fall because it has nowhere to fall to. There is no reason at all to be afraid of that happening! And the sun, moon, and stars seem to just float on top of the sky like ducks floating on a pond. None of them have ever shown any signs of falling before, and they surely never will. They are the way they are because it is the way they are meant to be. That will never change, and you really don't need to be afraid that such a permanent arrangement will ever suddenly end." And with those words, the man from Ch'i's fears began to ease, he began to eat and sleep again, and soon he was as happy and as healthy as he had ever been.

When Ch'ang Lu Tzu heard about all this, he smiled and said, "The Earth, sky, moon, and stars are all products of Tao, just like everything else, and therefore they will cease to exist someday, just like all other things. But I'm sure that won't happen for many centuries and that the man has nothing to worry about in his life-time, or even in the lifetimes of his children! But his friend was wrong to assume that they will remain where they are forever. And if there are still people on Earth when they do someday fall, those people will certainly be in danger!"

But then, when Lieh-Tzu heard the story about the man from Ch'i and Ch'ang Lu Tzu's response to it, he laughed out loud. "It's foolish to even consider whether or not the Earth, sky, sun, moon, and stars will someday perish," he said. "If they do, it's likely to be in the far distant future, so we will not be alive to care about it. And even if they were to surprise us all and collapse tomorrow, there would be nothing we could do about it, and we would cer-tainly perish right along with them, so there would be no need at all for a place afterward for our bodies to dwell!"

. . . .

Lieh-Tzu #8

. . . .

Mr. Kuo and Mr. Hsiang had been friends when they were both young men but had not seen each other for many years. Then one day they happened upon each other on a street in the town of Ch'i. Mr. Hsiang had become rather poor, but Mr. Kuo appeared to now be quite prosperous. He wore nice silk clothing with fancy embroidery and some expensive-looking jewelry, and he was ac-companied by several servants.

Mr. Hsiang was impressed by his old friend's apparent success and asked how he had achieved it. "First, I studied the Tao in general for several years," Kuo said, "and then I gradually became adept at the art of 'using what I need from Tao.' Within a year I could support myself, within two I was quite comfortable, within three I was flourishing, and lately I have been wealthy enough to sometimes even help some of my neediest friends and neighbors." And after that brief conversation and a little reminiscing, the two old friends parted ways.

Mr. Hsiang went home and thought about the words of his old friend Kuo and decided to try to improve his lot in life by reproducing his old friend's strategy. He felt like he already knew enough about Taoism itself, so he decided to focus on the "taking what I want from Tao" aspect of it. He learned to climb over walls and to break into houses. He became quite good at choosing which houses to rob, when to rob them, and what to take; and he was successful enough to become rather affluent himself after a short while. With his newfound wealth, he bought a nice home, hired servants, dined at only the finest restaurants, and drank only the best beverages.

But then one day Hsiang was caught breaking into a home and was thrown in jail. Only luck and a corrupt magistrate saved him from being hanged for his crime, and even though he did escape the most severe of punishments, between the bribery, fines, and restitution to his former victims, Hsiang found himself poorer than ever.

Several months later, Mr. Hsiang happened upon Mr. Kuo once again on a street in Ch'i and once again he was broke. In fact, this time he was even worse off than before because of the wear and tear from his various legal problems, while Kuo, on the other hand, appeared to be even richer than before. "How do you continue to rob people without ever getting caught?" he asked Kuo after explaining what had happened to him since their previous encounter.

"What makes you think I rob people?" Kuo asked quizzically.

"You said you specialized in 'taking what you want from Tao,'" Hsiang answered. "What else could you have meant?"

"I said I had become adept at 'using what I need from Tao.' That is quite different than 'taking what you want,' and it does not involve robbery! Stealing from people hurts them and endangers yourself, while just using the manifestations of Tao that don't belong to anyone else to help accomplish your goals hurts no one at all. Tao does not care if you use it. And by the way, you can't ever really take anything from Tao at all. You can use its manifestations, you can change them from one form to another, but nothing is ever really lost except the form they happened to first be in, I suppose.

"But understanding any application of Tao does always require recognizing and considering the possible consequences of your actions. You can use and alter any of Tao's various manifestations anytime you want to, and Tao will not care, but doing so will always result in consequences. That is just a reality of the universe. All things are interconnected through Tao, so anything you do to one of its manifestations will result in changes to others, and that is what causes the consequences. And in some cases, the consequences can be significant. When planning out a strategy in advance of doing something consequential, one must always be careful to balance the possible benefits of the proposed action with its possible negative consequences.

"And that, my old friend," Kuo went on, "is why robbery is not a good way to practice the art of 'using what you need from Tao.' While Tao doesn't care what things you use or what you use them for, people definitely do. And when you take things from people against their wishes, the consequences, as you have seen, can be quick and quite severe!"

. . . .

Lieh-Tzu #9

. . . .

For the first fifteen years after the Yellow Emperor came to the throne, he enjoyed his newfound wealth and power by living a life of excess and gluttony. He suddenly found that he could have anything he ever wanted, and so for all those years, he took on as much each day as his body could endure, and gradually his ravaged flesh began to darken, he became soft and puffy, and his senses dulled and stupefied.

Eventually, though, he began to realize how destructive and meaningless such a lifestyle was and therefore changed his focus. For the next fifteen years, the Yellow Emperor concentrated on ruling his country as well as he possibly could. He had the magistrate of each district report to him directly and regularly about all significant events in his region and took an interest in resolving all important conflicts. New laws were passed, and he concerned himself with every aspect of the kingdom's income and expenses. But though he was no longer living a decadent lifestyle, he grew neither happier nor healthier. Instead, he found himself becoming demanding and irritable. Those who worked under him came to avoid him whenever possible, and instead of appreciating his efforts, the citizenry seemed to become ever more sullen and rebellious. It became painfully obvious that he was still doing something terribly wrong.

So the Yellow Emperor determined that he had no choice but to try to find a way to become a better king as well as a happier and healthier person. He delegated temporary management of the kingdom to his ministers, dismissed his orchestra, his concubines, and all his attendants and went off to live for a while all alone in a cabin in a nearby forest reserve. There he fasted and meditated for several months and considered the life he had led so far and the choices he had made.

One pleasant spring afternoon, the Yellow Emperor fell asleep under a tall gingko tree and had a remarkable dream in which he visited and explored a mystical country far from his own. It was the country of Hua Hsii, and it was impossible to even get to it by any means other than a journey of the spirit.

In Hua Hsii there was no all-powerful single ruler at all, and those who were chosen by the people to lead were chosen because they always put the interests and personal development of the people they served above and beyond their own. In this magical place, he found that no one ever had any uncontrollable cravings for things that were self-destructive or that belonged to someone else. All people seemed to love life but did not cling desperately to it, and neither did they fear death, and each one seemed to care at least as much about the welfare of those around him or her as they did about their own. No one seemed to even be able to conceive of themselves as being separate from those they lived among. No one ever confronted anyone else with complaints or about personal slights, and neither did they ever turn their backs on one another.

Things were accomplished and progress was made not by standing stubbornly against the tide of events nor by going mindlessly with the flow but instead by moving with the current and guiding it gently in advantageous directions at propitious moments to achieve their desired ends. In that way no one ever had an emotional stake in specific outcomes and decisions could always be based on the most reasonable choices and best compromises as agreed to by all. Egos, regrets, fears, and envies seemed not to even exist in that unusual place.

Much of what the Yellow Emperor experienced in the country of Hua Hsii was beyond words and explanations, as seems to always be the case with dreams, but somehow it seemed to him that because of their personal freedoms, senses of community, lack of self, and the absences of detrimental emotions, the people of Hua Hsii all seemed to always be joyously happy, fearless, and boundless in vision and spirit. The country just seemed to be much like what one might expect heaven to be like.

When the Yellow Emperor awoke, he realized that his strange dream had somehow changed him into a different and better person. He returned to his palace and summoned his ministers and told them, "For three months now I have stayed alone in a cabin in the forest, and I have fasted and meditated in order to come up with new and better strategies and policies for conducting myself and our government. I did not find any of those things that I can lay out to you in any detail because the utmost Way can never be fully explained with words, logic, and policies, but I now know what it is that we must do, even if I cannot actually describe it to you."

And so, over the next twenty-eight years, the Yellow Emperor slowly came to model his country to be as much like Hua Hsii as possible, and when he died, the people did not stop wailing over their loss for more than two hundred years.

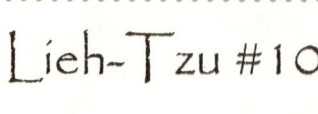

Lieh-Tzu #10

When Lieh-Tzu was young, he studied Taoism for many years under Old Shang and while doing so also formed friendships with several other notable Taoist scholars. From that long and full emersion into the philosophy, he learned how to live life fully and most effectively through Taoism's tenets. Eventually, though, it seemed that he had learned all there was to learn in that environment, and so he returned to his original hometown to be among his old friends and family and to teach his understanding of Taoism to eager young students.

One day a young man came and asked to be included as a student in Lieh-Tzu's school. Yin Sheng, as he was named, was an enthusiastic but rather impatient student. Within only a few months, he began to approach Lieh-Tzu every time he noticed that the sage was idle and beg information about advanced Taoist beliefs and practices, and each time he did so, Lieh-Tzu politely turned him away and declined to discuss the topic with him. After a dozen or so such incidences, Yin Sheng became indignant about Lieh-Tzu's lack of cooperation, and eventually he just packed up his few belongings and returned to his home.

But it was not long before Yin Sheng began to question his decision. Had Lieh-Tzu really been rude to him or had he, himself, been impatient and unrealistic in his expectations? Eventually he realized that the important thing was that he really wanted to learn about Taoism and that Lieh-Tzu was recognized by all to be the wisest sage of the philosophy in the region, and so several months after leaving Lieh-Tzu's school, Yin Sheng returned and asked once again to be admitted.

"Why do you come, and then go, and then come back again?" Lieh-Tzu asked him.

"When I was here before," Yin Sheng admitted, "I became upset because you would not answer my questions, and that is why I left, but after thinking about it, I decided I had been unreasonable and, besides, I really would like to learn about Tao from you and that is why I have come back!"

"I used to think you were intelligent but now I'm not so sure. Are you really as petty as that?" Lieh-Tzu asked. Then after a short pause, he continued. "OK, I'll tell you some of the secrets of Taoism that I've learned over the years from my studies.

"The first three years I studied under Old Sheng, I gradually learned not to allow my mind to consider who was ever 'right' or 'wrong,' or what might 'harm' or 'benefit' me. Only after I had done so did he ever give me so much as a glance.

"After five years, my mind had once again begun to think of 'right' and 'wrong' and of 'benefit' and 'harm,' but from a totally different perspective than before, and the day the master realized I had learned this was the first time he ever smiled at me.

"After seven years of study, I had come to think whatever came into my mind to think and to say whatever came to my mouth to say without any regard at all as to any 'right' or 'wrong' or 'harm' or 'benefit'" that might come from it, and that was the first time the master allowed me to sit on his mat with him."

"After some nine years, I thought without any restraint at all anything that came into my mind and said without any restraint at all anything that came into my mouth without ever even knowing whether any possible right or wrong or harm or benefit from doing so were mine or someone else's because, after all, we are all one in Tao anyway.

"By that time, it had become irrelevant that the master was the master and that my Taoist friends were my Taoist friends. I had come to the end of all that was inside of me and all that was outside of me, and I was no longer even a barrier between the two. My ears, eyes, nose, mouth, and mind were all one. All of everything, in fact, was one! It no longer mattered where my mind was or what ground my feet trod upon. My mind drifted with the wind east or west like a leaf from a tree or a dry husk, and I never even knew or cared whether it was the wind that rode me or I that rode the wind.

"Now you come to be my student and after only a few months are indignant because I won't immediately tell you all the teachings of Taoism. So now I will tell you the first and most important lesson of all, and that is that very little of Taoism can even be taught with words. Most must be gained over the years through a long process of observation, dedication, self-awareness, discipline, and then finally through a total loss of self. The concept of 'you' and 'I' as separate entities is only an illusion. I did not answer your questions earlier because there wouldn't have been any benefit to anyone at that point in doing so." And then Lieh-Tzu turned and walked away.

And after hearing all this, Yin Sheng was so embarrassed about his earlier behavior that he hardly spoke to anyone at the school at all for the next six months and just watched and listened.

. . . .

Lieh-Tzu #11

. . . .

Those who are adept at following the Way of Tao can accomplish great things. They move confidently and effectively amid all other manifestations of Tao without ever even a tremble!

Every person, plant, animal, and object in the universe is a thing of Tao equal in origin to all others. Some are soft and others hard, some come and go quickly and others endure for eons, some are animate and others inanimate, some can be dangerous and others beneficial, but despite all such superficial characteristics, they are all just manifestations of Tao—each only superficially different within the totality of Tao than any other.

How can it be, then, that people who know Tao best and are most in tune with its Flow are different than those who are not? How is it that such people tend to distinguish themselves from the rest? How is it that the one can affect or influence change more effectively than the other? Why do such people usually succeed at whatever they do while others more often do not? The answer lies in their ability to maximize the bodily energy they hold within themselves and then to use it most effectively to fulfill their objectives!

Those who are good at following the Way of Tao take care of themselves. They eat healthy foods and get the exercise their bodies require. They don't overindulge in destructive habits. They learn what they need to know about the things they do before they do them. They don't waste thought about themselves, about what others think of them, or about insignificant things like attaining wealth, power, or fame. Because they don't do things that might cause them guilt, they never need waste their time in contemplating it. And because they are in tune with, or (even better) are one with the Flow of Tao and avoid going against it, whatever they do can be done most easily and effectively.

Such a person will learn and become comfortable with his capabilities and will always stretch but never exceed them to any dangerous level. He will quickly sense what needs to be done next in any ongoing process and how best to accomplish it. When necessary, he will stand back from the chaos and tumult of any social interaction likely to distract and waste his energy and allow his mind to roam calmly back to the place where all myriad things first start and eventually end. From that perspective, such a person can keep his being unified with the Flow of Tao, can keep aligned with what is truly important, can assess how best to utilize his energy, and can more easily maintain his virtue. When one has a firm connection to the source of all people, all things, and all actions, how can anything else defeat him? What can hurt him?

When a drunken man falls off a horse-drawn carriage, he is less likely to be hurt by the fall than is another man who is sober. His bones and joints are the same as any other's, but the alcohol has numbed his self-awareness. He rides without caring that he is riding. He falls without caring that he is falling. He is not limited by any love of life nor by any fear of death. And when he hits the ground, he is loose and limber and therefore avoids injury. Since this is true of a man who has numbed his senses with alcohol, imagine how much more powerful the effect can be instead for one who loses his sense of self due to a unity with the ultimate source of all being and all action!

. . . .

Lieh-Tzu #12

. . . .

There was once a rich and powerful businessman in the country of Chin named Tzu Hua who was much beloved by the country's prince. Although he held no official title, he sat to the right of the three ministers, and those he favored tended to prosper while those he disliked, the state was likely to punish. There were almost as many visitors in his audience chambers as there were in the royal court, and he even maintained his own personal little army consisting mostly of the sons of local noblemen.

One day, two important clients of Tzu Hua who were returning to the city found themselves late in the evening to be short of their destination, and so they sought shelter for the night at the hut of a poor peasant named Shang Chiu Kai. There they ate a quick meal, drank some of the wine they had brought with them, talked for a while about the wealth and power of Tzu Hua and how he could save or ruin or enrich or impoverish anyone he chose to, and then the two travelers fell asleep on mats on the hut's floor.

That night, while his two unexpected guests were drinking wine and talking, Shang Chiu Kai was sitting quietly outside a window listening carefully to their conversation. He had lived a meager, cold, and isolated life thus far in his little hovel beside his stingy fields. He had never had enough to eat, and none of the few unmarried girls he knew had any interest at all in marrying him. He had always dreamed of living a more satisfying life, and now he was hearing of a man who might supply a means for him to do so. And so, for several days afterward, he considered what he should do and finally decided to gather his few useful possessions, put them in a basket on his back, walk to Tzu Hua's gate, and ask for employment.

Shang Chiu Kai presented a rather comical figure as he sought a position as a man-at-arms in Tzu Hua's audience chamber. Everyone else was clean, well groomed, and dressed in fine white silks, while he wore dirty, ragged clothing, spoke with the rustic accent of a peasant, and had no experience at all as a soldier. But he did speak with confidence and sincerity and said all the right things, and Tzu Hua's small army just happened to be short-handed at that moment, anyway, and so Tzu Hua surprised even himself by agreeing to give the peasant a trial period in the position he'd requested.

At first things did not go well. Tzu Hua's other men-at-arms all saw Shang Chiu Kai as a man of low birth who would never be able to fit in with the rest of them. He knew nothing of current fashion or of any of their other interests, and he also knew nothing of warfare, even though he did admittedly work hard at the training that was being provided for him. They scorned and shoved him and stopped at nothing to insult and make him look silly, but despite their rude behavior, Shang Chiu Kai never showed the least anger, and eventually the retainers tired of their sport and just tried to ignore him as best they could.

Then one day the group was on top of a high terrace laughing, bragging, and insulting one another and one of them offered ten gold coins to any other who would jump off the wall down to the next level. As tempting as the prize was, as the challenger had expected, no one was willing to accept his dare. It was a long drop, and it seemed impossible to jump so far down without incurring a serious injury. But then Shang Chiu Kai suddenly leaped over the edge. Everyone gasped in surprise, but he seemed to float almost gently down to the ledge below, where he landed gracefully and then ran back up to collect his prize.

As surprising and impressive as Shang Chiu Kai's feat was, no one thought much of it until several days later when the group was gathered near a deep bend in a nearby river at a location where the current ran especially hard and fast, and someone commented that there were said to be gigantic pearls in some of the freshwater mussels on the riverbed below, available to anyone able to swim down and stay long enough to collect them! Immediately after hearing that, Shang Chiu Kai disappeared into the water and several minutes later reemerged holding a large pearl that he had liberated from a mussel down in the depths. Once again everyone in the group was surprised, and when Tzu Hua heard about it, he granted Shang Chiu Kai an allowance of meat and silk for the first time, just as he gave to all his other soldiers.

Not long afterward, Tzu Hua's warehouse caught fire and he arrived at the blazing building at the same time as his men. Seeing a fortune's worth of his silks and brocades about to go up in flames, he offered a large reward to anyone willing to rescue the goods. Fearful of the fire, everyone except Shang Chiu Kai hesitated to act, but he immediately ran into the burning building and began carrying out bundles of cloth. And so, as his fellows contented themselves with carrying up buckets of water to throw on the flames, Shang Chiu Kai ran into the inferno again and again until he had saved most of Tzu Hua's valuable goods. The soot did not even seem to stain his clothing and the flames did not scorch his body!

Shang Chiu Kai's actions during the fire finally convinced everyone that he was an extraordinary individual. He collected a generous reward from Tzu Hua, and immediately became the patron's favorite, while his fellows in the small army all became convinced that he must be a sage of Tao. One day they all approached him to apologize for their previous behavior.

"When you first joined us," they told him, "We played tricks on you and humiliated you, not knowing that you followed the Way of Tao, but then none of us could have ever done the things you did. You must have thought us stupid, deaf, and blind! Please forgive us for our ignorance and be kind enough to teach us what you know of Taoism!"

"I know very little about the Way of Tao," Shang Chiu Kai responded. "Until now I didn't even know that I had been doing anything special. Before I came here, I heard two men talking about the wealth and power of Tzu Hua, and I believed what I heard them say with all my heart. That is why I came. When I arrived, I believed that everything you all said was true and feared only that I might fall short in acting on it as you would do. I never even thought about where my body was or what it was doing or about what might benefit or harm me. I was completely single-minded about doing the things I did, and I guess that was why I kept being successful! Now that I know that what I did was unusually difficult and dangerous and that none of you would have ever done it, I consider myself lucky not to have been injured, drowned, or badly burned. From now on I will probably never again be able to leap from high places, swim in swift streams, or be near hot flames without being afraid.

Sometime later, when Confucius heard the story of Shang Chiu Kai, he commented that "all aspects of Tao seem to naturally react in helpful ways to those of perfect faith. Such people just move heaven and Earth aside and fill the universe all around them with themselves, and then there is nothing left to stand in their way!"

. . . .

Lieh-Tzu #13

. . . .

King Hsuan of Chou had a servant named Liang Yang who had a unique talent for taming and raising wild animals. He collected and fed them in the king's royal gardens and kept animals together there even as potentially ferocious as tigers, wolves, and eagles. Males and females of each species were comfortable coupling and raising their young in his and each other's presence, and the animals of the various species lived side by side without ever attacking and injuring each other.

The king was most impressed by Liang Yang's talent and loved to visit the gardens and witness the many wild beasts living together in harmony. The only problem was that Liang Yang was getting old and the king feared that the secrets of his art would be lost upon his death. Therefore, King Hsuan ordered a younger servant named Mao Chiu-yuan to become Liang's apprentice and learn his skills.

When Mao Chiu-yuan arrived and told Liang Yang of the king's instructions, the old man at first modestly denied that he had any significant skills at all, but then after a moment's reflection said, "It is the nature of all beasts of vigor and intelligence to be tolerant of those who treat them politely and respectfully and who do so without fear."

"It pleases them to be allowed to have their own way and they are inclined to become angry whenever they are thwarted from their natural needs and desires. And, especially for carnivores like wolves, tigers, and eagles, anger must be avoided. Whenever tigers get angry and kill people, it is almost always because the people thwarted them in that way."

"One who keeps tigers must be especially sensitive to their moods and must learn to understand the motives behind any danger-ous mood they might feel. Feeding tigers correctly is especially important for keeping them happy. One certainly never wants to allow them to become too hungry. I never give tigers live animals to eat because they tend to get into a rage killing them. I also do not dare give them entire carcasses because they might get into a rage just tearing the meat apart. Instead, I give them chunks of meat at regular intervals so that they are always calm and con-tented."

But, at the same time that one does not want to allow tigers to become enraged by thwarting them, one also does not want to spoil them by giving in to every one of their more whimsical de-sires, either, for when joy reaches its climax, it is likely to revert to anger; and when anger reaches its climax, it is likely to revert to joy. It is a matter of always trying to keep the moods of the an-imals in balance! If I never spoil them by giving them their way too often, or anger them by thwarting them, the animals begin to regard me as one of their own, and therefore they are always happy roaming on our gardens, and never even miss their deep forests, marshes, and lush mountain valleys!

. . . .

Lieh-Tzu #14

. . . .

Anything with flesh and skin upon a human frame, with hands designed to grasp, with feet and legs formed for upright walking, with most of its hair on the top of its head, with eyes on the front of its face, and with the ability to speak a language is automatically considered by most of us to be a human, and yet such a person might well have the mind and manners of a beast. On the other hand, anything that walks on four legs or flies with wings, that is covered with fur or feathers, and that does not have the ability to speak a language is labeled a beast and will be treated as a lesser being, even though it might well be just as wise and noble as any human being.

It is said that in ancient times there were gods and godlike men with the bodies of animals and the heads of humans, and others with the bodies of humans and the heads of animals, and that all were wiser than any normal person. It is also said that in ancient times Emperor Chou of the Yin Dynasty, Emperor Chieh of the Hsia Dynasty, Duke Huan of Lu, and King Mu of Ch'u all looked like and were generally considered to be human beings, but that all had the minds and manners of beasts—so it is clearly difficult sometimes to tell who or what is human and who or what is beastly!

It is true that there are obvious ways in which animals differ from people—they look different and animals cannot speak with words, but there are many more ways in which the intelligence of animals is naturally similar to our own. Each individual creature wishes as much as any person to maintain his or her own life; they all seek good partners to mate and to create their young with; they all look for fertile, healthy, and safe places to bear and raise their families; many value the companionship of others of their own kind and defend one another from enemies; and many, like many people, grow with age and experience to eventually become wise.

Long ago, men and wild animals lived and walked side by side. Even though people had to hunt animals for food, and some animals hunted people, there was a mutual understanding and respect between the people and the animals. Most people knew the habits of all the creatures they lived among and could interpret their sounds. People often came to know specific animals as individuals and learned their personalities. Now, sadly, many such animals must hide in their lairs by day and can only safely venture out at night to live and hunt for their food, just because of all the dangerous activities of so many of us human beings. Today, most people do not really know wild animals and the wild animals do not really know us.

And so, while most people judge others of all species by their exterior appearances, the sage looks beyond that shallow facade and searches for wisdom within. It can be found in many surprising places by those willing to look deeply enough to find it.

Lieh-Tzu #15

Lao Ch'eng Tzu had studied for several years under a few notable Taoist masters, but he was an active man with many ambitions, and he sought a deeper and more practical understanding of the Way of Tao than he had found so far, in hopes that he would be able to apply it in achieving his many long-term goals. To satisfy that desire, he went to learn from Wen Tzu, who was said at the time to be the wisest sage of Tao of them all.

For the next three years, Lao Ch'eng Tzu studied the Way with Wen Tzu and his other students. The group ate together, meditated together, visited other schools in other towns, and had many long conversations about the Way and how best to live their lives in harmony with Tao's Flow. Being together as much as they were, they became quite close, but while Lao loved the school and appreciated the people he studied with, he still did not feel that he was gaining knowledge that he could use to help him accomplish all he eventually hoped to, so one day he approached Wen Tzu and told him about his concerns and announced that he had decided it was time to return home to his family and friends.

Hearing this, Wen Tzu bowed deeply and expressed his sorrow that Lao was leaving and that he had not learned all he had hoped to learn. But later, just as the student was about to walk out the door, Wen Tzu added, "Perhaps this will help you in your search—when the positive and negative energies that make up the great void of Tao interact with each other, they often create forms. Those forms include ourselves and all the other people and things we recognize and experience in the world around us. Each form comes into existence and lasts for some period of time, and then eventually fades away and disappears back into the void of Tao. Sometimes the period during which one exists seems short to us and sometimes it seems quite long, but for as long as each form does exist, it will constantly be changing, and no form ever lasts forever. When the forms are living creatures, we call their emergence into the world 'birth,' the changes that take place to them during their existence 'growing up' or 'aging,' and the inevitable final cessation of their life 'death.' On the other hand, when the forms are inanimate objects, we describe the changes by such words as 'evolution,' 'formation,' 'erosion,' 'decomposition,' and 'destruction.'

"During the periods of their existence, forms interact with each other, and as they themselves change, the nature of the interactions between each one and the others change as well. Whatever people choose to call the constant changes that take place to and between the forms of Tao, the complexity of it all is quite profound and is not easily understood or applied. But if one only latches on to the superficial effects of it all rather than trying to understand it more deeply, he or she will only be playing with the minor effects of illusions, and anything that they are able to accomplish, even if it might perhaps appear to be dramatic, will not endure for long. To make long-term, significant changes in anything, one must come to understand the complex relationships and interactions going on in the Flow of Tao behind the forms.

"It's important to remember that all we ever experience of the forms of Tao are only illusions generated by the abilities and limitations of our eyes, ears, noses, and other sensory organs. Our five senses can only provide us with simple representations of an infinitely more complex reality. Only when you delve deeper and consider the sciences of structure, creation, change, dissolution, and other such subjects can you really begin to understand the deeper reality behind what is going on and from that deeper understanding institute any real and long-term changes you might wish to make to the reality you live.

"And remember also that not only are your experiences of other forms around you shallow impressions only simplistically representing their actual reality, your impressions of yourself, your impressions of other individuals, and everyone else's impressions of you are also illusions only vaguely based on any actual reality! Those facts must be more than just vaguely recognized by you, they must be deeply ingrained, and their implications acknowledged if you hope to ever be successful doing anything involving intricate interactions with other people or things. And, of course, the first and most important step in understanding anything realistically is to prevent any distortions in your perceptions caused by the emotional effects of your ego."

Lao Ch'eng Tzu took those words of wisdom home with him when he left the school and thought deeply about them and their implications for the next three months. During that time, he focused on ridding himself of his illusions of self, on trying to make his understandings of others as realistic as he could, and on focusing on the complex realities of the changes constantly going on in the Flow of Tao around him related to the things he hoped to do. And later, when he finally immersed himself in his business and political activities, he went on to do many important things and to satisfy most of his many ambitions.

Years later, Lieh-Tzu is said to have commented, "Those who have gained a deep understanding of Tao often do not casually reveal the significance of the understandings they have gained. Therefore, the things they do are often not attributed to Taoist thought at all. It is generally believed, for instance, that the ancient kings and conquerors accomplished all that they did as a result of their bravery, virtue, and ordinary intelligence, but who can say that they did not also use their own especially deep understandings of the Way, or that of their advisors, to help them accomplish all that they did?"

· ·

Lieh-Tzu #16

· · · · · · · · · · · · · · · · · · · ·

Mr. Yin of Chou had become a very successful businessman. He had originally inherited his estate from his father but through hard work and a perfectionist attitude had also amassed a considerable fortune of his own to add to it. Unfortunately for his employees and servants, though, he demanded at least as much effort from them as he did from himself, and for some of them, it was very difficult to constantly satisfy his many expectations.

One such person was an old servant who had worked for Yin and his father all his life and who had gradually become beaten down in body and spirit by the constant demands being put upon him. Each day he trudged through his assigned chores, only to often then be browbeaten for the time it took him to do them or for some little mistake he had made in the process.

But while the old servant's days were miserable, his nights were not. At the end of each day, he would happily crawl into his bed, fall immediately to sleep, and dream the most delightful dreams wherein he was always in charge and all those around him loved him, comforted him, and happily fulfilled his every desire. And when, on occasion, some friend would console him for some harsh treatment he had received on that particular day, he would often reply that even though his daytime life was certainly less than ideal, he was a prince by night and felt no need overall to complain.

Troubled by the demands of running his extensive worldly affairs, Mr. Yin, on the other hand, often had trouble falling asleep at night at all, and while his old servant's dreams were always pleasant, his own when he did sleep were not very pleasant at all. He often dreamed that he was being presented with impossible tasks to accomplish and had to perform them just right or some dire punishment would be inflicted upon him. In those unpleasant dreams, he was always fearful and stressed.

One day, after a particularly bad night, Mr. Yin decided to talk about his problem with a Taoist friend who had some remarkable insights as to the world in general and as to the emotional problems of people in particular. After hearing about Mr. Yin's nightmares, the friend pointed out that the most pleasant condition a person could experience is when he is at peace with himself and is enjoying his life. That condition usually occurs when the person feels loved and appreciated by others, when he or she is healthy and having fun, when all his basic needs are being fulfilled, and when he enjoys whatever it is he is doing in his work. But, when some of those factors are not being met, the pleasant condition quickly starts to become lost, an imbalance is created, and the person becomes unhappy. The further such factors move away from the ideal and the longer they remain so, the worse the imbalance becomes, and often, when they get that bad, some extreme opposite factor will naturally be formed to reestablish some kind of balance.

"In your case," Mr. Yin's friend concluded, "it seems that your unpleasant dreams are occurring for that reason. Determine which factors in your daytime hours are out of balance and are taking you so far from life's most pleasant condition and change them, and I suspect the nightmares will soon go away."

So, Mr. Yin went home and considered his friend's words and the realities of his life, and soon knew exactly what he needed to do. He realized that he really had no need at all to amass even more power or wealth than he already had, and that it was time for him to start focusing on having more fun in his life instead. And so, starting the very next day, he stopped pushing himself and his workers so harshly. He lessened everyone's workloads, including his own, and he started being much more involved and compassionate about everyone who worked for him and their personal needs, and in no time at all he was no longer having nightmares, and everyone else in his company began to enjoy their lives much more than before. But after several weeks, his old servant started to notice that his dreams were no longer nearly as vividly idyllic as they had been before.

. . . .

Lieh-Tzu #17

. . . .

Mr. P'ang of Chin and his wife had a son who had been quite clever as a young child but seemed to become ever more confused about everything as he grew older. He began to see black as white and white as black. To him, what others thought pleasant was offensive and what they thought offensive was pleasant; what every other person saw as good, he thought bad and what all others saw as bad, he thought good. It seemed that no matter the topic, his views had become the opposite of every other person's viewpoint in the village.

Mr. P'ang and his wife became very concerned and wondered aloud to their friends about what they should do. Someone pointed out that the Confucionists of Lu were said to be quite wise and to have many arts and skills and that they might be able to help with the boy's abnormality, and so P'ang set out for Lu to inquire from the Confucionists what he might do to help the child. But along the way, P'ang happened to stay one night at the same inn as the well-known sage Lieh-Tzu, and over the evening meal, they discussed the problem.

Lieh-Tzu listened carefully, thought for a moment, and then asked, "How do you know that your son's thinking is abnormal? It seems nowadays that everyone has a different opinion about what is right and what is wrong and what is good and what is bad. What really is normal and what really is abnormal, anyway, and who are we to try to make the final decision on such things?

"Besides," Lieh-Tzu continued, "one man's different opinion about something isn't usually enough to corrupt his family, and even if they did eventually come to agree with him, that family's different opinion would surely not be enough to corrupt the whole village, and should the whole village slowly come to agree with the family, that village's different opinion would probably not be enough to corrupt the entire nation, and even if it were to do so, that nation's different opinion wouldn't likely corrupt the whole world; and even if it did somehow change the world's opinion, then the new differing opinion would no longer be abnormal, would it? What if everyone in the world except you came to agree with the 'abnormal' views of your son. His views about things would become the normal ones and yours the abnormal ones!

"All such things are just matters of opinion based on personal experience. There can be no final determining judgment about them."

"Thinking about it, I'm not even sure that these opinions of mine are normal rather than abnormal, let alone any opinions of the Confucionists of Lu. Those people, in my opinion, have the strangest views on things of anyone. I think you should just go home rather than wasting your time and money consulting with them. That's my opinion!"

. . . .

Lieh-Tzu #18

. . . .

An official of Ch'in was on a state visit to Lu, and while in town he dropped in to visit an old acquaintance named Shu-sun who happened to live there. In their conversation, it came up that the famous sage Confucius was a resident of the town.

"How do you know for sure that Confucius is really a sage?" the high official wondered.

"I once heard his student, Yen Hui, say that Confucius was able to shut off his mind and use his body to know and understand things," Shu-sun answered.

"We have a sage in our country too," the high official replied. "He is a student of Lieh-Tzu called Keng-sang Tzu, and it is said that he can see with his ears and listen with his eyes!"

Shu-sun was quite impressed by the idea of a sage being able to do such an unusual thing and so he mentioned it later to the marquis of Lu, who was equally impressed by the strange talent. He was so fascinated in fact, that he sent an official emissary to Keng-sang Tzu to humbly request that he visit the marquis sometime when he was available to discuss his Taoist talents.

Several weeks later, when Keng-sang Tzu arrived at the court of the marquis of Lu, he quickly pointed out that it was only a rumor that he could see with his ears and hear with his eyes. He stated that he was, instead, able to look and listen without using his eyes or his ears, though.

"But that is even better!" replied the marquis of Lu. "Please tell me more."

"My body is in tune with my mind, my mind is in tune with my personal energy, my personal energy is in tune with my spirit, and my spirit is in tune with the interconnectedness of the Flow of Tao," Keng-sun Tzu explained. "If anything is happening, or even the faintest sound that affects or relates to me, whether it is far away or as close as between my two eyebrows, I will know it. But the thing is, whenever that does happen, it is hard for me to tell for sure whether I perceived it somehow with my five regular senses or through my heart or belly. It always just seems to be a sort of self-knowledge or a sixth sense!"

The marquis was fascinated to hear that and thought about it frequently for the next few days. And then sometime later when he was with Confucius, he told him what the sage from Ch'in had said. Confucius just listened, smiled, and nodded, but there was nothing that he really had any desire to say about it!

Lieh-Tzu #19

Tzu Hsia was visiting from out of town, and he asked Confucius about his current group of students. "What sort of man is Yen Hui?" he wondered.

"For kindness, he is a better man than I," Confucius responded.

"What about Tzu Kung?"

"For eloquence, he too is better than I!"

"Tzu Lu?"

"For courage, he is much braver than I could ever be!"

"Tzu Chang?"

"For dignity, he is a much more impressive person than I am!"

By that point, Tzu Hsia had passed looking surprised and was now looking obviously annoyed. He stood up from his mat and asked, "Since your students are all so much more talented than you, why are you the teacher here and they the students?"

"Please sit back down and relax and I will explain," Confucius answered calmly. "Yen Hui is naturally kind, but he is unable to be firm when being firm would be more appropriate. Tzu Kung is eloquent but has trouble holding his tongue when it is silence that is really called for. Tzu Lu is very brave but is often not cautious enough, and he often gets himself into trouble because of that. And Tzu Chang is quite dignified but is unable to ever just relax and enjoy himself.

"Every person has a complex personality made up of many characteristics—some perhaps seen by others or by themselves as beneficial and some as problematic. The combination of them all is what defines who we each are. Because of circumstances that have occurred here in recent years, along with some people's appreciation of my understanding of Tao and certain favorable aspects of my personality, I guess, I have been chosen to be the teacher here recently and they the students. But who knows? That could change tomorrow!"

. . . .

Lieh-Tzu #20

. . . .

Lung Shu and an old friend were getting together for the first time in several years. Lung Shu had been studying Tao with a well-known sage, and his friend had been studying medicine at a school in a different region. Lung Shu's friend was excited about all he had learned as a doctor and commented that he now thought he could diagnose and treat almost any common ailment, and so Lung Shu decided to test the claim.

"I've actually been suffering from a strange medical problem myself lately," he said, attempting to look concerned.

"Well, tell me about it," his friend responded.

"It's affecting my emotions," Lung Shu said. "They seem to be receding, almost like the shoreline in a waning tide. I no longer care whether those around me like or dislike me. I am who I am and do what I think I should do. That's all that seems to be important to me anymore. I no longer care if I win or lose, I simply enjoy whatever I'm doing no matter the outcome. I no longer become distressed when events go against me or overly excited when they bring me success. I control what I can and want to control in my life but know that all the interacting parts of Tao are far too complex for me to be able to fully manipulate anything. I just do what I can do and then accept what comes afterward.

"Life and death, riches and poverty, fortune and misfortune all now seem irrelevant to me. I hardly ever even see or feel myself at all anymore. I'm you, I'm my teacher, I'm my wife, I'm the peddler selling fish in the market, and I'm even that bird on that tree over there. I find myself becoming everyone and everything everywhere!

"Ever since I came down with this crazy illness, I've lost all interest in wealth or fame and I've found myself even more unwilling to follow all the silly rules and regulations made by selfish officials for self-serving reasons. It's affected my relationships with the government, my family, and my friends and even changed the way I run my business. What do you think might be wrong? Do you think you can help me?"

The new doctor could tell where Lung Shu was going with his dissertation, but he decided to play along with the premise, so he said, "Okay, let's check you out and see if we can figure out what's happening with you!" And then he proceeded to check Lung Shu with every test and procedure that he had so recently learned. He poked and prodded. He looked at his eyes, ears, and mouth. He tasted his blood, smelled his urine, and listened to his heart. He even had Lung Shu stand with his back to the late afternoon sun in a small doorway so he could use the light to help gauge the state of his internal organs.

Finally, the doctor relaxed and with a straight face said, "Well, I can't find anything seriously wrong with you, Lung Shu. For the most part, you seem to be in excellent health. You do still have a heart, it seems, and it is beating well enough. As near as I can tell, you are simply moving along on your path toward enlightenment. I did notice a small blockage in your heart region though, and that might explain why you seem to view enlightenment as a strange ailment that needs to be cured. If that is indeed the case, I'm afraid there is really nothing I can do to help you!"

Lieh-Tzu #21

King Hsuan of Chou was fascinated by physical strength and often hosted competitions between the strongest men in his kingdom during which they would perform amazing feats to demonstrate their abilities for his amusement and that of his friends. Then, over the course of several months, the king began to hear rumors about the ruler of a nearby country who was called the Earl of Kung-yi, who was said to be an incredibly strong man. Intrigued, King Hsuan invited the earl to come to visit his palace in Chou so that the two could get to know each other and perhaps become allies.

But when the Earl of Kung-yi arrived, the king noticed immediately that he was not a very muscular man at all. In fact, he seemed to be quite puny! Surprised and disappointed but trying to be diplomatic, King Hsuan said to him politely, "I was told that you were a very strong man. Are you able to perform any unusual feats of strength?"

The earl was, in turn, surprised by the king's question and replied, "I've certainly never claimed to be especially strong. I can barely even snap the leg of a grasshopper in the springtime or pierce the wing of a cicada in the fall. I don't know why anyone would tell you that I could perform amazing feats of strength."

"I have men in my kingdom who can rip the hide of a rhinoceros apart or can drag nine oxen by their tails. I wonder how such an inaccurate rumor about your strength ever got started," the king said.

After a moment's pause, the earl answered, "Perhaps we can trace it back to my old teacher of Tao when I was just a young man. One day I risked my life on his behalf and as a reward he gave me some especially wise advice.

"He told me that most people compete with each other to try to guess what will be coming in the distant future or what is currently happening in faraway places, but that in his experience it was much wiser to focus instead on seeing, knowing, and understanding well the world that is close at hand. He said that people focusing on the faraway tend to often miss completely what is happening right under their noses.

"He also said that most people also tend to compete on accomplishing the very difficult or even the unattainable, and that he had found it to be much wiser to become adept at accomplishing what is more easily achievable but that others usually don't even think of or don't bother to do.

"He suggested that I should train my eyes, ears, and brain to see, hear, and examine the mundane things that surround us all but that others don't even notice, like carts loaded with firewood rolling down the street or the clanging of a neighbor's bell down the block. He pointed out that when a person focuses intently on all aspects of what is going on around him in the here and now instead of on the yet to come, the faraway, or the barely attainable, their lives become easier, their objectives become more achievable, their problems become more resolvable, and their self-confidence becomes healthier."

King Hsuan listened to the earl's words with curiosity mixed with frustration and then interjected, "That's very interesting and sounds like excellent advice, but what does it have to do with the rumors of you being one of the strongest men in the region?"

"Well," the Earl of Kung-yi continued, "I took my teacher's advice very seriously and have been training myself ever since to do as he suggested. As a result, I've become strong in my confidence, determination, and abilities, and my country has grown strong economically and militarily as well. Perhaps the 'strength' the rumors mention became confused in the retelling and originally referred to that. That's all I can suggest!"

King Hsuan agreed that the earl's theory made sense and was probably accurate, and during the next few days and then over the course of the next few years, the two men became good friends. They did eventually form a formal alliance between their two countries and then negotiated a trade agreement that benefited the citizens of both for many years thereafter.

. . . .

Lieh-Tzu #22

. . . .

Find and follow the Way and it will light up your path,

But then if you lose it, your path will be even darker!

The Way is not something you can find and then just forget,

Nor will it come to you if you don't even try to find it.

Look for it in front of you, and it might be behind or off to the side,

Because you can never find it with your eyes or your ears, or in a book.

It can only be found and followed with a quiet and determined mind,

And then with patience, its presence can slowly grow within you.

The small you looking outward will become a new, more inclusive you.

You will find access to whatever you determine to find access to.

Your only limits and boundaries will be those you've agreed to accept.

When active, you will flow like a river, when still you will be a mirror,

And when acted upon by others, you will become their echo.

You might at times find yourself moving counter to the Flow of Tao,

But the Flow of Tao will never purposely move counter to you!

. . . .

Lieh-Tzu #23

. . . .

Long ago, in a village surrounded by mountains, an old man lived with his wife, two sons, and his sons' young families. Many in the village thought of him as being an old fool and even called him that behind his back because he always seemed to be coming up with outrageous and impractical ideas for doing things in new and unusual ways.

One day, tired of having to take the long and circuitous multiday trip around the nearby mountains to get to the nearest market town by the sea, the old fool suggested to his family that they build a road over the steep and rugged gap between the two nearest peaks so that they could more easily get to the town on the other side. The old fool's sons and their families thought it was an excellent idea and started discussing how it might be accomplished, but his wife was more skeptical. "You're an old man," she protested. "You have trouble even pulling out the weeds in the garden. How could you possibly build a road over a mountain? Besides, what would you do with all the rock and rubble you would be creating?"

"We would help him," the sons answered enthusiastically, in support of their father. "And whatever rock and rubble we can't use, we could throw into the ocean as soon as we get across to the other side."

And so, the very next day the old fool, his sons, and a neighbor's boy who had heard of their project and decided to help headed out to the foot of the mountain with picks, shovels, axes, and a wheelbarrow and started to build a road.

Throughout that summer, anytime they could spare a few hours, they returned to the project, but even so, as the summer waned and the weather started to turn cold, little obvious progress had been made.

Most of the people in the village just shook their heads and chuckled about the old fool's latest scheme. It wouldn't be long, they felt sure, before he tired of the work and abandoned it for some other new and crazy idea. An old friend of the fool and one of the wisest men in the village even approached him one morning as he was heading out to the project with his tools and told him, "At your age you should know that it's crazy to try to build a road over the mountains. No one has ever been foolish enough before to even try that. It's impossible, especially for you! Why, you're so old and weak you can hardly even pull out the weeds growing in your garden!"

The old fool just sighed sadly and said, "You know, your head has grown as hard as one of the rocks sitting beside our new road. Even my neighbor's young son has more insight than you do. It doesn't matter that I'm old and weak. My sons are committed to the project. They will help me now and when they grow old and weak themselves, their sons will help them. It might take many years, but the goal is worthwhile, and it will get finished eventually." The wise man could not really argue with his friend's optimistic belief, so he just shook his head doubtfully and then walked away.

Over the following years, the roadbuilding project continued. Eventually the old fool died, but his sons remained committed and worked on the project every chance they got. Often their friends would help them, and soon their own sons were old enough to help as well. After a few more years, it even became somewhat of a community project. Villagers began to use whatever length of road had already been completed to access untouched areas for hunting and fishing, and then they used it to get access to good timber for building materials and firewood.

As the villagers approached the top of the pass, people from the other side even started building their own road upward from the market town that eventually met the other one near the top. Valuable ore was found along the way and mines were dug. One day, the elders of the market town decided that they needed a breakwater for their harbor, and so the unused rock and rubble from the roadbuilding began to be used for that.

Over the years, the road continued to gradually be improved and widened. In some areas it was rerouted to create a gentler grade. Eventually it became much more practical as a route to get from the old fool's village to the market town than the old route had ever been.

In all the years since, traffic has steadily increased on the new road, and the little village behind the mountain has prospered. It became a hub for new roads that radiated outward from it to even more remote places beyond. But despite all the changes that have occurred over the many years to the road over the mountains, its name has always remained the same. To this very day, it is still called "the old fool's road!"

. . . .

Lieh-Tzu #24

. . . .

Hu Pa was very good at playing the lute, but he was not content with just being very good—he wanted to be great. He had heard of lute players so skilled that birds danced in the trees and fish leaped joyfully out of their ponds when they played, and he dreamed of having that kind of talent with his own instrument.

So, Hu Pa went to study at a school run by the famous musician, Music Master Hsiang.

But after three years, it seemed that study at the school was not helping Hu Pa's abilities at all. In fact, it seemed to be harming them! It was as though he had lost the ability to even complete a song. Repeatedly he would start to play a piece, get part way through it, get a disappointed look on his face, and then set his lute down and stop playing.

Finally, Music Master Hsiang himself asked for a meeting with Hu Pa in the school's courtyard and said to him, "Your instructor tells me that your talents with the lute seem to be diminishing with his instruction rather than increasing. Perhaps it would be better for you to quit the school for a while and try to regain your abilities at your home."

"I have not lost my ability to pluck the lute's strings nor to complete a song," Hu Pa answered firmly. I have not lost any of my abilities. I simply have not yet gained what I hope someday to gain—the ability to not just play the lute but to become one with it and its music when I do play. Only when I've accomplished that will I be able to become a truly great musician. I just get frustrated by so many failed attempts. Please let me stay in your school a little longer. I believe that the talent I seek will come to me soon.

So, Hu Pa continued to study at Hsiang's school and soon his skills did, indeed, finally begin to improve. In fact, they began to improve so dramatically that one day in the fall, Music Master Hsiang once again asked Hu Pa to meet him in the school's courtyard. "Your instructor tells me that your lute playing has improved dramatically in the past few months," he said. "How do you feel about that?"

"Yes, I believe I have truly made a breakthrough," Hu Pa replied happily. "Let me show you."

Hu Pa then picked up his lute and began to play a tune designed to represent the autumn season. His fingers gently touched each string with beautiful precision. The timing and mood of each note was perfection itself. Suddenly, a chilly breeze blew through the courtyard. Autumn leaves fell from the trees, and in those that bore fruit, the fruit began to ripen noticeably before Hsiang's eyes.

Then, when Hu Pa had finished the autumn song, he began to play another written to represent the springtime. Again, he played the piece flawlessly, and this time as he played, Hsiang noticed that the clouds parted in the sky, the chilly breeze died away, and the courtyard filled with sudden warmth. In the very same trees wherein fruit still hung from the branches, new flowers suddenly budded and then began to blossom.

Then, after the end of that song, Hu Pa played another that represented winter, and immediately a thick, dark cloud blew across the sun, casting the courtyard into shadow. A gust of frigid air slapped their faces, scattered flakes of snow drifted to the ground, and Hsiang noticed ice crystals beginning to form along the edges of the courtyard pond.

Finally, Hu Pa strummed a playful summer tune and the dark cloud scurried away, the sun again shone warmly, a frog began to sing its raspy song in the pond, and Hsiang felt an incredibly joyous feeling welling up from deep within himself.

"Your lute playing has truly become sublime!" Music Master

Hsiang told Hu Pa with heartfelt sincerity. "You have far sur-passed your goal of becoming one with your instrument and its music. You now seem to be able to reach through it to not just af-fect the Flow of Tao around you but to actually become one with it. Your skill with the lute is now the best I have ever known!"

. . . .

Lieh-Tzu #25

. . . .

When Tsau Fu was young, he wanted to become a great chario-teer, so he apprenticed himself to the most legendary charioteer of the time, T'ai Tou. For many months, Tsau Fu was only in-structed to run errands, take care of the horses, clean stalls, and otherwise help around the facility. He received no instruction on chariots at all, but he did not complain or become bitter. Instead, Tsau Fu remained humble and cheerful, and after two years had passed, the master finally decided that the boy was worthy and started his formal training.

So, one day, Tsau Fu was called to the training yard and T'ai Tou said to him, "To be a master bowmaker, one must first learn how to be a basket maker; to become a master blacksmith, one must start out by learning how to make coarse chisels; and to become a master charioteer, one must first learn to run across the tops of posts." And with that, T'ai Tou led Tsau Fu to a row of ten upright posts sunk partially into the ground, each a long stride from the next. Then he leaped onto the first, balanced on one foot for a second, and then proceeded to run down the row, leaping effort-lessly from the top of one to the top of the next. When he reached the end of the row, he turned and ran back again. Then, as if that was not enough of an achievement, he folded his arms in front of him, started to sing a song, and did the same thing all over again. Leaping then to the ground, T'ai Tou said to the boy, "When you can do what I just did, we will move on to the next phase of your training," and with that, he turned and walked away.

Tsau Fu wondered briefly what running on post ends had to do with charioteering, but then started considering the task before him. Jumping cautiously from the top of one post end to the top of the next did not seem too difficult, but running quickly back and forth, especially with his arms folded in front of him, seemed nearly impossible! Nevertheless, that was what he was expected to do, so he had to learn to do it!

Each post end was only wide enough for one foot, so Tsau Fu quickly realized that the only possible way to pass down the row successfully was to leap quickly from each to the next. The first few times he tried, he quickly fell and was lucky not to have injured himself. It took half a day of repeated attempts before Tsau Fu was able to run down the post ends from beginning to end and back for the first time without falling, but by the end of that first day, he could do so fairly consistently. The second day, he continued practicing, and when he felt ready, he tried doing it again with his arms folded in front of him. Again, he fell may times but eventually was successful, and by the end of the third day, he was singing as he ran and decided that he had finally mastered the art of post-end running!

The next morning, when T'ai Tou watched Tsau Fu demonstrate his new skill, the master charioteer was obviously pleased. "You're quite agile," he said happily. "You picked that up quickly. There are several basic physical abilities essential for becoming a good charioteer—agility, strength, stamina, balance, and eye-body coordination are examples. When driving a six-horse chariot hour after hour in all sorts of situations, charioteers need all of them. You have now demonstrated that you have those abilities in good measure, so now we can move on to actually teaching you about chariots.

"As you probably already know, a charioteer drives the six horses that pull his chariot by means of twelve reins—one for each side of each horse. One end of each rein attaches to one end of the bit of each horse's bridle and the charioteer holds the other end in one of his hands—the left hand for the left-side reins of the horses and the right hand for the right-side reins. It is by means of the twelve reins that he communicates his instructions to the horses as to where he wants to go and how fast he wants to get there.

"What makes the system complicated is that each of the six horses is an intelligent living creature. Each one has a personality, good and bad days, and personal likes and dislikes. Some may get along well with all of the other horses, while others may not. Some may do better in front while others do better behind. One horse might be quite sensitive to his driver's instructions while another might sometimes be inclined to resist them. As a charioteer, you must know your horses and be sensitive to their needs and personalities, while still maintaining total control over them, and for the most part, that is all done by means of the reins.

"When one is first learning to be a charioteer, he must listen and learn and focus with his conscious mind on all the details of the job. He must concentrate on getting to know and understand the personalities of his horses as communicated through the reins, and on how to use those reins to control them most effectively. But you, as a student of charioteering, must be aware that your ultimate objective is to do all those things without using your conscious mind at all, because when a charioteer knows his horses and his chariot well enough, and when his horses know him, his job can best be done by intent alone. His hands, holding the reins, respond directly to his intent, and the horses then respond to the pressures they feel from the reins. Without ever even needing to use a whip, he can therefore guide his chariot forward or backward, or turn to the right or to the left without thought or effort.

"The good charioteer controls twelve reins, six bridles, two wheels, and twenty-four hooves all at the same time with precision and without confusion on steep and narrow mountain roads just as easily as he does on flat meadowland. Whether on long and boring journeys or maneuvering on frantic, fast-changing battlefields, he melds as one with his vehicle and his horses and can drive them any which way effortlessly.

"So, now that we have tested your personality, gauged your physical abilities, and gone over what you need to know intellectually, all that remains is for you to absorb it all deeply within yourself by means of constant practice. Let's go for a ride!"

. . . .

Lieh-Tzu #26

. . . .

Personal Virtue approached Destiny one day and said rather arrogantly, "I'm much more important in people's lives than you are."

Destiny was taken aback by Personal Virtue's unexpected comment, but then asked, "Why would you even say such a thing?"

"I say it because it's clear that the key to long life, success, and happiness for people is to work hard, live a virtuous life, and to be careful to make wise decisions when faced with important life choices!" Personal Virtue answered. "Their final destiny will just come as a result of that!"

"I disagree," Destiny responded confidently. "You give yourself too much credit. That may often be true, but it also often isn't! There have been an almost infinite number of businessmen, politicians, and bureaucrats in the world who have used corrupt means to become rich and powerful, and there have been just as many wise, virtuous, hardworking people who have remained poor and powerless all their lives. Old Peng is said to have made many foolish choices when he was alive and yet he lived a long and prosperous life, while Yen Hui, Confucius's wisest student, died a miserable death when he was only eighteen. Confucius himself was far more virtuous than the notorious feudal lords of his time, but compared to them he lived a life of destitution. The emperor Shang Tse was horribly cruel and immoral but became immensely rich and powerful, and he also lived to be quite old, whereas his ministers tried to be virtuous but met with violent early deaths. If you were truly so much more important than I in determining long life, success and happiness, why is it that so many virtuous people led short, miserable lives and so many contemptuous people turned out to live long and be successful?"

Personal Virtue was surprised and dismayed by all this evidence against his assertion and found himself answering meekly, "Well, maybe you're right! I guess I don't have quite as much impact on people's lives as I thought I did. But since you seem to be the one, then, who determines long life, success, and happiness, why do you allow so many undeserving people to be successful and so many deserving people to be unsuccessful?"

Destiny laughed and said, "Now you're giving yourself too little credit and me too much. Besides, you really don't understand me, at all, it seems. I can't just determine the future, nor purposely create specific outcomes for specific people. Listen, and I'll try to explain.

"I am not some inevitable determinant of the final tally of each person's life, as some people portray me," Destiny continued, "All I am is the series of situations each person encounters from moment to moment throughout their lifetimes. And that's where you—Personal Virtue—come into the picture, because each individual who has gained any control over his or her life at all will react in his or her own way to all those various situations I present to him by means of the decisions they choose to make. And their decisions are determined by their relationships with you! While each person may or may not have much control over what I create for them, they do have control over their relationship with you and the choices they make because of it, especially as they mature and establish themselves in society!

"And so, it is no-doubt true that if a person always makes wise and moral decisions when dealing with the situations they experience from day to day, it will increase the odds of them encountering increasingly more favorable situations in the future and therefore of them being able to attain long life and success. But if, on the other hand, I—Destiny—were to only present the person constantly with miserable and impossible choices, I think there would be little opportunity for you to ever help them. It seems then that you and I are of somewhat equal importance in people's lives, but each in our own way!

"And as to happiness, while I'm sure it's always easier to be happy when Destiny smiles on you and Personal Virtue eases your path forward, I also think happiness in many cases is just a matter of each person's natural temperament—no matter what they happen to encounter in life!"

. . . .

Lieh-Tzu #27

. . . .

Pei Kung met Hsi Men on the road one day, and on this occasion Hsi Men agreed to sit down for a while to chat. The two had been the best of friends when they were young, but their lives had diverged dramatically as adults, and they had not spoken together for several years.

After a few minutes of catching up on the affairs of mutual friends and the events going on in each other's lives. Pei Kung commented despondently, "You and I are the same age and grew up together, but people have always been more willing to help you succeed in what you do. We look and act very much alike, but it's always you that everyone loves. We are both good, honest people and hold the same values, and yet it is always you that they trust. And when, long ago, we both held office in court, you were promoted and I dismissed, even though I was always very good at my work. When each of us trade, you make a profit and I lose money. When we farm, you harvest a big cash crop and I'm lucky to even break even.

"Look at us now!" Pei Kung continued with rising passion. "I wear coarse wool and eat millet. I live in an old, thatched hut on the edge of town, and I must go everywhere on foot. You, on the other hand, wear brocades and silk and eat meat and expensive grains. You live in a fancy house near the palace, and if you want to travel any distance, you ride in a beautiful carriage with four beautiful horses. Nowadays, when we pass each other on a street, you usually ignore me. It's been years since we've sat down together to visit or share a meal! Have you decided now that you're better than I am?"

Hsi Men was embarrassed and annoyed by his old friend's outburst. "I really don't know what to say!" he answered. "Whatever we undertake, you seem to fail at, and I succeed. I guess in that one respect, at least, I am better than you!"

Pei Kung could not think of anything more to say, so he just got up and started walking back to his home, feeling humiliated and discouraged. Along the way, he met another old friend, Master Tung Kuo, who noticed that he was upset and asked what was wrong, and so Pei Kung told him what had happened.

Master Tung Kuo thought for a moment and then said, "Hearing about your conversation, I must say first of all that I'm surprised by the resentment you feel about your old friend's success at accumulating wealth and prestige. Those are only two of many different measures of success in life. Hsi Men is lucky to have developed a friendly and outgoing personality and it seems to have served him well in business and government, but I have known you for many years and I know that you too have many personal strengths and blessings. Your house may not be as big and fancy as his, but it is a nice house. You have a beautiful family that loves you. You earn an adequate income, and while the food on your table may be plain, it is ample and nutritious. Your friends may not be as plentiful or as illustrious as his, but there are many of us, and perhaps our friendships are more sincere than those of his friends. You would do well to recognize what you do have and learn to appreciate that rather than bemoaning the fact that someone else has a few strengths and blessings that you don't have."

"How can you compare lives with someone when you are both so young anyway? Most people's lives are long and subject to many changes. Your friend could live his entire life being successful in business and government and you might always have to struggle to support your family, but who knows what might happen tomorrow or the next day? It's just as possible that in a year of two, Hsi Men will be feeling resentment about your success in some aspect or other of life. You have been assuming that Hsi Men will always be more successful in general than you will be, but so far he has only been more successful in a couple of aspects of life for a couple of years! It's just silly to compare your life, or even a segment of it, with another person's, anyway. You and your friend are each just equal parts of the whole of Tao, only superficially even separate from each other. You each only have one life to enjoy in whatever way you decide to before you eventually return to the great void. Don't worry about what other people are doing or thinking. It's irrelevant. Concentrate on making the most of this one incredible life you now get to experience!"

Pei Kung walked the rest of the way to his humble house deep in thought. When he got there, he kissed his wife and children and realized that he was happy to be home. Over the course of the next few days, he discovered that his wool clothing was actually quite warm and comfortable, and that his bean and millet meals were both delicious and nutritious. One day he realized that he really had everything in the world that he ever actually needed. He began to dedicate himself completely to his work, family, and friends and soon found himself to be the happiest man on Earth.

"He has been asleep for a long time," Master Tung Kuo said later, when Pei Kung's name came up in a conversation, "but a man who wants to listen and understand is easy to awaken."

Lieh-Tzu #28

Yang Pu was curious about the differences between people's lives, so he asked his older brother, Yang Chu, about it.

"How is it that two friends who are the same age and grew up together in the same town, who have similar parents, look the same, shared most of the same childhood friends and experiences, and believe in much the same things can then grow up to have totally different adult lives than each other?" he wondered. "Doesn't that seem strange to you?"

"A lot of it has to do with each person's personal destiny," Yang Chu answered. "Personal destiny is what just happens to occur to each person every day and affects them in all sorts of unexpected and obscure ways, and each of us has our own personal destiny due to our unique situation within the Flow of Tao. Even people who grew up with similar childhoods and had the same friends will each have a different personal destiny."

"Isn't it frightening to think that such important parts of our lives will always be beyond our control?" Yang Pu asked with concern.

"That's just the way life is!" his brother answered. "You must remember that each of us is just a tiny part of the entire Flow of Tao. It's natural to want to control everything around you, but Tao is complex and constantly changing, and your personal destiny is just that minuscule part of its Flow that touches you most directly. You are always subject to whatever it happens to bring you. Whatever aspects of it you can't control, you must just come to accept! The thing that you do have control over, though, is how you choose to react to what happens!"

"That is what the Way of Tao is all about. You must first learn to understand Tao and how it works, and then you must learn to accept its Flow and whatever it happens to bring you. Learn to have faith in your ability to respond to what happens in ways that will bring you successes later that you can be proud of. In your responses to what the Flow of Tao brings you today, you gain some control over what it might bring you tomorrow and in all the days after that.

If you decide to build your house out of stone or adobe because you know someone whose house burned down and you don't want that to happen to your house, for example, you will lessen the likelihood that your own will ever burn down. If you make a point of learning to farm and hunt because, as a child, you were sometimes hungry and don't want your family to ever be hungry, you lessen the likelihood that they will ever need to be. In such ways you can guide your future destiny in the direction you want it to go. But you can never totally control it because the Flow of Tao is just too complicated and difficult to predict."

For the person who has learned the Way of Tao and gained faith in his ability to deal with his destiny, there is no difference whether it happens to bring him a long life or a short one, between gaining wealth or remaining poor, between here or there, companionship or solitude, or other people's approval or their disapproval. There is never anything to regret nor to celebrate. It is all just his destiny, and only his choice of responses matters.

"The greatest of all such men in that regard are the sages," Yang Chu continued, "because they choose their responses not to benefit themselves but to benefit all of Tao that they have come to know and love. That is the best anyone can ever do!"

. . . .

Lieh-Tzu #29

. . . .

The *Book of the Yellow Emperor* says:

"The sage at rest is as relaxed in body and mind as if he were not even conscious. He feels no exultation, anxiety, regret, or fear. His thoughts deal calmly with memories, possibilities, the needs of others, lessons learned, the movement of the Flow of Tao, objectives and how best to achieve them, and likely desirable and undesirable outcomes.

"The sage in motion is as confident, focused, and as powerful as a dynamo. He knows where he wants events to go and efficiently aims them in that direction in a way that is aligned with the Flow of Tao. He feels no need to change his expressions, opinions, or actions when others watch him because his conscience is clear. Such a man is true to what he believes in. He is genuine. He need never fear or desire anything on behalf of his ego because that is never his concern. And nothing can ever really obstruct him, for he will simply find a way around it!"

Lieh-Tzu #30

King Ching of Ch'i and his royal retinue went on an excursion to Ox Mountain one summer to visit a beautiful mountain meadow overlooking the county's main river valley. He, his father, his grandfather, and probably all their ancestors for centuries had come to that same spot on occasion to look down on their capital city and much of the kingdom that stretched out for hundreds of miles behind it. From that meadow they could see rivers meandering through lush green valleys separated by wooded hills and ridgelines, villages, smoky towns, and mile after mile of fertile farmland. It was truly an awe-inspiring sight, but on that day, the elderly king suddenly grew sad. He sighed and said, "What a pity it is that I shall have to die someday and depart from this beautiful kingdom. I wish death never had to come and I could enjoy these beautiful valleys and mountains—in fact, all of my wonderful kingdom—forever!" And then a tear ran down his cheek.

Two of the king's servants and his chief minister, Yen Tzu, happened to be near him at that moment and heard his sad words. The two servants grew sad along with their king, and one of them said, "That is so true, my lord. Even we who have so little and who must eat only coarse grains and tough meat would like to live forever. Death must be even more difficult for yourself, who has a beautiful kingdom and so much wealth." But then the two servants and the king all noticed that the chief minister standing next to them had a look not of sadness but of amusement on his face.

"My servants and I are saddened by the prospect of death someday," King Ching said to Yen Tzu, "But you seem to find it amusing. Why is that?"

"I'm very sorry," Yen Tzu answered. "I did not mean to be rude, but it occurred to me that if each of your ancestors who had come to this meadow and wished for eternal life in the past had had their wish granted, what a strange and different world it would now be. T'ai Kung, the founder of your lineage, would no doubt still be king, and his sons would still be alive but would only be dukes. Their sons would still be alive as well but would only be mayors and magistrates; and their sons would still be alive too but would only be businessmen and landlords. Your grandfather might be a servant to one of your ancestors, and your father only a serf farming someone else's land. You, if you had ever even been born at all, might be the lowliest of peasants not even able to feed yourself and your family, and praying, perhaps, not for eternal life but for a quick and painless death to end your misery. I apologize again for my rudeness, but the irony of those thoughts just somehow struck me as amusing.

King Ching felt a rush of various emotions flood through his head as a result of Yen Tzu's explanation. He was certainly not used to being made to feel foolish by his chief minister, but he could not in all fairness justify being too angry at him. The man had seemed sincerely contrite in his apology and had merely been honest about his thoughts. Finally, the king said, "I suppose you're right, Yen Tzu. All good things must eventually come to an end or at some point they would no longer be good things anymore at all!"

Lieh-Tzu #31

Yang Chu noted that a ninety-year lifespan might seem like a long existence, especially to a person who is still young, but that if you break the ninety-year lifespan down and examine it, there is actually very little time in it that is truly one's own. As much as a third of a person's life takes place at the two ends when the person is likely to be either too young and inexperienced or too old and feeble of mind or body to make important life decisions and then to be able to carry them out. Roughly a third or so of what is left is lost to sleep. A third or so of what is left after that is taken up by doing whatever one must do to earn a living so that they can purchase necessities like food and shelter—usually accomplished by serving the demands of someone else. And then of the little remaining time, a third or more is often taken up by such routine and necessary chores as running errands, cooking, cleaning, washing, and taking care of children. After the removal of all that time that is not entirely one's own, the average person will be lucky to have the equivalent of eighteen years or so remaining of their entire lifetime to do whatever each, personally, wants to do to satisfy his or her own desires and pursue his or her own dreams.

And, of course, the time doesn't come in a solid eighteen-year block; it comes in the form of a few hours here and a few hours there, parts of days, weekends, and perhaps occasional short vacations. Since those little blocks of time are the only periods in one's entire life when he or she has both the total freedom and the ability to really do whatever they want, it could be said that out of a whole lifetime, that eighteen years of time, broken into short periods, is the real nexus or highlight of it all. Given its importance from that perspective, what should one do with it? What would be most meaningful? What would bring the most joy?

Many people very pointedly do very little of any consequence with their free time at all. They use it to relax, to idle away the hours, to socialize with family and friends, or to amuse themselves with trivial pursuits.

Other people have hobbies or activities that they enjoy spending time on, they work on projects around their houses or gardens, or they work on community projects or do things to help their families and friends.

Many people spend every free moment doing things they think might eventually help bring them more wealth, power, or fame. Wealth might bring them a nicer home, luxuries, beautiful carriages and fine horses, the most delicious foods, servants, and clothing of the finest materials. Power might bring them control over social, political, and business events, assets, and people. And fame amounts to public recognition of their talents, hard work, beauty, or cleverness and is likely to increase their self-esteem.

There is no right or wrong answer as to what someone should do with the few years' worth of precious self-directed time they are allotted in their lives. It is their own time to do with as they wish. But there are considerations to point out.

One problem with spending one's precious personal free time pursuing the goals of wealth, power, and fame is that if the person does so by working extra hours at his usual workplace, or even somewhere else, under the direction of someone else telling him what he must spend the time doing, isn't he voluntarily giving away the very same personal free time that is so short and precious—that same free time that is arguably the nexus of the person's very existence? And for what? Are the benefits of wealth, power, and fame worth that cost?

And has the person decided to devote his few decades worth of personal free time trying to attain wealth, power, or fame because he made a conscious decision on his own to do so, or is he doing it because it was expected or demanded of him? If so, then the person has agreed, perhaps unwittingly, to surrender that most significant portion of his life to benefit those other people in hopes that it might also benefit him!

The most meaningful and self-defining part of your life is actually quite short and is widely scattered into little parcels here and there. It is yours to do with as you like, but be sure to recognize it for what it is and also be sure that what you do with it is truly what you and not others with power over you want you to do with it!

Lieh-Tzu #32

We all know that many people around the world live short and miserable lives due to poverty. Poor people usually don't get enough nutritious food, they might not have warm and safe places to sleep at night, they are often victims of abuse of one sort or another, and they probably don't have access to good medical care when they need it. What is less well-known is that people who are overly obsessed with the accumulation and maintenance of wealth often live short and miserable lives too because of their obsession.

People who are so driven, at first, often work too hard and play too little. They worry too much about financial gains and financial setbacks and tend not to appreciate and enjoy the little things in life that make it truly worthwhile. Too often they underappreciate the importance of the people around them, sacrifice their personal relationships for opportunities to advance themselves, and find themselves lonely and surrounded only by sycophants like themselves. The importance of moral principles becomes undervalued because it so often gets in the way of economic opportunity, and therefore they must also live with compromised consciences. And once wealth is finally attained, if it ever is, it becomes much too easy for such a person to drown out their unhappiness and guilt by overindulging in a decadent lifestyle that too soon damages their health.

So, what is the happiest and healthiest way to live one's life? The answer lies in simply enjoying it and keeping oneself free from guilt. If you have something worthwhile you want to achieve, achieve it. If you need to earn money to support yourself, find a way you can enjoy earning it. If you need something extra you can't afford, work a little harder so you can buy it—but enjoy yourself while doing whatever it is you decide to do, and don't compromise your values in the process. Challenge yourself to be successful because it's fun, rewarding, and makes life worthwhile to do so. Those who are good at enjoying life are rarely poor for long!

. . . .

Lieh-Tzu #33

. . . .

Yen Tzu and Kuan Chung were having a conversation over tea, and Yen Tzu asked Kuan Chung about his philosophy of "maximizing life" that many people had been talking about lately.

"You only have one life, and it only makes sense to live it to the fullest," Kuan Chung commented. "Maximizing life means living it without constraint or suppression."

How does one do that?" Yen Tzu asked.

"You must never let foolish fears hold you back. Give yourself up to whatever your ears find most pleasing to hear, search out and see whatever it is your eyes most want to see, follow your nose wherever it takes you, discover the places where your mind and body find the most comfort, say all the things that you feel you should say, and achieve all the things you are driven to achieve! If you don't fully explore everything in your lifetime that you want to explore and do everything that you want to do, you will have allowed your one and only life to be constrained.

"And when you hear, see, and smell your world, be sure that you hear, see, and smell what is actually there and not just what you've been told by others that you should expect to hear, see, and smell!

"Your only constraints should be your own logically derived constraints conceived within you. For example, you must always consider the effects and consequences of your actions on yourself and on others, especially those who are good, those who are innocent, and those you care the most about, and you must always avoid what would sully your conscience—but beyond those consciously chosen limitations, in order to maximize your life, you must not allow either your personal fears or the requirements of others to restrict you, for if you do, you will not be experiencing fully the one and only life you have been given. One day of full life is worth more than a hundred years of a lifetime that is being constrained or suppressed!"

At that point in the conversation, Kuan Chung paused for a moment and then said, "Now I have told you about my philosophy of 'maximizing life,' tell me your feelings about death. What do you think about proper funeral ceremonies and burials? What would you prefer for yourself, hopefully many years from now, when the time comes for you to pass?"

"None of that matters to me at all. I have nothing to say about it." Yen Tzu responded.

"Please! I answered your questions, now you must answer mine," Kuan Chung prodded. "You must have some opinion!"

"Once I am dead, what difference will any of that make to me? It is the same to me whether you bury me or burn me, whether you put me under the ground or throw my body in a ditch. It will make no difference to me whether I'm in a marble coffin or a wooden box—whether I'm draped in an old sheet or dressed in an embroidered silk shirt with a dragon-emblazed jacket over it. I do not care now, and I will certainly not care then. Burial and funeral ceremonies are for the benefit of those who are still alive, not for those who have died."

And with that, Yen Tzu and Kuan Chung looked at each other and nodded in agreement. Between the two of them, it seemed, they had said all there really was to say about both living and dying!

Lieh-Tzu #34

Tuan Mu Shu was the descendent of Tzu Kung who had been a student of Confucius and a very successful businessman. As a result of his ancestor's success, Tuan Mu Shu inherited a large fortune and was a very wealthy man. But unlike Tzu Kung, Tuan Mu Shu had no interest in doing any kind of work at all. He enjoyed the good life and followed wherever his fancy happened to take him.

Tuan Mu Shu had a huge mansion built of the very finest materials and decorated by the most skillful artisans. He ate the best foods and wore clothes of the finest quality. He traveled in fancy carriages pulled by beautiful horses, and he was always accompanied wherever he went by the most beautiful young women in the region.

Tuan Mu Shu always pursued whatever stimulated his senses, aroused his curiosity, and excited his mind. He collected rare artifacts and treasures from foreign countries. He traveled to exotic places, was entertained by the best musicians and dancers, and never denied himself anything that he ever desired. He lived an extravagant lifestyle that was envied by kings and noblemen alike.

Unlike many wealthy people, though, Tuan Mu Shu was never tight-fisted with his money. Instead, he was always generous and spent it as freely to help others as he did for himself. He often threw huge parties and invited hundreds of people to come and enjoy the best foods and the finest entertainment. He shared his wealth with relatives, neighbors, and even with strangers he noticed who obviously needed his help. His generosity was so great that there was not a person in his town or even in the region who did not benefit directly or indirectly from it.

But by the time Tuan Mu Shu was sixty years old, his health was beginning to fail, and he had either spent or given away much of his wealth and possessions. Within another year the rich man had become a poor man, and when he finally became very ill, he couldn't even afford a doctor and soon passed away.

It was then that his children realized how desperately poor he had become. There was nothing left at all for them or their children, and not even enough to pay for his funeral.

Fortunately, those who had benefited the most from Tuan Mu Shu's generosity over the years heard of the family's financial problems and stepped up as a group to help the family out. Together, they paid for his funeral and even pooled enough together to return some of the money Tuan Mu Shu had given them over the years to assist his children and their families.

When one prominent scholar of the time heard Tuan Mu Shu's story, he declared the man to have been a degenerate madman. "Tzu Kung would have rolled over in his grave if he heard how his wealth had been squandered," the scholar said. "Tuan Mu Shu abandoned his family and did not even provide for the welfare of his descendants." But another scholar commented that "Tuan Mu Shu was an enlightened man. He was sincere in everything he ever did. There was no pretense, no scheming, and no ulterior motives in his actions. He followed his heart and was not constrained by social conventions. He enjoyed himself freely, gave freely, and never did anything that went against his nature."

Tuan Mu Shu, being deceased, did not care at all what the scholars thought about the life he had chosen to live!

Lieh-Tzu #35

A student asked Yang Chu one day, "If a person were to take great care and always do everything he could to keep his body healthy, do you think it would be possible for him to live forever?"

"It's impossible to live forever," Yang Chu answered curtly.

"Do you think that valuing one's life greatly and treating it with extreme care might at least prolong it?"

"I think that valuing your life too much and being overly cautious with it is more likely to shorten it than it is to prolong it. Doing what you reasonably can to try to stay strong and healthy might prevent you from dying earlier than you might otherwise, but there is nothing you can do that would keep you alive much beyond the usual top human lifespan of ninety to a hundred years. When people are meant to die, they will die. There is nothing that can be done to prevent that.

"Why would you want to prolong your life beyond a hundred years anyway?" Yang Chu went on. "By the time a person has lived a hundred years, what more is there for him or her to experience? By then he will have felt all the emotions there are to be felt thousands of times over. By that age he will have already discovered what he likes and what he doesn't like. He will have done all he can do. He will have tasted all the flavors, smelled all the smells, heard all the sounds, seen all the sights, and felt all the sensations.

"Life amid the Flow of Tao is a repetition of cycles anyway. There is a period of good government, then a period of bad government, and then one of good government again. There is a period of prosperity, then one of hard times, and then of good times again. Fads come and go, and then come back again in a somewhat similar fashion. There are times of good luck and then times of bad luck. By the time one approaches one hundred years of age, he has seen them all and his body is becoming more of a burden to him than a blessing. By then most people are readying themselves to move on and leave this world to their children and grandchildren to do with as they will."

"If old age is so unpleasant and meaningless," the student then commented, "perhaps the elderly should just purposely end their lives with knives or by running into burning buildings rather than doing anything they can to prolong them!"

"No, that is not the way either. As long as you live, experience as much as you can experience, do as much as you can do, learn as much as you can learn, and then teach as much as you can teach. Just let your life run its natural course. Satisfy all your desires for as long as you are able and then wait patiently for the end. There is no need to try to delay that nor to hasten it. Life's end will come when it is time for it to come!"

Lieh-Tzu #36

Yang Chu was visiting the king of Liang and commented that ruling an empire properly should not be difficult at all. The king, who was a good-natured man and liked Yang Chu, smiled and said, "Chu, I have heard that you have both a wife and a mistress and that you cannot seem to control either one of them, and that you have a small garden that you cannot seem to keep weeded. Do you really feel qualified to comment on ruling empires?"

At that, Yang Chu chuckled and agreed that he was not much of a gardener and also that he had given up even trying to keep track of his wife and mistress, but then he pointed out that managing an empire was quite different from managing one's domestic affairs.

"The whale is the master of the ocean but does not presume to be good at swimming around in shallow water, and the swan, who looks down from lofty heights and could choose to land anywhere is never comfortable dealing with the small puddles and ponds and therefore always chooses the larger bodies of water to float on.

"There is an old saying in my country that 'one who focuses on great enterprises will not want to concern himself with trifles.' And another that states that 'in order to gain great victories, one must usually first endure many small defeats.'

"Along similar lines," Yang Chu continued, "Yao and Shun are still known centuries after their deaths as having been among the greatest of all emperors, and yet if either one during his lifetime had been put in a pasture and forced to try to round up just one ram to drive into a pen, I doubt if he could have done so, even though a ten-year-old shepherd boy with a stick over his shoulder would have no trouble at all gathering and leading a flock of a hundred sheep to any pasture or pen.

"That, by the way, is how I, liking to focus on big projects, suggest that you manage your empire, Your Majesty—like the shepherd boy—using comfortable expertise to gently nudge your flock with only a small stick in any direction you decide you want them to go!"

Lieh-Tzu #37

Yang Chu once said:

"The events of the distant past have long since vanished from the knowledge of everyone. No one in the very early days even knew how to record them. The actions of the very first emperors are only legends now, more lost than really known. And of those emperors who came soon after them, we know only a few names and dates and a little of what some of them did—nothing more—all really more fantasy than fact!

"Of the multitudes of other people who have lived and died since then, even since the invention of writing, we know only a very little about a very few. The rest lived and then died and were all then eventually forgotten, along with all the events they ever experienced and all the accomplishments they ever achieved.

"And even of the billions of people alive at this very moment, very few of us will ever know more than perhaps a few dozen very well. Some few more we might recognize and say hello to on a street corner and know, or think we know, a little about. Of those currently alive who are famous, we might know of them, but it's unlikely we will ever actually know them. But in truth, all we can ever really be certain of is what we, ourselves, have experienced. Beyond that, we can choose to believe or not to believe whatever we are told by others!

"From the most distant past all the way up until just a century or so ago, every single actual memory of the achievements and follies, inner merits and flaws, personal successes and failures, sins and virtues, hopes and fears, and loves and hates of every person who has ever lived have all without exception been lost. There is no way at all, of course, to preserve them. All that is left are legends, stories, and perhaps biographies or autobiographies of a few of the most famous. All just words!

"In truth, all that ever really matters is the impact that each person's life has on society and on those around them, whether credited to them or not. Do they improve the lives of those who know them, or do they damage or disrupt them? Do they advance knowledge or improve the realities of the world around them in some way, or don't they? The concept of one's personal "legacy" is a fraud! If a person is remembered at all for any length of time after his or her death, it will only be some pale recognition of their prior existence along with a list of their supposed accomplishments, devoid of all else that made the person who he or she really was. And being dead, it will be of no value to them, anyway.

"Each person should just live his or her life each day in such a way that he experiences and enjoys it as much as is possible and in such a way that those who interact with him realize that they can safely value, trust, and perhaps admire him for who he is and what he does. That is all that really matters!"

Lieh-Tzu #38

When Lieh-Tzu was still quite young, he studied Taoism under the famous sage Hu Tzu. "When you have learned how to follow the Flow of Tao," Hu Tzu told him one day, "I can start to teach you the Way, and with the Way, you will learn how best to be able to do all the things you ever hope to do in your life."

"Then please tell me how to follow the Flow of Tao," Lieh-Tzu replied.

"Go outside and observe your shadow for a while and then you will begin to understand."

So Lieh-Tzu went outside and watched his shadow. When he bent over, his shadow bent over, too. When he stood up straight, his shadow stood up straight. Every movement that his body made his shadow made as well.

When he went back into the room, Hu Tzu said to him, "Your shadow is perfectly attuned with the movement of your body. Your task, now, is to learn to be as attuned to the movements of the Flow of Tao as your shadow is with your body. It will not be a quick or easy job, though, because the Flow of Tao is infinitely complex and incorporates an almost infinite number of aspects—social, biological, economic, climatic, environmental, and all the many other things that are a part of it. And there are some that you will never be able to predict at all because they are unpredictable, like sudden acts of nature, the weather, and unexpected actions by strangers you find yourself affected by.

"Learning to attune your mind to the Flow of Tao will involve a lot of conscious thought at first, and your perceptions of it will never be perfect because of its unpredictable nature, but over time and with practice, you will eventually learn to be able to often sense the movements of the Flow, and your understanding of what is likely to happen next will someday become largely intuitive.

"And after you begin to sense the Flow of Tao and to follow its movements, the next thing you will start to learn is how to do what you want to do in alignment with it, and even eventually sometimes to do them in front of it—for that is what this is really all about. To be most successful and effective in doing the things you want to do in life, your timing must always be in tune with, and sometimes even just slightly in front of, the Flow of Tao!"

Lieh-Tzu #39

Kuan Yin said to Lieh-Tzu:

"If your words near others are enthusiastic, bitter, happy, or sad, they will create an echo.

"If your moral standards are notably high, indifferent, or lacking, they will create a shadow.

"The opinions of others who have heard you will be the echoes, and their actions will be the shadows.

"Hence it is said:

"Be careful with your words, for some who hear you are likely to agree with you.

"Be thoughtful about your morality, for it will affect what takes place around you!"

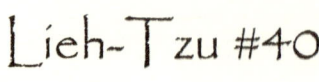

Lieh-Tzu #40

The sage considers what is likely to come out by noting what went in. He also considers what is likely to come next by noting what has passed before.

He makes tentative assumptions based on those observed effects by light of his own experiences but then verifies those assumptions by considering the experiences of others. And when both his experiences and his verifications concur, he knows that acting on that basis will almost always take him where he wants to go, whereas being afraid to act is akin to fearing to follow a well-trod path aiming directly at his destination!

Lieh-Tzu #41

Yen Hui said to Lieh-Tzu:

"The only reason for studying the Way of Tao is to learn how to be successful so that you can earn lots of money, but getting money that way requires years of study. I might get richer quicker by winning the lottery or by finding buried treasure. Why bother?"

"I disagree that that is the reason for studying the Way of Tao, entirely," Lieh-Tzu answered. "Anyone who is a dedicated student of Tao studies it for the wisdom it imparts and for the understandings of life and of their own life's purpose that they gain from it, not for the sake of wealth. If some should ever attain wealth as a result of it, that is a secondary benefit—if one even wants to think of wealth as a benefit at all!

"Those whose highest concern is chasing after wealth are much like chickens scratching around a farmyard for a fat seed or a juicy bug, or like a dog wandering through the woods looking for a bone. Like wild animals, they lock their horns and fight for scraps—and to the winners go the spoils! How can one expect others to respect him or her if they live their lives like such creatures?"

Lieh-Tzu #42

Lieh-Tzu decided to learn archery, and after practicing for a few hours had hit the bullseye several times, so he went to tell his instructor, Kuan Yin, who asked him, "Do you know why you hit the bullseye when you did?"

"No, not really," Lieh-Tzu responded honestly.

"Then just keep practicing."

So Lieh-Tzu continued to practice with his bow and his arrows every chance he had. For more than a year he shot at targets at different distances, at different times of the day, and in different seasons. He shot up hills and he shot down hills. Eventually he came to be able to hit the bullseye most of the time, so he went back to Kuan Yin and told him about his progress.

"And do you have an understanding now of why you hit the bullseye when you do and of why you miss it when you don't?" Kuan Yin asked him.

"Well, I can't put it into words, but yes, I think I do!" Lieh-Tzu answered.

"That's perfect! Then you are truly learning archery," Kuan Yin told him. "Hold on to that understanding and do not lose it. That is the kind of understanding that applies not only to archery but to all aspects of life."

Lieh-Tzu #43

Lieh-Tzu said:

"It is difficult to teach the Way of Tao to many who are young. Those at the peak of their attractiveness tend to be proud and those at the height of their vigor tend to be impetuous. And when a person is young and proud and impetuous, he or she often tends not to value the opinions of others. And if one does not value the opinions of others, then he or she will usually choose to make decisions and act solely on the basis of their own often limited judgement.

"More mature and wise people value the opinions of others. Because of that, their power does not diminish as quickly as they grow older, and they are not thrown into confusion when their own knowledge and cleverness sometimes happen to fall short.

"The difficulty for such older and wiser people when they reach positions where they manage others, then, becomes not so much their own limited knowledge and cleverness as it is their ability to determine the true knowledge and cleverness of those they end up working with."

Lieh-Tzu #44

Lieh-Tzu and his wife had moved to Cheng, and the transition had not been an easy one. Food and money were in short supply, and their bodies had begun to grow lean and their faces gaunt. An acquaintance who worked in government mentioned their problems to Tzu Yang, the prime minister of Cheng.

"Lieh-Tzu is known to be a sage of Tao and yet he and his family are quite destitute right now. If you help him in his time of need, you will be seen by the people as being a generous patron of an important scholar," he told Tzu Yang.

Tzu Yang immediately saw the possible political benefits of helping Lieh-Tzu and ordered a gift of grain to be delivered to his door. But when a messenger arrived bearing the gift, Lieh-Tzu bowed twice, asked the messenger to express his profound gratitude to Tzu Yang for the offer of the grain, but then refused to accept it, asking that it be given to some more deserving family instead. After the messenger left, Lieh-Tzu's wife was furious because of his action. "I have heard for years about the benefits of your study of Tao, and yet when we need help the most and it is offered because of your reputation, you reject it. Why? Are we destined for some reason to have to live our lives hungry and destitute?" she asked angrily.

But Lieh-Tzu just smiled and said, "I would have accepted the gift under different circumstances, but in this case it would have been unwise to do so. Tzu Yang is in trouble politically. The people do not like him, and I am told that he is falling out of favor with the king as well. He is only trying to bolster his situation in the king's court by assisting us. But if we had accepted his gift, we might be seen as encouraging his patronage and as being his supporters. And if he is ousted someday soon, it could then go badly for us! That is why I did not accept the grain. Don't worry, we have other safer friends who will help us until we become more established here!"

And as things turned out, not long afterward there were violent demonstrations against Tzu Yang and the king decided to remove him from office. Some months later, he was deemed to be a threat to the kingdom and was then executed, and Lieh-Tzu's wife became extremely grateful that they had not become associated with the man!

. . . .

Lieh-Tzu #45

. . . .

Mr. Shih of Lu had two sons, one who had chosen to become a student of the Way of Tao and one who had chosen to become a student of the Way of War. When the two boys grew up, the first presented himself to the marquis of Ch'i and sought a position as a teacher of Taoism. The marquis was pleased with the young man and hired him to be a tutor for his sons. Mr. Shih's second son went to Ch'u and presented himself to the king as a military strategist. The king was impressed by his knowledge of warfare and ideas on strategy, and it was not long before he had advanced to where he was put in charge of the king's entire army. The two men's salaries helped enrich their family, and their high positions honored their parents.

Mr. Shih's neighbor and friend, Mr. Meng also had two sons who were several years younger and had similar interests and abilities as those of Mr. Shih—the one a scholar of Taoism and the other adept at military strategy. When Mr. Meng's sons came of age, the one went off to Ch'in to offer himself as a teacher of Tao to the king, and the other went to Wei to seek employment as a strategist to the marquis of Wei.

When the first entered the great hall in the palace of Ch'in, the atmosphere was decidedly tense. The lad had barely begun to tell about his understandings of Taoism when the king stood up and said, "Young man, I have one army threatening me on my northern border and another amassing strength to the west. I don't have time to worry about your 'Way of Tao,' and I could not care less about ruling my country according to some moral Taoist philosophy. I am entirely focused right now on arming and feeding my troops." Then the king turned to his captain of the guard and said, "Take this boy and enroll him in the army—and make sure he learns how to swing a sword." And so Mr. Meng's oldest son was then dragged off to be a soldier in the king of Ch'in's army.

When Mr. Meng's second son spoke of his ideas on military strategy with the marquis of Wei, the ruler listened patiently and then said, "You seem to be well versed on the subject and to have some brilliant ideas, but I have no need at all for your services. Wei is a small and weak country trying to survive amid a number of larger and stronger ones. We do so by placating and paying tribute to our strongest neighbors and by forming alliances with several of our fellow weak ones. I survive through diplomacy, not through military might. If I were seen to be developing a stronger army, I would be crushed in no time at all. Now, my young friend, what am I to do with you?" And with that, the marquis of Wei turned to his captain of the guard and said, "Take this boy to the prison and put him behind bars until I decide what to do with him. I can't have him going off and selling his talents to any of my aggressive neighbors!"

When Mr. Meng heard of the fates of his two children, he went next door to lament the situation with his friend Mr. Shih. "My sons have the same talents and abilities as yours and went off to seek employment in the same manner they did, but look at what has happened to them. Instead of being given good jobs in their chosen fields, they have been treated most callously. Why?"

Mr. Shih was very sympathetic to his old friend but then sighed and said, "There is an old saying—I'm sure you've heard of it. It says, 'Pick the right time and place and you will prosper! Pick the wrong time or place and you will perish!'

"It seems that picking the wrong time and place is the reason your sons went astray. There is no principle or strategy that is right at all times or in all circumstances, and few that are always wrong at all times or in all circumstances. The method we used successfully to do something here yesterday might not work here again tomorrow but might be effective over there in a week or two. The ability to pick the right time and place to optimize each opportunity that presents itself is a matter of sensitivity to the Flow of Tao and also of a certain special type of wisdom. If you have not attained that sensitivity or that wisdom, you could otherwise be as wise a scholar as Confucius or as brilliant a strategist as Sun Tzu and still only find trouble wherever you go!"

Lieh-Tzu #46

Duke Wen of Ch'in was on the way to his southern border with his army to meet his allies and with them attack the neighboring state of Wei. One evening, next to the campfire, he noticed his advisor Kung Tzu Ch'u look up at the sky and smile his biggest smile. Curious, he asked the man what he had found so amusing.

"I was just remembering a story my neighbor told me once about something that happened to him late last summer, my lord," his advisor explained. "He was taking his wife to go visit her family and happened to notice a young woman picking mulberries in an orchard next to the road. He found her attractive and paused for a few minutes to ask her about the harvest, but when he turned back around, he found his wife standing on the other side of the road talking flirtatiously with another man. For some reason I was thinking about that story and found it to be funny."

Something about Kung Tzu Ch'u's story struck Duke Wen as strangely interesting, so he thought about it off and on for the rest of the evening, and then, early the next morning after a flash of insight, he ordered his army to turn around and head immediately back to his capital city. But later that same day, a messenger on an exhausted horse white with sweat galloped up to tell him that another neighboring state had just attacked Ch'in on its northern border!

Lieh-Tzu #47

The state of Ch'in was infested with robbers, and the marquis of Ch'in was determined to solve that problem. One day he heard of a man named Hsi Yung who had the ability to look at another man's face and tell whether that man was a thief, so he interviewed Hsi Yung, reassured himself that the man's skill was reliable, and then added him to the roster of the state's sheriff's department. And in no time at all, the jails in the kingdom were filling up and incidences of robbery were down.

Ecstatic, the marquis summoned Chao Wen Tzu so he could tell him of the success of the program, but Chao Wen Tzu was not impressed at all. "I am happy to hear that you have been able to reduce the number of robbers in the country lately, my lord," he said, "but I fear the technique will not be successful for long. We have a couple of sayings in Chou that will illustrate why that is:

"Techniques that reveal the locations of fishes hidden in the watery depths are very unpopular with the fishes!

"And:

"Knowledge of deep dark secrets is likely to be hazardous for those who are known to know them!

"Soon it will be known by all that Hsi Yung is responsible for catching the robbers and having them thrown in jail, and I'm afraid he might not be with us for very long after that happens!"

Sure enough, a few weeks later, several robber gangs joined together to develop a plot to rid themselves of Hsi Yung. They soon waylaid and murdered him, and none were ever even caught and punished for doing so.

The marquis of Ch'in was devastated by news of the man's death and summoned Chao Wen Tzu once again. "Events have turned out just as you predicted they would," he said sadly. "Hsi Yung is dead! Now, how are we ever going to catch all the robbers?"

"My lord," the sage answered, "with Hsi Yung you were trying to solve a problem by eliminating its symptoms rather than by correcting its causes. If you really want to minimize robbery, your best course of action would be to introduce many worthy men to office in your government. Honest and dedicated officials would enlighten those above them and would also reform those below. If the people are led by a government that demonstrates honesty and creates a thriving economy, few people would ever want to become robbers in the first place, and those who are already robbers might decide to find a safer and higher paying real job, instead."

And not long after that, the marquis made Chou Wen Tzu himself prime minister of Ch'in, and because of his new policies, the robber gangs slowly began to dissolve.

Lieh-Tzu #48

The countries of Ti and Ch'u were at war and Prince Chao, the young new ruler of Ch'u, sent his army to Ti to try to win the final victory. When both of the two largest cities of Ti finally fell in defeat on the same day, the general of the army sent a courier to notify Prince Chao of their glorious victory.

The prince was having dinner with a few guests when the courier arrived and made the announcement, and the room immediately erupted with happy excitement. Voices rose in loud conversation, glasses were raised, and toasts of victory were drunk, but one guest noticed that the prince himself was not celebrating at all. Instead, he sat quietly on his throne in deep thought. "My lord, why are you not celebrating our great victory?" she asked him politely.

"Madam," he said, with a smile on his face, "I am certainly delighted that the war is over and that we have won, but now that the first phase of our conquest of Ti is over, it is time to begin implementing the second phase!

"When the fierce storms of springtime rage with high winds and ferocious downpours, and the mighty rivers flood, we all focus intently every long second on the damage being done and on surviving the onslaught, but each of those storms only lasts a few hours and even the floods only last for a few days. When it all finally ends and the skies clear and the waters recede, then what? The answer is that then we breathe a quick sigh of relief and immediately start to clean up the mess, repair the damage, and figure out ways to try to minimize the problems that will occur the next time it happens. And all that must be done quickly or disease will spread, crops will fail, people will go hungry, and valuable things will become damaged even more than they already are."

"Our war with Ti has been like the storms and the flood, but now that the time for focusing on the events of war is over, we are faced with the time for cleaning up, repairing, and incorporating Ti successfully into our kingdom. And if we don't do that quickly, our great victory could turn, in just a few months, into a horrible loss." And with that explanation, the dinner guest nodded and understood.

When Confucius later heard of the prince's words, he said, "It seems that Prince Chao will become a great king. Winning the great victory is only the first step in any long campaign. The even greater step is making the victory last through time. Many noted leaders enjoyed a great victory or two that then ended eventually in defeat because they did not quickly move on to the next phase that needed to be accomplished. Prince Chao did not want to be known forever just as the prince who once defeated the kingdom of Ti!"

Lieh-Tzu #49

King Chuang of Ch'u asked Chan Ho, the court philosopher, "How can I ever straighten out all the problems in my kingdom? The harder I try to make things better, the worse it all seems to get!"

"I'm sorry, my lord," Chan Ho answered, "but my expertise is in helping people to understand their lives and how to make them better. I have no knowledge at all about running a country."

"We are being threatened on our borders by our neighbors, the shrines of my ancestors are being desecrated by angry citizens, the economy is in a shambles, and everyone is just generally angry all the time. Surely you must have some advice that might help me. You're my court philosopher!"

"I can only say that in all my years, I have never known of a ruler whose personal life was happy and in order while, at the same time, his country was in turmoil, nor one whose personal life was in turmoil while his country was happy and prosperous. Therefore, I would speculate that perhaps that might be at the root of your problems—but I would not presume to speak about the trunk or the tips of the branches!"

"Good," said King Chuang, annoyed!

Lieh-Tzu #50

When Sun Shu-ao was growing old and approaching the end of his days, he warned his son:

"The king has offered me large parcels of land several times as a reward for my lifetime of service to him, but I never had any desire for land and never accepted his offer. After I am gone, he is likely to make the same offer again to you. If he does and you decide you want land, do not accept strategically vulnerable land near our borders or you will not be likely to be able to hold it for long. I have found land that is fertile and available that I suggest you ask for. It is at a place called Cemetery Hill. The people of Ch'u fear ghosts and the people of Yueh believe in omens so, between its location far from any disputed territory and its inauspicious name, I think our family would be able to prosper there for many generations to come!"

And when Sun Shu-ao did die soon after that, the king did offer his son his choice of several large and bountiful estates in strategically vulnerable locations, and his son did politely request the land on Cemetery Hill instead, and his ancestors still live there happily to this day!

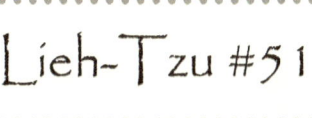

Lieh~Tzu #51

Yang Chu said:

"It is natural for the young adult to reflect back toward the world the treatment he feels he received from it earlier as a child.

But the mature adult must realize that what emanates outward from him toward others will come back to him in kind.

If kindness and benefit emanate outward from him, its fruits will usually be returned by others in answer.

If dislike and resentment go out from him, it is dislike and resentment that is most likely to be returned.

So, the sage is cautious of how he acts, and what he says and does to others, for in that way he does not defeat himself!

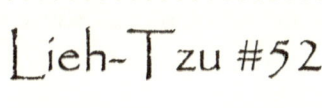

Lieh~Tzu #52

Yang Chu's younger brother, Pu, went out one afternoon wearing a white silk jacket, but it rained and the white jacket got wet, so Pu took it off and replaced it with a black one borrowed from a friend. A few hours later when Pu came home, his dog did not recognize him at first and barked and growled viciously. Yang Pu became angry at the dog for his hostile welcome and scolded him indignantly because of it.

But Yang Chu, hearing all the commotion, came out the door and understood immediately what had happened and said, "Don't be angry at the dog. He just did exactly what you or I might do. If he left home with white fur and then came back a little later with black fur, wouldn't you be startled?"

. . . .

Lieh-Tzu #53

. . . .

T'ien of Ch'i was going on a long journey, so before leaving, he hosted a huge banquet for over a thousand guests and sacrificed a lamb in order to honor and please the god of the roads. As he stood there admiring the many platters of fish, fowl, venison, pork, lamb, different types of bread, rice, and jugs of rice and millet wines, he sighed and commented to those standing near him, "How generous the gods have always been to humankind. For our benefit, they have created all these wonderful kinds of meat, the five grains, and even a wide variety of different beverages!"

All the adult guests who heard him echoed his praise of the generous gods, but one impulsive twelve-year-old boy of the Pao family who also happened to hear his words said, "That's not really the way things are at all, your lordship. All the many creatures between the heavens and Earth are born in the same manner that humans are and do not differ from each other or from us in any type of natural hierarchy. None is more noble than any other; it's simply that the stronger and more intelligent are able to take advantage of those that are weaker and less intelligent. Some creatures are able to capture, kill, and eat others, but that does not mean that those who are eaten were created by the gods just for the enjoyment of those who eat them. Besides, gnats eat our skin, mosquitos suck our blood, and tigers eat our flesh anytime they get a chance. Does that mean that the gods created humankind for the benefit of gnats, mosquitos, and tigers?"

T'ien was very concerned that the boy's impudent outburst might offend the gods and put his journey at risk, but he left on schedule anyway and did not have any significant problems at all while he was away!

Lieh-Tzu #54

There used to be a very poor man in the city of Ch'i who was a beggar at the city market. He had begged there for so long that those who shopped there regularly had grown tired of seeing him and had stopped giving him their coins. So, hungry and desperate, he went off to look for regular employment somewhere— anywhere—and finally found work as the servant to a local horse doctor.

Those who were used to seeing him in the market soon found out where he now worked, and a few of those who were young and cruel, seeing him occasionally on the streets, began to make fun of him over his new job. Being a horse doctor's servant was certainly not considered to be a very desirable profession. His pay, after all, was quite low and much of his time was spent cleaning out horse stalls.

But the former beggar from the city market could not understand why the boys were teasing him at all. "Before, I was just a beggar," he thought to himself. "I had no steady income, I did not have a warm and safe place to sleep at night, and more often than not I was hungry. Now I always have a warm bed, and I have at least one meal each and every day. What's wrong with them? I am finally beginning to move up in the world!"

Lieh-Tzu #55

There was a man who could not find his axe and suspected that the boy next door had stolen it. Whenever he watched the boy, everything the lad did seemed to confirm that he was, indeed, the thief. His walk, his expression, the things he said, and even his mannerisms all seemed to betray his guilt. All the man needed was some sort of tangible proof, and he was prepared to confront the boy and his parents and demand that they return his axe.

But then the man was weeding his garden and found the axe half buried behind a bush and remembered that he had used it there several days earlier. And the next day, when he noticed the boy outside his house, he realized that there was actually nothing about the child and his behavior that seemed so suspicious to him after all!

Lieh-Tzu #56

There was a man in Ch'i who lusted for gold. One morning he put on his hat and his coat and went to the market. He was wandering through the stalls looking for a few groceries for his kitchen when he noticed that the gold dealer was distracted for a moment and was not watching some coins that sat on his counter. The man quickly scooped up the coins and ran off, but the police soon determined who he was and went to arrest him.

"Why would you steal gold coins in front of so many witnesses?" the policeman asked him. "Some of those people knew exactly who you were!"

"When I took the coins, I didn't see any people at all," the thief replied. "I only saw the gold!"

Words of Wisdom Attributed to Lieh-Tzu

- Death is a rest for the weary, peace for the pained, and a release from guilt for those who have lived a life of bad decisions.
- Life is a journey, and every part until its end has good characteristics and bad. Each should be experienced and appreciated fully.
- Reality is too diverse and ever-changing to support most opinions for long.
- When joy reaches its climax, it is likely to revert to anger, and when anger reaches its climax, it is likely to revert to joy. It's better to just keep one's emotions in check.
- Not all beasts walk on four legs. Check for the humanity within.
- The most important step for understanding things realistically is to prevent distortion of perception from emotion.
- You might sometimes find yourself moving counter to the Flow of Tao, but the Flow of Tao will never purposely move counter to you.
- Manage your personal empire like a shepherd manages his flock—using comfortable expertise and a little stick to move it gently in the direction you want it to go.
- Be careful with your words, for some who hear are likely to agree with you. Be thoughtful about your morality, for it will affect that which takes place around you.
- Those chasing after wealth are like chickens scratching for fat seeds or dogs wandering through woods looking for a bone.

- With the right time and place, you will prosper. Without them both, you will not.
- Knowledge of deep dark secrets is likely to be dangerous for those who are known to have it.
- Winning the great victory is only the first step. The next is making the victory last through time.

SECTION III

Modern Taoism

"The reality of the world today is that grounding ethics in religion is no longer adequate. This is why I am increasingly convinced that the time has come to find a way of thinking about spirituality and ethics beyond religion, altogether." The Dalai Lama

Passages of the Taoist Sages by Topic

About Tao:

Lao Tzu, passages 1,4,6,14,25,34,42A,51,62,73

Chuang Tzu, passage 39

Lieh Tzu, passage 2

About the Flow of Tao:

Lao Tzu, 4,5,14,16,25,32,34,42A,51

Lieh Tzu, 3,4

The Way of Water:

Lao Tzu, 8,78, plus brief mentions in other places

The Way of Little Ego:

Lao Tzu, 3,13,19,24,48,65,66

Chuang Tzu, 35,38,40

Lieh Tzu, 29

Achievement with Little Friction:

Lao Tzu, 21,36,40,43,45,63,64

Chuang Tzu, 7,9,14

Lieh Tzu, 23,24,25,26,28,29,38,40,42,45,46

Benefits of Following the Way of Tao:

Lao Tzu, 18,35,37,38,52,54,55,56,65,66,67

Chuang Tzu, 11,32

Lieh Tzu, 11,12,21,22

The Ideal Society:
    Lao Tzu, 81

On Life and Death:
    Lao Tzu, 3,36,52,73
    Chuang Tzu, 5,8,10,13,27,33,35,48
    Lieh Tzu, 1,4,5,8,16,19,27,28,30,31,32,33,34,35,37,44,46,50

Note to the Reader

Lao Tzu states emphatically in the very first chapter of the *Tao Te Ching* that "the true Tao can never be grasped with words. Even its name is just a sound!" That is certainly still true in the strictest sense, but it is not as true now as it was twenty-three hundred years ago. The reason for the difference is that the basis of Taoism, although they didn't know anything specific about it at that time, has always been the science of physics, the interrelationships of primary particles, and the way those interrelationships all come together to create us all and the universe we are each a part of. The ancient Chinese, of course, could only sense and experience the Flow of Tao as evidenced by the processes of nature and experienced with their five senses. They did not have the background of knowledge we now have nor the scientific instruments present today. And while the Flow of Tao is still much too complex to ever fully understand and explain with words, because of the scientific progress we have attained in recent centuries, we can certainly do a better job of that now than Lao Tzu and the other ancient Taoist sages could all those many centuries ago!

6

The Physical Basis of Tao

Tao and Taoism

I suspect that most American adults today have some knowledge of Tao and Taoism. In the 1980s and '90s there was an upswing in interest in it as a result of several popular books on "The Tao of (various topics)," with *The Tao of Pooh* by Benjamin Hoff being the most popular and the longest enduring. It was on the *New York Times* Best Seller List for forty-nine weeks, has sold millions of copies through the years, and is still a popular purchase today because it illustrates some of the basic concepts of Taoism in a comfortable and easily understood manner.

Other people have been exposed to Taoism and other Eastern concepts as a result of their interests in martial arts, yoga, and Buddhism. I would guess that, as a result of all those influences, most American adults have at least heard of Lao Tzu and the book attributed to him—the *Tao Te Ching*! Many fewer people, certainly, know the other two Taoist books highlighted herein that are from roughly the same period of ancient China and that also illustrate and define the ancient philosophy of Taoism—*The Book of Chuang Tzu* and *The Book of Lieh-Tzu*. Between the three, though, the basic concepts of ancient Taoism can be rather well understood and appreciated by modern readers. "But why bother?" you might ask. "It's just ancient Chinese philosophy; why is it important to me? I live in today's world!"

The easiest way to answer that question is to point out another book written much more recently (in 1975) called the *Tao of Physics* by Fritjof Capra, which points out in exquisite detail the basic accuracy of what the ancient Taoists perceived as the physical underpinnings of the universe upon which the philosophy was based.

The ancient Chinese knew nothing about modern physics, of course, but they did believe that there must be an unseeable physical structure to the universe behind and below what they were able to experience with their five senses—behind and below even their gods. They called it Tao. And even though they were unable to experience this unseeable physical structure directly, they made some assumptions and engaged in some speculation as to what it might be like. Those assumptions and speculations became the basis of Taoism and are briefly described in several passages of the Tao Te Ching and other two books. And although their understandings were very basic and primitive, they are remarkably accurate according to our current understandings of physics.

Today, physicists obviously have a much clearer comprehension of the foundation of the universe than the ancient Chinese philosophers did. Our understanding of physics takes us down with apparent accuracy as far as the level of the quantum field. Behind and below that, little still seems to make much sense even to the most brilliant modern scientific minds. But at the level of the quantum field and above, we know that several basic forms of energy somehow interact to form a variety of what are called subatomic particles. Some of those types of particles are attracted to each other to form protons and neutrons. Protons and neutrons along with electrons (which seem to be elementary particles in and of themselves) interact to form atoms, and there are only about ninety-two different types of naturally occurring atoms (elements) on Earth (the exact number depending on what you consider to be "naturally occurring")—each with characteristics different than any other. Only twenty of those elements make up 95 percent of what we find on Earth, the others being present but relatively rare. And the different characteristics of each element come only as a result of the unique number of protons, neutrons, and electrons that it contains. Molecules are formed by atoms that are naturally inclined to attract more electrons than they already have and that they can find available in isolation. Because of their need to overcome that deficiency, they join together with other deficient atoms to share electrons. And when they do, each different combination of protons, neutrons, and shared electrons exhibits unique characteristics different from the characteristics of the individual atoms they are composed of.

All we experience of the physical world during our lives is a result of these various forms of energy, the various particles composed of the energy, the ninety-two or so different types of atoms (elements), and a multitude of different types of molecules formed from atoms sharing electrons, and the various characteristics of them all. And since molecules are composed of atoms and atoms are composed of particles and particles are expressions of energy, we can say that all we experience of the physical world—what we are able to see, touch, hear, smell, and taste—are expressions of energy! The "things" that surround us in life, including the ground we stand on, walls we walk around, objects we make in our factories, plants and animals we live with and around, moon and sun and planets, friends and strangers we know and meet, parents who conceived and bore us, and even we, ourselves, are all comprised of atoms and molecules made out of energy clumped closer together than usual to form what physicists call "matter." And matter is defined as "mass that takes up space," and as Einstein famously demonstrated, M (mass) =

E (energy) × c² (the speed of light squared). Everything in the universe, therefore, including you and I, are ultimately all about energy and the movement of energy!

Nothing of what we know today discredits the conclusions Lao Tzu, Chuang Tzu, and Lieh-Tzu and their fellow philosophers made over two thousand years ago regarding the basis of reality and what it means with regard to people's lives and behavior. In fact, the findings of modern physics confirm the underpinnings of their ancient philosophy.

But, as human beings, we are affected and influenced by much more than just physical reality. Our thoughts, our emotions, the words and actions of others, social realities, and governmental policies are all also important parts of our lives. These must also be included in what Tao is interpreted to be because, even though they are not physical products of the physical universe, they are creations of humankind, and humankind is a product of the physical universe, and therefore all those nonphysical things are indirect products of Tao. And they, like all aspects of the universe Taoists call Tao, are constantly moving and constantly changing.

The Universal Flow of Tao

Today it is generally accepted that our universe began as an "initial singularity," which means it was a massive black hole of infinite density that contained within it all the energy and space-time of the universe as it is now. That initial singularity was then somehow triggered into what has been labeled the "big bang." CERN, the European Organization of Nuclear Research, describes what happened then like this:

> In the first moments after the big bang, the universe (expanded and) cooled, and conditions became just right to give rise to the building blocks of matter—the quarks (a type of sub-atomic particle), and the electrons of which

we are all made. A few millionths of a second later, quarks aggregated to produce protons and neutrons. Within minutes, those protons and neutrons combined into (atomic) nuclei.

As the universe continued to expand and cool, things began to happen more slowly. It took 380,000 years for electrons to be trapped in orbits around nuclei, forming the first atoms. These were mainly helium and nitrogen, which are still by far the most abundant elements in the universe. Present observations suggest that the first stars formed from clouds of gas (of mostly helium and nitrogen) around 150–200 million years after the big bang. Heavier atoms such as carbon, oxygen, and iron have been continuously produced in the hearts of stars and catapulted throughout the universe (ever since) in spectacular stellar explosions called supernovas.

Subatomic particles, being expressions of energy, are always compelled to move, most fundamentally outward from the original size and location of the initial singularity but also for shorter distances in other directions as a result of interactions with other particles or as a result of one or more of the four basic forces of physics: gravity, the strong nuclear force, the weak nuclear force, and electromagnetism. Such interactions cause them to either alter course or to join and form a bond with the other particles.

Two of the basic forces of physics attract some particles to certain others (i.e., gravity and the strong nuclear force), one is a factor in the decay and gradual destruction of radioactive elements; (i.e., the weak nuclear force), and one can either attract particles to other particles or repel them depending on electrical charge; (i.e., electromagnetism).

The movement away from the universe's point of origin, the four basic forces of physics and other fundamental characteristics of particles all result in a variety of characteristic "movements" and tendencies for movement. Most particles tend to spin, for example. That is thought by many to be a result of the fact that the initial singularity was spinning rapidly at the time of the big bang. The strong nuclear force causes a tight bond between the protons and neutrons in the nuclei of atoms, and when they are bonded together in the center of a nucleus, they can spin at speeds of around 25 percent of the speed of light. Electromagnetism tends to capture electrons into a sort of orbit around the bonded-together protons and neutrons, and the resulting relationship and interactions of those three types of particles form what we call atoms. But when electrons for one reason or another are able to escape their bondage with nuclei and travel freely, they become photons and result in what we experience as heat and light.

Gravity is the primary force-related fundamental interaction involved in drawing atoms and molecules together in large and dense quantities. The bigger the grouping of such atoms and molecules gets, the stronger the gravitational attraction becomes and so too does the resulting pressure for anything near the center of the cluster (resulting, as CERN pointed out, in the creation of heavier elements). If enough atoms and molecules composed of particles group together under the right circumstances, such clusters can eventually grow to become what we call moons, planets, stars, solar systems, and galaxies, and all the various movements and forces that characterize such massive clusters of particles result in phenomena we experience as rivers, lakes, and oceans; night and day; the seasons of the year; tides; phases of the moon; our comfortable attraction to the ground beneath us; and an almost infinite number of other such things.

The tendency of some types of atoms to bunch together, share electrons, and thereby form molecules is of special significance to us and all other life forms because the interactions that are characteristic of molecules and their electron sharing result in chemical reactions, and life forms are little more than collections of organic self-replicating chemical reaction systems in the form of trillions of bodily cells composed of molecules working together by means of their chemical reactions to maintain the continued life of the organism they are a part of. It is the chemical reactions of the molecules in our bodily cells resulting from their interactions with other molecules in the food we consume, along with water and oxygen, that are the processes that maintain the human life within us.

We must regularly supply our bodies with those molecules from the world around us, or the chemical reactions within us will stop and we will die. Protein from meat, eggs, dairy, and some beans and seeds; carbohydrates from grains, fruit, and root crops; and vitamins, minerals, and fiber from plant life are all needed to keep our cells healthy and functioning properly, and all are molecules except for some of the minerals. And of course, in order to consume them, we must first locate and kill them. For that purpose, in order to be able to defend ourselves from predators who would prefer to consume us rather than be consumed by us, and to find partners to mate with in order to perpetuate our species, we and all other advanced creatures have evolved five different means of sensing what is going on in the world around us—sight, hearing, smell, taste, and touch. The two we humans happen to use the most for those purposes are sight and hearing, and interestingly, those two sensory organs both work in curious and roundabout ways.

We don't actually see objects, for instance—at least not in any direct way. In fact, there aren't really any objects at all to see in the way normally imagined by the minds of people. What does exist are large and densely packed clusters of atoms and molecules formed of moving particles composed of energy, and each separate atom and molecule is actually almost entirely just empty space. The actual particles that make up each atom are incredibly small compared with the size of the atom they comprise. If you could magnify an atom so that its nucleus was the size of a basketball, for instance, the rotating electrons around it would be several miles away, and all the space between would be nothing but empty void. The area within an atom is, in fact, 99.99999999999 percent empty space.

What you do see when you are out hunting for food, whether out in the woods or at your local grocery store is light (photons) reflecting off the electrons circling the nuclei of large numbers of densely concentrated atoms on the exterior of your prospective meal's skin, fur, feathers, scales, or (if at the grocery store) manufactured packaging material. The electrons circle the nucleus in broad waves and wide dancelike movements at such a high speed that the photons cannot pass through but instead reflect off them and into our eyes. The frequency it does that at determines the colors you see, and that is important because plants can usually be recognized because we see them as being green, and fruits and vegetables can usually be easily recognized because we see them as being a variety of other bright colors. After our eyes detect the patterns and frequencies of the photons that have been reflected into them, they send the information via neurons to our brains which then have the job of creating the images of reality that we recognize and then deciding what they are and what, if anything, we should do about them.

Hearing is the other interesting tool our bodies have evolved to use frequently to detect and understand our environment. Other than sounds made by animal life forms, there are few natural movements of clusters of atoms and molecules that create the kinds of vibrations we experience as sound. Waves pound onto beaches, an occasional rock will roll down a hill, a dead branch will fall to the ground, wind will make noise when it blows through trees, and thunder booms, but when animals are present, they are the usual cause of most such sounds, and animals also just happen to be the best source of vital protein molecules for our bodies. Being able to detect such sounds provides another important way for hunters to find sources of food to provide those essential chemical reactions our bodies require for their continued survival.

Movement causes vibrations, especially if one cluster of atoms and molecules strike or rub against another. Those vibrations are passed along to atoms and molecules in the air, and then from those to others, and on and on until eventually vibrating air finds its way into our ears. Our brains can recognize patterns and frequencies in the characteristics of those vibrations that they are likely to be able to recognize if they have ever heard them or anything like them before.

Probably the most central tenet common to all Eastern religions is a common belief in the basic unity and interconnectedness of all things in the universe. All physical phenomena and events are seen as various manifestations of this basic oneness. Recent realizations in the sciences of physics and astronomy are bringing today's scientists to a similar conclusion. The universe we live in is most fundamentally a construct of particles, but the particles have been found not to be separate, individual, and permanently definable types of energy at all. Instead, their properties are all turning out to be interconnected, and seem to be definable and observable only through their interactions with each other. Nothing in particle action and interaction is predictable with any certainty or for any length of time on their own because all particle actions seem to always be influenced by the actions of all others that happen to be nearby. In other words, the interconnectedness of the universe of particles seems to be its most basic reality.

This has recently proven to be true at the galactic level of particle construction as well as at the subatomic level. Until just a few decades ago, galaxies were seen to be mostly isolated gigantic assemblages of stars and their planets associated with each other within the galaxy because of gravitational attraction. In general, each moved away from the origin of the big bang, and each was somewhat attracted to other nearby galaxies due to gravity, but otherwise each seemed to be quite separate and independent of the others. But about forty years ago, the first clues began to emerge that the generally accepted separateness of galaxies might not be entirely accurate. Due to the advent of ever more powerful and precise equipment, astronomers began to notice patterns in the arrangement of clusters of galaxies. They then began to detect wispy connections between the clusters. By focusing on those connections and bringing their instruments to bear, they began to realize that galaxies and galaxy clusters all seem to be interconnected by what has been labeled "galactic filaments" creating what appears to be a three-dimensional latticework interconnection between them all. Exactly what that web of filament is and what it signifies is still entirely unknown.

The takeaway of all this is that the reality we each experience is just our own brain's interpretation of the incredibly complex interactions of an infinite number of tiny bits of energy around and including each of us. The physical world of objects, people, and events we know is not unreal, but it is only a very simplistic representation of the totality of all that is actually taking place behind and below whatever it is we are able to experience. The actual reality is a massive and continuous interconnected flow of movement and change and events taking place, leading from what was in the past, through what is in the present, and into what will be the future. That flow is a logical transition leading from the beginning of time to its end. We are each affected by that logical transition, and we each in turn also affect it. Within it, there will be cycles of similar but always somewhat different occurrences. There will be creation, change, and eventual destruction. Nothing will ever remain the same for long! We are each blessed to be able to experience and interact with what will take place during our lifetimes, and as we do, we will be experiencing and interacting with all the various people and creatures living concurrently around us, as fellow time travelers—interconnected in the universe we call Tao. That is the universal Flow of Tao. It is in some respects logical and predictable for us, despite our limited ability to perceive it, and we are each a tiny but important part of it all!

Each Individual's Personal Experience of the Flow of Tao

The earliest bilateral creatures that scientists have discovered fossil evidence of so far were small, simple worms that lived on the ocean floor about 555 million years ago. Those ancient worms or others like them were probably the ancestors of all the complex animals alive on Earth today, and with regard to their basic form and biological processes, they were little different from those of us who have since evolved through the eons from them.

Food was gathered and ingested on one end of a central food processing tube, the molecules necessary for the chemical reactions required to keep the worm's own body cells alive were separated from what was unusable and were distributed from there throughout the worm's body, in each cell the organism's molecules exchanged electrons that allowed the cells to continue to live, and then unwanted waste products from those chemical reactions were passed back to the digestive tube to join the non-nutrients for excretion at the opposite end from where it had all originally been ingested. Today, after 555 million years of evolution, there is considerably more complexity in almost every aspect of almost every organism, but the basic system still works in exactly the same way.

The first such creatures could get away with being quite simple and generalized because at that time there were many nutrients available on the ocean floor, and few other animals were competing for it. But that certainly didn't stay the same for long.

The number of different habitats early organisms were able to survive in multiplied, new genetic variations evolved, populations found themselves competing for ever more scarce resources in ever more hostile environments, predators evolved that sought to eat the worms for nutrition instead of the nutrients on the sea floor, and specialization became ever more necessary for continued survival and for reproduction in adequate numbers. All those many millions of years of evolution have led to the world of creatures we live in today.

To compete successfully in a world with limited resources and many thousands of different species challenging each other for them, it was important for each one to have unique characteristics that gave its members an advantage for obtaining nutrition, for defending themselves, and for reproducing adequately so that they could outcompete both their competitors and their predators. Some animals came to blend in so well with their environments that prey or predators could rarely ever even detect them, some came to have potentially deadly claws or teeth, some ran extremely fast, some reproduced at a prodigious rate, birds and bats came to be able to fly, and some creatures developed extraordinary sensory abilities, etc. Almost every species that survived the eons and evolved into the creatures we know today did so because of unique impressive abilities and continuing adaptability.

We humans don't have exceptional fangs or claws. We don't naturally have extraordinary sensory abilities. We can't naturally fly, run particularly fast, or stay underwater for extended periods. We don't have camouflaged fur or skin. And our females don't bear extraordinary numbers of babies. In truth, we are rather unexceptional creatures in all respects except for one—that of course, being our uniquely large and powerful brains paired with hands that have opposing thumbs. The combination of brain and hand we humans have at our disposal as tools for understanding and manipulating our environment is our own species' special survival trait. It allows us the means to understand things and events taking place around us, especially regarding prey and predators, and to think up ways to outsmart and outmaneuver them especially, as it has turned out, through the process of tool-making.

The general Flow of Tao, as we have seen, involves the movement and interactions of an almost infinite number of particles and things made from particles across time and space. If it were possible for any one individual's sensory organs to detect every particle in the region around him, as well as all the atoms and molecules created from those particles, and was then capable of telling what each was doing, what their interactions with others were, what their current statuses were, what form they were recognizable as having at the human level of recognition, etc., and if that individual also had the mental capacity to process all that data in ways that would help it meet his biological needs, that individual would be an invincible hunter, gatherer, and survivor indeed. He would know everything that was going on around him and would be able to predict with prodigious ability what all was likely to happen in the immediate future! But that, of course, is all impossible and would be impractical as well. No creature and no human individual could ever possibly have the sensory organs to gather all that data, nor the mental capacity to ever process it. Each person, instead, must make do with whatever his sensory organs are capable of gathering and whatever his brain is capable of deducing from that information.

The very limited amount of information that each individual person can and does detect and process of the universal Flow of Tao around him or her is what I call his or her "personal experience of the Flow of Tao." Someone in a coma in a hospital bed, for instance, even though alive, would be having no personal experience of the Flow of Tao at all because he or she would be neither experiencing nor processing any information about it, while another person with an active and adventurous lifestyle who also kept up faithfully with current events, had received a good education, and who was dedicated to his or her career using modern investigative equipment, would be able to have as full and complete a personal experience of the Flow of Tao around them as it would ever be possible for a person to have.

All that each of our most ancient proto human ancestors were able to perceive and process of the Flow of Tao millions of years ago was the natural physical world the people lived amid because at that time that was all there was on Earth for them to perceive. The world they experienced consisted of what was occurring to them each day of their lives involving such things as weather, the different seasons of the year, other natural phenomena, interactions with wildlife, the physical changes of aging in themselves and other members of their tribe, and their social and familial interactions. Other than the basic and primitive conversations such people probably had and other social interactions, all such experiences involved the detection and manipulation of "things" made out of particles and particle constructs that they needed to interact with for their continued survival. Those first proto humans lived completely natural lives interacting with the physical realities of the Flow of Tao. And they did not alter it significantly any more than any other animal did.

But then, some 2.5 million years ago, some of our ancestors began making simple tools out of rocks and sticks, and then somewhere around a million years ago, some of them learned how to control and use fire, and ever since, our species has continued to advance their tool-making abilities until today many people live lives in which they rarely interact intimately and exclusively with the natural physical realities to the Flow of Tao at all.

Today, as a result of the use of technology, many of us live our lives almost entirely surrounded by products of our own human manufacture. Such objects are made of particles and particle constructs but are artificially made by people to suit human needs and desires and with few exceptions are unlike anything that might ever arise through any natural process without human intervention. Such objects include our houses, almost everything in our houses, cars and other vehicles, tools and other devices, clothing, and the very cities and towns that most of us live in.

All those many things that we make, all the changes that occur to our planet in the processes of making, using, and disposing of them, and the extended time it takes for many of them to decompose and return to a natural state, together affect us and other lifeforms on the planet dramatically. They alter the natural Flow of Tao of planet Earth and the personal experiences of the Flow of Tao of each of us, and none of those changes would ever take place at all if we had not created them.

The personal experiences of the Flow of Tao of people changed even more dramatically between seventy and thirty thousand years ago with what Yuval Harani calls the "cognitive revolution" in his book *Sapiens*. That period of human history is significant because it was characterized by seemingly dramatic changes in human mental abilities that resulted in an increased capacity for people to live more complicated lifestyles, have more extensive imaginations, and have more complex languages. During that period, the average human life transformed from being that of a nomadic hunter-gatherer into that of a resident of a long-term human community. People began to develop much more advanced and complicated inventions, and not long afterward we find the first evidence of agriculture. Most significantly of all, people rather suddenly seem to have gained a new ability to conceive of, share, and complete complex community designs-of-the-mind such as long-term construction projects. They seem to have first developed complicated social constructs and imagined realities like formal fixed laws and political structures. They first conceived of complicated religions, shared myths, and business and economic structures. And none of those new, revolutionary concepts were directly based on any physical reality of the natural Flow of Tao at all.

It was a rather rapid and dramatic transformation of human nature and human culture, and as yet there is no clear explanation as to why it even came about at that time. Was there some genetic alteration that spread quickly throughout the human population and gave our species a new and advanced mental ability, as Harani suggests, or did the changes just come about naturally due to necessity as a result of increasing population and dwindling resources? We just don't know.

Regardless of cause, ever since this cognitive revolution, human society has been changing ever more dramatically and imagination-driven realities have become a more and more dominant part of our lives. And when writing was invented some six thousand years ago, the changes became even more pronounced. As Harani noted, human history has become separate from biology, and it can easily be said that the most dramatic period of change in human history has been the past few tens of thousands of years of the cognitive revolution.

Most human beings today live in or near cities and towns that, in addition to being man-made physical structures themselves, are full of human manufactured objects and are also remarkably complex social constructs only tangentially even related to physical reality. To a large extent, the physical and natural Flow of Tao today has become little more than a source of resources for manufacturing products and a setting for recreational activities. Other than a few unavoidable natural realities related to aging, other problems with our bodies or resulting from weather extremes or natural catastrophes, the personal experiences that many people most often have come not from the physical and natural Flow of Tao but from physical or mental constructs that were designed and created by the human mind.

Some people—scientists, farmers, and doctors, for instance—still spend much of their lives focusing on one aspect or another of physical reality related to particles and particle constructs and their movements and interactions just because it is their occupation to do so, but for many, the personal experiences of the Flow of Tao they know and pay attention to today relate almost exclusively to things that are manufactured by people or that are mental constructs and social fictions—realities formed by words and imaginations based only vaguely and indirectly on physical reality. That list includes most experiences related to such employment concepts as teaching others, politics, law, business, fashion, status, entertainment, history, economics, finance, and countless others.

And since it is in this disconnected-from-physical-reality world that most modern men and women live and experience their lives, it must also be in this same disconnected-from-physical-reality world that students of Tao must now learn and try to understand Taoism, form their personal objectives, and learn how to live happy, successful, and productive lives.

7

The Way of Tao

The Way of Water

The ancient sages of Tao appreciated the characteristics of water, particularly the water they knew so well in the Yellow River and its tributaries, which dominated the part of what is now China that they lived in. The Yellow River Valley was huge and complex, but it seemed like a comprehensible and representative part of the whole of Tao that they could study and come to know as a small reflection of Tao's entirety. From their knowledge of the river, for example, they knew that both the river and surely the whole Flow of Tao started in particular places and proceeded in one direction until their end, and they knew that both were ultimately unstoppable in their progress along the way. Barriers might temporarily slow the flow of the river's waterways, diversions might send water for some period of time to other places, but eventually, by one means or another, that water would all end up back in the river heading downstream. The greater Flow of Tao, they determined, must be like that, too!

They knew that the rules of Tao and the rules of its echo, the Yellow River, were rules of nature, not rules of man, that those rules ultimately controlled everything, and that both the flow of the river and the Flow of Tao tended to be most stable and most peaceful when allowed to flow unimpeded on their natural courses rather than being altered or constrained by the actions of man.

They knew that the shape of the water in the river was flexible and always changing. In some places it would be narrow, deep, and quickly moving—in other places wide, shallow, and sluggish. It always adapted itself to its environment. During times of late summer drought, the water level would be low, while during springtime there would often be floods. Usually in the winter, ice would form in some places.

The Yellow River always altered the landscape around it, just as the Flow of Tao constantly changed the realities of the world they lived in. The solid rock of mountains near the top of the watershed and in gorges along the way slowly eroded and broke into smaller pieces, and those were carried downstream by the water. Over time, those pieces became even smaller and were carried along even further, and eventually they became fertile soil lower down the valley. In places with rapid currents, sand and soil were constantly being picked up and taken away, while in other places calm eddies allowed them to settle and be dropped, and so over time the riverbed changed. Nothing ever remained the same for long.

But most important of all, the Yellow River, like Tao itself, allowed and supported life. Because of its water, the valleys it and its tributaries passed through were filled with an abundance of it. Forests and fields of crops flourished. Wild and domesticated animals were everywhere, and people generally prospered. The Yellow River Valley owed its life directly to the water of the river, but all of it, of course, was ultimately just a small part of the bounty of the Flow of Tao.

The ancient Taoist sages saw other aspects of the water in the valley that they found appealing and Tao-like as well. Despite its importance to all life and all that it did to support it, the water never asked for anything from that life in return, and it was always generous with itself. It gave all lifeforms, including every individual human, whatever they needed of itself equally, regardless of species or even of merit. It took the snow and rain supplied by Tao, gathered it together and distributed it to whosoever and whatsoever needed it without discrimination, and it was never itself diminished by all that it did give. And the water had no sense of self. It never felt anger, arrogance, humiliation, insecurity, sadness, envy, or any other ego-driven emotion. It just went about its unstoppable and inevitable business as it seemed to naturally be meant to do.

The sages appreciated the fact that water in general was shapeless. It would fit effortlessly into any container big enough for it. And it was formless in other ways, too. If one looked at the surface of a pond casually on a nice sunny day, he or she was likely to simply see the world around them reflected on its surface, but on the other hand, on a cloudy day or if the person just chose to do so, he or she could look down into its depths and see all details of whatever was there. For one willing to take the effort to look deeply into it, water was transparent.

The Taoists especially liked the strategies that the water in the river used to transform the world as it irresistibly flowed from the mountains toward the sea. They seemed to, likewise, be admirable strategies of the greater Flow of Tao as well. The water, for instance, never tried to rise above anything else, always being content to flow along at the feet of all who stood beside it. The river waters normally flowed easily around all obstacles that tried to stand in its way. And it normally provided little resistance to any person or creature that tried to move through it. When forced to travel underground, it just seeped slowly but inevitably through tiny cracks in the rock or between the particles of sand or dirt, and it gradually, over time, made the cracks in the rock it passed through larger so that it might flow through them more easily in the future.

Water was usually much more passive than it was aggressive, but when circumstances were just right, floods could suddenly occur, and when that happened the water was capable of raging. Rocks were sometimes torn from cliff faces. Trees were sometimes uprooted. Riverbeds were sometimes quickly altered. And the entire valley was sometimes changed dramatically because of it. No matter what, it seemed, the water always won in the end, just as did the greater Flow of Tao!

The ancient Taoists were so impressed by the traits of the water in the Yellow River Valley as a reflection of Tao that they decided that they, and in fact any person, would benefit individually, and that the entire society would benefit as a whole, if those traits could be emulated. After all, the river was usually humble, flexible, patient, selfless, and generous, had no fear, and yet always prevailed in the end. The only problem was that for whatever reasons, most people did not naturally live, act, and treat others with the same admirable traits that were so characteristic of the river. So, the sages determined that they needed to learn how one might become able to do so!

The Way of Little Ego

"A human being is a part of the whole called by us 'Universe'; a part limited in time and space. He experiences himself and his thoughts and feelings as something separated from the rest, a kind of optical delusion of his consciousness. This delusion is a kind of prison for us, restricting us to our personal desires and to affection for a few persons nearest to us. Our task must be to free ourselves from this prison by widening our circle of compassion to embrace all living creatures and the whole of nature in its beauty." Albert Einstein

In trying to understand why it was difficult for them to learn to follow the admirable qualities of Tao, it must have been as obvious to ancient Taoists as it is to us today that the primary problems came from the fact that people were living creatures with intelligence, emotions, agendas, and self-interests and tended to act accordingly, whereas Tao had no intelligence in any human understanding of the word, no emotions, and never chose actions on the basis of any self-interest. Tao always just did the next things that needed to be done based on what had happened before. And the actions that motivated Tao and the reactions it responded with were not affected at all by factors of limited time and location as those of humans always were. Tao and the time and geographic horizons it worked within were infinite, whereas human horizons in those regards were always quite limited.

All but the most primitive creatures observe the world around them as they are able to experience it with their sensory organs and nervous systems, then compare those experiences to memories and lessons learned from similar past circumstances and interpret them, and from that determine the reactions that seem most appropriate and effective for the current situation. And the most fundamental basis for doing that has always been the recognition of whether or not the particulars of the Flow of Tao experienced at the moment: 1) appear to be dangerous in some way to its physical well-being; 2) seem to provide some opportunity that could satisfy biological needs such as food or opportunities to mate; or 3) do not seem to present any unusual circumstances for danger or opportunity and therefore do not require any action. Evidence of each of the first two circumstances would trigger whatever response seemed appropriate and most beneficial for the creature's continued survival and reproduction.

In the case of the earliest and simplest creatures, reactions to dangerous situations or opportunities were quite simple and reflexive or were instinctual in nature and related strictly to basic survival and reproduction, but as environments gradually became more challenging through time due to competition and the need to live in ever more marginal but less populated environments, those simple reflexive and instinctual reactions became inadequate for meeting the more complex circumstances. More and more complicated choices needed to be made for continued survival and therefore brains came to have to make more complex critical life-affecting decisions between ever more complex possible choices of action.

That, I suspect, was when the first egos began to develop. For a species to continue to survive into the future while making complex life-critical decisions, its individual members had to have a strong will to survive and to reproduce. Each had to be willing to fight for its life ever more assertively and to demand its claim to both scarce resources and to preferred mating opportunities. By doing so, the most successful members of each species were able to survive and reproduce and the species as a whole could continue to adapt, endure, and perhaps even proliferate. All that could best take place if each individual had a "hard-wired" sense of self-identity from which to make all the decisions necessary to best react to both dangers and opportunities. As the decision-making part of creatures' brains became ever more sophisticated through time along with their other body parts, so too that "hard-wired" sense of self-identity became ever more sophisticated, leading up eventually to ourselves—human beings—with our most advanced and complex brains and also the largest and most complex egos of all.

Thus, the source and cause of what we call the ego is undoubtedly a natural part of the human brain and is therefore impossible to eliminate completely, but Taoists believe the illusion that the ego creates that each of us is separate from all other people and things is not only false in light of the realities of Tao, it is also counterproductive in many ways to human society today and to the world in general, especially in the post–cognitive revolution world we now live in.

Except in the poorest and most primitive societies on Earth, relatively few people these days need to vie directly and desperately for sufficient food, shelter, clothing, or any other basic necessity needed for survival unless they are physically, socially, or mentally disadvantaged in some way. At the same time, most wars and other types of physical violence occur not because of a need for basic survival but because of a desire by some person or government for money, drugs, more possessions, valuable territory, or power over others. And those things are all needs of the ego and advance the desires of the ego of an aggressor at the expense of victims and of society and the world in general.

Taoists are realists. We don't deny what is known to be true and would certainly not deny the lessons of true (as opposed to politically motivated or commercial) science, so if the ego is a natural, organic part of each of us, no Taoist would try to deny its existence, but in today's world of human supremacy over other creatures and the world in general, many of the ego's effects are unrealistic and counterproductive, and so Taoists seek to recognize the effects of their own egos within themselves and of those within others in order to understand them, control them, and reduce their negative influences.

As understood by Taoists, the truth is that each of us is a collection of tiny biochemical factories that have somehow formed out of particles and particle constructs and came to be joined together because of the biochemical realities of DNA to form one large living entity. The complexity of the human biological machine, though amazing, is not significantly different in kind from that of a dog, a cat, a moose, or even a mouse. Each species has simply evolved in its own way to best survive in the circumstances its ancestors lived within. The adaptations that worked for our humanoid ancestors just happened to be powerful brains and hands that were able to be used as tools to manipulate the environment. As constructs of Tao, other than being alive and self-aware, people are not otherwise much different than a storm cloud, a fish, a tree, or even a rock. We only think we are because of our egos.

People live amid and are parts of Tao just like any other of its constructs. Given that reality, Taoists study the universe and its relationship to their philosophy and try to personally emulate Tao's most desirable characteristics while avoiding or minimizing characteristics that are unlike Tao's—in particular, those attributable to the human ego. By doing so, we find that we are happiest and most productive and are able to live our lives with as little detriment to ourselves, society, and the world in general as possible.

Tao has no ego. Nothing it ever does is personal. It had a beginning long ago and it will ultimately have an end, and between the two, it will accomplish what it is destined to accomplish and be what it is destined to be. But as it does so, it will not be driven by any preset agenda. It will always just do those things that are the next best things for it to do. Because of that, it does not get upset by failures, nor does it glorify its successes.

Tao provides for and affects all life equally. It doesn't play favorites, and it doesn't expect quid pro quos for what it does. It would never hurt anyone maliciously, but it does what it must do and accepts what must be done without questions or regrets. Because that is the natural Way of Tao, that is also the preferred way of the Taoist.

But people cannot be Tao. They are human, and as humans they do have egos. They can't eliminate those egos altogether and therefore must accept at least some of their effects. All they can do is minimize and marginalize them.

How does a Taoist minimize his or her ego? By reminding

themselves frequently that they are in reality only parts of the whole of Tao, equal to but not more nor less than any other part, including any other person or creature. Only in their own imaginations and perhaps in the imaginations of other people are they any more or any less than that. Then, by looking for, recognizing, and trying to reduce the number of their ego-driven thoughts and behaviors.

What kinds of things do they look for? For one thing, they look for general nonproductive criticisms of themselves or of those that they interact with. Everyone is different, everyone has strengths and weaknesses, everyone makes mistakes sometimes, but there are very few people that are valueless or who are inherently "bad!" Criticizing yourself or anyone else in general, as opposed to noting mistakes related to specific foolish decisions or behaviors for the sake of improvement, is ego-driven and unproductive. And overemphasizing the significance of specific mistakes or failings related to oneself or any other person is as well!

Likewise, and for the same reasons, glamorizing someone else or being egotistical or prideful about oneself is not realistic and instead is also ego-driven. Just as very few people are totally and inherently flawed, similarly, no one is even close to being perfect! We all have things to learn to become better and becoming better for the purpose of doing better is what life is all about! And, of course, we are all just equal parts of Tao.

Trying to impress someone by showing off to him or her is ego-driven behavior caused by feelings of inferiority relative to the person he is trying to impress. If he accepted the fact that they were both totally equal, it would not seem necessary to try to impress him or her. Instead, the one who is trying to act impressive is obviously concerned that the other person will not think highly enough of him. He is therefore unwittingly inflating the other person's importance relative to his own in his own mind and probably in the other person's mind as well. In reality, only in terms of social status (a human created fiction) is one person superior or inferior to any other, and no one, from a Taoist perspective, need try to impress anyone else for such an artificial reason. Keep in mind though that "trying to impress" is different than "being respectful." It is not only okay but also appropriate to be respectful toward anyone who is older, wiser, or more experienced than yourself! Taking that stance makes it easier to learn from the one who is older and wiser!

In the case of jealousy, the jealous person feels that it's unfair that someone else appears to be more successful in some aspect of life than he or she is. The person's ego feels wounded because all egos would always prefer to be the most successful one of all. Jealousy is a foolish ego-related emotion for several reasons. First, it presumes inferiority when there is actually no such thing except in terms of social expectations. Second, it assumes that the impression the jealous person has of success by the other at that moment implies success in all important aspects of life forever. The reality might be totally different. Who knows what might be going on in the life of the person one is jealous of that is undesirable, unknown, and unseen. And third, it must always be remembered that time changes all. The person one is jealous of on one particular day might fall into hard times the next, while the jealous person might, through some unexpected twist of fate, suddenly become far more successful in one way or another the next day. So, success and failure are both not only illusionary but subject to change from day to day!

Especially when one person feels inferior or jealous toward another, it is not uncommon for him or her to try to increase their own self-esteem by trying to put down or trip up the person they are jealous of. By bringing the other person "down," their ego hopes to raise itself "up." Any success using that strategy is bound to be short-lived, though, because no one can ever really fool themselves, and others are bound to see through the ploy quite quickly.

Selfishness is the classic generalized expression of ego-driven behavior. The selfish ones care only about their own needs and desires without any concern as to the implications to anyone else. They see themselves as uniquely important and their desires as being of far more consequence than those of anyone else. Taoists, of course, understand things quite differently.

Emotions are the easiest way to tell reactions that are related to the ego. Experiences that deflate the ego and therefore one's self-identity initiate sadness, anger, or other unhappy emotions. Experiences that reinforce the ego's desire for a positive image of itself, such as praise, honors, the love and respect of others, and other such pleasant happenings cause happiness and pride—all the positive emotions. But while positive emotions are certainly preferable to negative ones, the Taoist recognizes that both are reactions of one's ego and therefore warrant scrutiny and caution for one trying to follow the Way!

Ambition is a complex topic when it comes to following the Way because, while it is certainly an ego-driven impulse, it is neither always necessarily "good" nor always necessarily "bad." Which one it actually is according to Taoism depends on what the ambition is about and how it is pursued. The drive to satisfy basic objectives is a natural aspect of life and survival, and ambition is certainly just the deep desire to successfully fulfill whatever objectives are being pursued, so in relationship to survival and the pursuit of success in the accomplishment of worthwhile goals, ambition is natural and "good." It becomes more problematic, though, when the objectives the ambition is related to are not so worthwhile, and when the means used to fulfill them are selfish and disregard the welfare of others. We are all equal interconnected parts of Tao and therefore no one ever really benefits in the long run by hurting others, though it might seem so temporarily. When one purposely hurts another person, he or she also hurt themself. So, ambition is "good" when it involves the satisfaction of worthwhile personal goals without hurting others but is "bad" if the goals being sought are not worthwhile or if the means used to satisfy those goals knowingly hurt others.

The ancient sages were especially wary of ambitions related to the accumulation of wealth, power, and fame! One reason, as they pointed out in numerous passages of the Taoist classics, was that they did not feel that the attainment of any one or more of those goals was worth dedicating one's life to, as so many people apparently were doing then, and as they also do today. Let's face it—many people dedicate their entire lives to the attainment of wealth, power, and fame but few are ever very successful at actually attaining them. Wealth, power, and fame are relative concepts anyway. No matter how rich or powerful or famous one becomes, it is rarely ever seen as being sufficient. And if you think about it, are rich, powerful, and famous people on average really any happier than those who are satisfied with living more basic lives? I would dare say that the evidence does not seem to indicate that they are! Many, if not most rich, powerful, and famous people seem to be rather shallow and miserable individuals!

Another problem with dedicating one's life to the attainment of wealth, power, and fame is that when success in those ambitions becomes important to one's ego, moral convictions seem to easily be cast aside. Attaining wealth, power, and fame too often requires a "tooth and claw" battle to the top, wherein any concern for the welfare and interests of others becomes a liability.

All that does not mean that a Taoist following the Way cannot seek success (as often defined today by means of financial rewards and notoriety). The differentiation is a matter of the ambitious person's goals and intent. For the follower of the Way, any wealth, power, and/or fame that might be attained through their actions is not the actual goal being sought but a secondary indication of success in some other different and more important objective—one that is more worthwhile, fulfilling, and noble than just seeking wealth, power, and fame! The ego of a successful follower of the Way is not gratified by the attainment of the wealth, power, and fame themselves—his or her ego is gratified by knowing that they have been successful in obtaining a more worthwhile, fulfilling, and noble objective! And if, by chance wealth, power, and fame come as a result of that, it can then perhaps be used as a powerful tool in the achievement of even more worthwhile, fulfilling, and noble objectives!

Each person who seeks to follow the Way is a separate individual and each has his or her own personal problems in trying to minimize the control, negative consequences, and other problems caused by their own individual ego. The answer is always for them to monitor their daily interactions with others and their private thoughts to look for, recognize, and learn to overcome ego reactions during those experiences. Sometimes they can be recognized by emotions that either trigger them or are triggered by them. Other times they can be detected by realizing that one is being selfish or is trying to impress someone else. When one realizes that their ego is controlling them and their actions and reactions, they must try to change their perspective and overcome it.

Then, at the end of each day, the Taoist reflects back on the events experienced earlier and tries to recognize and note times when their ego controlled their actions and affected their thoughts and motivations. When one makes a note of recognizing and trying to avoid similar ego-driven experiences each and every day, he or she can often eventually learn to minimize them. By making this all a normal part of their personal daily routine and doing so regularly, they train themselves to reduce and control their egos gradually over time, until eventually doing so just becomes a part of who they are! It is then that they first start down the road toward becoming a sage of Tao!

The Way of Achievement with Little Friction

The accomplishment of objectives is much of what life is all about. Inanimate objects never need to do anything to continue being inanimate, but all forms of life must, at the very least, do what they must do to keep their biological engines functioning so that they do not also become inanimate objects. Animals have always had to try to satisfy the basic objectives of finding food, avoiding or defeating predators, and finding partners to mate with so that they can each, individually and as a species continue to exist. And over the eons, as most creatures gradually became ever more complex in general, the number and complexity of the objectives they needed to and became able to satisfy gradually increased as well. Especially in the case of human beings.

The earliest humans were little different from any other animal in that regard, even after they first attained the abilities to make fire and create simple tools. But today, that has changed significantly. A typical member of our species these days rarely needs for the objectives he or she pursues to be directly oriented toward protecting themselves from immediate danger or for hunting in woods or grasslands to satisfy their hunger. Most of us do our hunting for food in grocery stores. Satisfying basic needs must still be accomplished, of course, but the world we live in today often puts multiple steps between the recognition of basic biological needs and how we are able to satisfy them, and that makes life for us much more complex, less intuitive, and therefore much more frustrating and emotionally stressful than human life ever was back in earlier times. Our bodies and minds originally evolved, after all, to satisfy the lifestyle of hunters and gatherers.

People's lives today are still all about satisfying objectives, but the objectives most of us live our lives satisfying since the cognitive revolution are now determined more by the realities of mental constructs set in place by our cultures than by the satisfaction of basic needs in basic ways as determined by the realities of the quantum field and the chemical needs of our biological molecules. A modern person must work at a job and earn a paycheck, for example, to buy food at the store. And, to find warm, safe shelter to sleep in, he or she must either fill out applications and have one approved by a landlord to live in an apartment or must qualify for a mortgage in order to buy a house. And to earn his money he must often buy, drive, and maintain a car, which might or might not be a reliable way to get to work each morning. All these new additional and often frustrating steps now needed to accomplish even the most basic of things creates an unnatural complexity to life for modern people that is quite different from what our minds and bodies originally evolved to cope with.

Objectives can be thought of as both the "big" needs and desires people want to achieve some day in their lives so they can feel happy and successful, and as the "smaller" plans for action created to satisfy those needs and desires. Without any such objectives, people (and other creatures) would just sit around starving and dying of thirst while doing none of the things necessary to save themselves. There would certainly never be any next generations!

For modern humans, as for simpler creatures, many "small" objectives are almost reflexive and are satisfied with little or no conscious thought. But more significant and complex objectives are consciously set. And if one includes both the reflexive and consciously set objectives, they represent a fundamental part of every aspect of each person's everyday life. Human objectives are of all kinds, sizes, urgencies, and levels of significance. Reflexive ones include such things as grabbing a tissue when one is about to sneeze or heading for the restroom when nature calls. Quick little objectives include such things as putting on a pair of socks or eating breakfast as parts of getting ready to go to work in the morning (a slightly bigger objective).

Intermediate objectives might include such things as working a little harder to earn the next promotion as a step in one's career path or getting a good education so one can obtain a desirable job after graduation. Usually, in order to satisfy any "big" life-defining objective such as reaching an upper management position in one's company, earning a degree, putting one's children through college, buying a house, or moving from one town to another, one must first satisfy a number of smaller intermediate ones, such as impressing the boss, passing essential classes, earning and saving necessary money, or raising one's credit score enough to qualify for a mortgage.

Ever since the cognitive revolution and our transition into a world based much more around social realities, many of each person's objectives have begun to be directed toward a variety of forms of ego enhancement. The focus of many objectives for many people today has changed from striving to continue to survive to seeking self-esteem and the esteem of others.

The truth is that today most people in modern society almost worship their egos. Ego enhancement drives a significant part of each nation's economy. The advertising campaigns that incessantly push the sales of many of our most common products often promote them by appealing to customers who want to be more impressive in one way or another than they already see themselves as being. Everywhere we look, we are besieged with calls to buy products that promise to make us look better, be smarter, get richer, own more impressive things, improve our social status, or attract more desirable lovers. When the focus of society in general in our post-cognitive revolution world is constantly aimed at everyone's relative esteem, it's hard for one not to form many of his or her personal objectives toward the goal of trying to raise his or her own!

But, as we have seen, the ego just creates a false impression of separateness. We are each really just one small part of the whole of Tao, separate only in our own imaginations and significant only in what we each accomplish during our time living in its Flow. The ego creates in each of us a false sense of separateness and self-importance. The truth is that we will each live a few decades and then die. And after each of us has gone, all the things we spent so much of our time doing for the purpose of building ourselves up and stroking our egos will disappear along with our bodies because those things never really mattered to anyone except ourselves anyway. At that point, only what we did for our children or for others or created on behalf of society or did to improve the world in general will live on. Each person's ego only directs his or her attention inward toward his or her own self and any self-perceived virtues or inadequacies, instead of outward toward doing things that really matter.

So, as you can see, there are significant reasons why it is difficult for many, and nearly impossible for some in modern society to set and then achieve their personal objectives in the most optimal manner and for the most optimal purposes. And apparently, that was already the case more than two thousand years ago when the three Taoist classics were written because the problem was addressed in Taoist philosophy in the form of what was then called "Wu Wei" – usually translated from the ancient Chinese to mean "doing without doing" or "actionless action". To me, that translation doesn't really create the proper image in the mind of the modern Taoist of what was originally intended as to how one should set and achieve their personal objectives, though, because it tends to create a picture of people sitting around doing nothing and waiting for problems to solve themselves, and that definitely does not describe the sages as they are presented in the Taoist classics. After studying references to Wu Wei in the Tao Te Ching, the Book of Chuang Tzu and the Book of Lieh Tzu, I have decided that the descriptive "achievement with little friction" provides a better conception of what Wu Wei was really meant to be about.

When "achieving with little friction", Taoists do not try to force things to happen with aggressive actions. Instead, they choose objectives that are in tune with the current Flow of Tao and then finesse the manner and timing of their accomplishments with sensitivity so that they are likely to be achieved in ways that are both natural and that create as little resistance as possible. That might sound complicated and perhaps even nonsensical when described in words, but with a little understanding and practice, one begins to realize how instinctive and effective the method is. It makes the formulation and accomplishment of objectives much simpler, more effortless, and more likely to succeed. And after a while, success often just seems to fall in place by itself at the right time and in the most convenient manner!

Briefly, "achievement with little friction" involves a blend of four different concepts: 1) knowing and accepting one's self for who he or she really is and how the person fits in with other things within the Flow, including consideration of such realities as his or her strengths, weaknesses, and interests; 2) paying attention to, understanding, and getting a sense of what is going on in the many aspects of the Flow of Tao and one's place in it all, including what has already happened and what seems likely to happen relevant to one's self and one's interests in the future; 3) picking "big" objectives that are both in alignment with one's own interests and talents, and that also seem most appropriate for what one understands to be happening within the Flow of Tao; and 4) determining how to achieve those "big" objectives that were selected with smaller objectives that are most appropriate and timely in relationship with the Flow.

Regarding the first concept of "achievement with little friction" - being able to know and accept yourself for who you are within the Flow of Tao becomes much easier after you have begun to minimize the influence of your ego. The ego acts almost like armor hiding and protecting all the self-declared vulnerabilities of the person it supposedly serves, but once people cast that armor off, accept themselves for who and what they truly are – vulnerabilities and all – they can realize that they are just like everyone else – strong in some ways and weaker in others, talented in some ways and clumsy in others, etc. It's okay not to be perfect because no one else is perfect either. There are no perfect people! There will always be some who are better looking or faster or stronger or who know more about some topic, but no one is better at all things, and everyone has weaknesses. What is important is that there will never be anyone else who has exactly the same combination of talents, strengths, weaknesses, and knowledge that you have! Your potential is what you can and do make of what you truly are, not just of what your ego is willing to let you and others see of you!

It is when a person is first being honest with himself about himself and is exposed in that way that the person can really begin to get to know and accept himself for who and what he or she actually is. And in order to practice what I call "achievement with little friction", the Taoist must come to recognize and accept his strengths and weaknesses, what he is good at and what he is not, what he likes and dislikes, what he dreams about doing and becoming in the future, and what he might feel guilty about from his past. With the armor gone, the Taoist becomes stronger, smarter, and better able to grow and develop into the future of his potential. When he is no longer focusing on hiding all his supposedly secret weaknesses, needs, and sensitivities, or pretending to be invincible, he can then focus much more profoundly on the world and people around him and on what he wants to accomplish. That honesty, understanding of self, and improved focus helps him be able to achieve objectives with little friction.

Regarding the second concept, (i.e. paying attention to, understanding, and getting a sense of the Flow of Tao), one must come to know and accept what Tao and the Flow of Tao are all about, what he or she are currently doing in it, and what that means with regard to his or her life and objectives. The practitioner is a part of Tao, as is all else, and all that he or she experiences are manifestations of it. All such manifestations are interconnected at their most basic level – the quantum field – and what the practitioner experiences are only surface effects of all that is going on at deeper levels – with many implications that are too subtle to be easily detected. It is important, nevertheless, for the practitioner of "achievement with little friction" to consciously pay attention to the Flow of Tao and its many aspects taking place around him as he can directly experience, and then to try to understand it to as deep a level as he is able.

He will never be able to experience everything that is going on, of course. He will be limited by the natural inabilities of his sensory organs and nervous system to sense things or events that are too far away, too minute, too unusual, seemingly too irrelevant, or that take place too slowly or subliminally to be consciously detected. And each person, of course, has a limited set of interests about what is taking place around them. Nobody can pay attention to everything about everything. Each has areas of personal interest related to their careers, areas of study, individual strengths and weaknesses, and other such things. Objects and events unrelated to those areas of personal interest are all likely to be ignored.

But one who has learned to "achieve with little friction" will know that even if he or she cannot consciously detect, understand, and express verbally all that is happening on the surface and at deeper levels of the Flow of Tao, his conscious mind only provides half of his total mental capacity. If he is sensitive, attentive, cares enough, and can focus without interference from his ego, his subconscious mind will often be able to intuitively understand and react properly to events taking place in the Flow that are not consciously apparent to him, or anybody else for that matter. Because of that, he is likely to have occasional surprising insights as to the Flow of Tao and be able to respond in intuitive ways to it. For those reasons, the Taoist will be able to achieve more of what he hopes to achieve with relatively little friction.

Third, as to what "big" life-defining objectives a person should pursue in his or her life, almost anything is acceptable, as long as it is something the person will be able to be proud of accomplishing (or trying to accomplish) if and when they are successful, also as long as it is something they will be able to enjoy doing, and finally, as long as it is not something they know will hurt others, society, or the planet in general. Taoists believe in striving for success, they believe in having ambitions to accomplish things they can be proud of, and when they succeed, they believe in being just a little bit pleased about what they have done. What they would never pursue are objectives for solely selfish purposes; to stroke their egos; for the mere accumulation of wealth, power, and fame; or for the accumulation of ever more meaningless material possessions.

In our modern human mental universe of social fictions untethered in large part directly by physical reality and usually not constrained by any serious concerns over basic survival, the possible life-defining objectives one might choose from are almost unlimited except by one's imagination, by likely undesirable consequences, by personal fears, and by the physical and social realities of the Flow of Tao. With regard to the Way, it is usually not so much a matter of what one chooses to direct one's objectives toward as it is why one has chosen to pursue them. We will discuss Taoist virtues in the next section, and they are certainly factors, but other than those considerations, if one's reasons for doing almost anything are well thought out and not directed toward the gratification of his or her ego, the results are likely to be in tune with the Way of Tao.

Sometime during their youth, most people first begin to imagine what they hope to achieve in their lives and sometime after that they will first begin to have thoughts as to how those dreams might be achieved. Those early fantasies become the genesis for each person's "big" life–defining objectives.

When most people first begin to formulate such hopes and dreams about their futures, though, they are usually still quite naïve about the world and few of them put much thought or do much research into the practicality, likelihood, or even the real desirability of what they are considering. The prospective futures envisioned are based on the romance of the thing in their young minds and reflect their limited experiences with the real world. Commonly, they are also influenced by the opinions of parents, friends, teachers, and the media. Therefore, they usually evolve, most quickly and substantially during the teen and young adult years as the young people get to know what life is really all about and how things work.

The world is always full of people trying to convince others as to what to do and who to try to be in their lives. Taoists listen politely and consider the possibilities of what's being proposed but are careful to always ultimately make their own decisions as to what feels best for them in light of their own interests, values, and personal visions. They know that this is their one life to live in their own way, so the choices they make for their objectives as they gradually form them must always be well thought out and, indeed, their own.

There are two most important factors Taoists will always naturally consider when making their big decisions, though: 1) who they really are, including their talents, likes and dislikes, personality, strengths and weakness, (which should all be much clearer to them after the masks of their egos have been lifted), and 2) the likely direction of the Flow of Tao relative to them and their interests (as mentioned above). All things will change including themselves, and therefore each person will want to choose his or her own personal path in a direction that will be likely to align favorably with those changes.

And then, because of all their carefully thought-out decisions, Taoists will afterward accept full responsibility for the choices they have made and their consequences.

Fourth, as pointed out above, life has gotten complicated, and the satisfaction of "big" life-defining objectives is almost certain nowadays to involve the satisfaction of an entire series of "smaller" intermediate objectives – almost like climbing a flight of stairs with multiple landings to finally reach one's destination on the top floor. The advancement from each step to the next and from each landing upward toward a person's big life-defining objectives is accomplished by a progressive increase in education and experiences related to relevant topics, by an increased awareness of and confidence in one's related strengths, by an increasing appreciation and recognition by other significant people of the person's abilities in the field, and by a gradual increase in seniority and status. Getting to know and following all the right steps is important for one's eventual success toward any major objective.

The most significant effect of this gradual movement toward the achievement of your big life-altering objectives will be the way in which each intermediate decision you make along the way will alter who and what you will become in the days, weeks, months, and years thereafter, and whether it will improve your likelihood of the achievement of the more important big objectives you have set, or will make it more difficult. Therefore, it's important for the ultimate fulfillment of your big life-defining objectives for you to put some thought into which little and intermediate goals you pursue each day and how you decide to achieve them. If you are conscientious about always doing things that are constructive toward achieving your long-term objectives and avoid non-constructive things, it will maximize who and what you will be in the future.

You will remember that the Flow of Tao consists of an infinite number of aspects all changing through time that might affect what the Taoist is trying to accomplish. They are all intertwined, but also somewhat separate and move at different rates and in different directions. The Taoist learns to look for cycles, patterns, and trends of events for each of the many social and physical aspects of the Flow he can identify that might affect him in the achievement of his objectives. Included are such considerations as the economy, politics, fashion, public opinion, related professional beliefs, business trends, international relations, and countless other possible things depending on the goals of the person. The Taoist factors in all those aspects of the Flow he can that matter when determining all that he hopes to do. Timing his actions relative to the Flow is important because he wants his activities to always work with the Flow and not against it. Anyone who becomes good at "reading" the Flow of Tao in this way and timing his actions accordingly can more easily be in tune with everything that matters when doing everything that he or she tries to do.

The biggest difficulty with remaining in tune with the Flow of Tao is that it is always prone to unexpected changes. Even the wisest and most sensitive sage will often be surprised by sudden shifts caused by the unexpected words or actions of influential people, unforeseen acts of government or other important groups, sudden events of nature, ongoing activities that they were unaware of, or any number of other possibilities that they did not expect. Therefore, while the Taoist tries to read and follow the Flow of Tao, he or she must always remain flexible and ready to make changes in strategy should that become necessary.

The Taoist accomplishes that flexibility, in part, by the manner in which he or she perceives and processes his objectives. He rarely plans out specific steps in words or writing toward the satisfaction of objectives in detail more than a few days or weeks in advance of carrying them out - if at all. The Flow of Tao is too unpredictable for that to be very useful and it encourages one to try to force things to happen according to the plan. Instead, he visualizes fulfillment of the various steps involved in their achievement on a day-by-day basis. That way he can keep track of what is going on that is related to his goals frequently and can continuously update and adjust what is next to achieve and how best to achieve it and can set in place any new intermediate objectives toward its achievement that seem helpful. And he joyfully anticipates upcoming successes because optimism is always a powerful aide in getting anything accomplished!

Then, with the successful achievement of each new little step, he quickly savors the moment. If others helped in its accomplishment, or if friends are happy along with him in his success, he makes a point of celebrating a bit with them.

But the Taoist does not gloat, brag, or posture. His successes are only significant because he has achieved something worthwhile toward the completion of his bigger worthwhile objectives. They have nothing to do with raising him above others or of putting others down relative to him. That would make the celebrations acts of ego rather than just incentives to go on to accomplish subsequent steps that can later be celebrated.

And on occasion, when the Taoist fails to accomplish his objectives, he does not become angry, sad, or resentful. And he is always honest about his failures because he sees each such experience as a lesson on what to avoid in the accomplishment of future objectives.

Visualizing the achievement of objectives in such ways and carrying out these steps enables the creative power of his subconscious mind with its natural flexibility to fully function and assist him in the fulfillment of his goals. When aspects of the Flow of Tao move in unexpected ways and affect one's short-term objectives, while keeping his long-term objectives in mind, the Taoist need only revisualize the intermediate objectives required to easily correct the direction of his progress.

But all the "big" life-defining objectives that anyone eventually achieves, and many of the intermediate ones, will always end up being at least somewhat different than the ones first imagined earlier in life. That is inevitable because everything is always changing in the Flow of Tao. You will have changed along with your hopes and dreams. Society and technology will have changed. And the world in general will have changed. That is all to be expected.

In the end, you will realize that enjoying your repeated, determined attempts toward fulfillment of your worthwhile hopes and dreams throughout your life – including all the joys, disappointments, and lessons learned – was your most ultimate objective of them all!

The Way of Taoist Virtues

Taoism is a philosophy of life and behavior based on physical reality. It is not a religion. The Tao is not alive and it is certainly not a god. Tao is simply the word followers use to refer to the physical structure of the universe—including the forces of physics that relate to its tiny particles and the forms they group themselves into. "The Flow of Tao" is the expression used to refer to the movements, changing structures, interactions (including, as we have pointed out, social interactions), and other phenomena that result from changes to it through time including, of course, ourselves.

Between those physical and social structures of the Tao and our usual conscious awareness, there seems to be a level of reality that we call the supernatural. Most people have experienced it in one way or another. It seems to sometimes supersede time and distance, involve morality and conscience and retribution, and occasionally bring unexpected awareness of distant events for which there is no logical explanation. That is the realm that religions seek to explain and concern themselves with. Taoism accepts the reality of that realm and the benefits of religion, but it is not within its purview to explore or try to explain it. For that, one should attend a church, temple, or mosque. There is wisdom there!

The only "motivation" (for lack of a better word) that Tao has for doing what it does is to continue progressing from the reality that existed at the beginning of the universe in an orderly progression as determined by the laws of physics toward the reality that will be present at its eventual end. But that process, despite the fact that Tao is not itself alive and is not intelligent, has created the universe we now live in, the beautiful planet we live on the surface of, the teeming life that shares it with us, the civilization our species has created, and the life that each one of us now experiences.

Having no intelligence or self-awareness, Tao could not care less whether or not a person chooses to get to know and follow the philosophy of Taoism. Tao also could not care less if one chooses to follow the tenets of Taoism while also being a Christian, Muslim, Jew, Hindu, Buddhist, or some other religion. It is, has always been, and must be, after all, behind and below all else, including God or gods. Therefore, Taoism is not a jealous philosophy. It does not demand loyalty, reverence, or obedience.

Any benefits one should happen to realize as a result of following the philosophy come as a result of the natural alignment of his or her Taoist beliefs and the objectives they pursue by acting in accordance with the Way of Tao, not because of any gift given as a result of loyalty or some sort of "acceptable" behavior.

Tao and its Flow set the backdrop for the world each of us knows. The events, environment, and people that we live in and around create us, shape us, and give us purpose. They limit us and they challenge us. Much of what happens to each of us as a result of the Flow of Tao we can only react to. It is the personal challenge of each individual to take as much control of events as possible that they want to within the Flow of Tao in order to improve the quality of his or her life, the lives of family members and friends, and of the culture we live in. The philosophy of Taoism helps us to do that in ways that are most effective and beneficial for ourselves, our society, and the world in general.

While Tao is not alive or intelligent, those who believe in Taoism are. And each Taoist is as much a part of the whole of it as is any other living creature, inanimate object, or system of structures. Therefore, each Taoist could be thought of as a tiny bit of intelligence and consciousness of the otherwise unaware Tao, much like a hippocampus or cerebellum is each a part of the intelligence and consciousness of the otherwise unaware body of a person. We Taoists, as a group, can therefore think of ourselves as Tao's intelligent representatives on Earth.

Each one of us, then, is a tool for Tao, helping to give it sight, sound, taste, smell, thought, and the use of our hands so that we can act on its behalf. And as such, each of us, though relatively tiny, is an integral part of the whole of it. Every person's life must always first and foremost be his or her own to do with as they choose, of course, but Taoists, no matter what else they might decide to do with themselves, must also always feel an obligation to consider the effects of their actions on the Flow of Tao taking place around them and on their possible consequences, especially to the environment that people on this planet must live as a part of.

Earth is one of what is probably a relatively small number of places, at least within this part of the galaxy, that can and does support life as we might recognize it. In fact, there may be no others. It has long been, and still is, conducive to the existence and proliferation of millions of species of plants and animals that live or have lived on it. It first became that way long ago as a result of the movements and realities of the Flow of Tao in this galactic region, and the life on the planet today is the result of billions of years of evolution since that early time. Earth can be thought of as a small irreplaceable and somewhat fragile haven of life in a mostly hostile universe. As intelligent representatives of Tao, then, it should be an essential objective for followers of Taoism, no matter what other objectives they might choose to pursue, to consider the effects of their actions on the preservation of the health of this precious planet and the balance of lives that live here.

Many forms of life on Earth have been suffering lately from the presence and resource use of an increasing number of our own species. As I write this, there are over 8 billion human beings on this planet, all requiring homes, food, water, manufactured goods, and the proper disposal of all their various waste products. As a result, some other species have gone extinct. The numbers of many others are dwindling. Some biological systems are failing or are in danger of failing. It is of special importance for Taoists to help keep the life that still exists here healthy and abundant until such time as our human population begins to decrease. Other species have a right to flourish and satisfy their needs with minimal interference from our own. Basic natural biological processes must always be allowed to function properly.

Intelligence to the level of our species is undoubtedly rare and precious in the whole of Tao, and it is therefore important to Taoists to do our part to keep our own species not only physically healthy but also emotionally and mentally healthy. Our knowledge and wisdom as a species must always be encouraged to grow, the strength and compassion of our societies must keep advancing, our personal freedoms must always be maintained, our economies must remain vibrant, our sciences and technologies must be kept developing, our political structures must always benefit citizens more than just politicians, and our boundaries must always be allowed to expand.

In general, each Taoist should strive to make the most of their own life and to fulfill their own destiny, but each must also consider the effects of their actions and make a point to do beneficial things rather than harmful ones. Balancing all these sometimes-contradictory expectations while pursuing one's own objectives is certainly always a challenge, but meeting challenges successfully and enjoying doing so is what life is all about.

The Inner Effects of Taoism

Taoists look for, understand, and accept the effects of the Flow of Tao on themselves and on the world around them. They understand that it is only a common egotistical illusion to consider oneself to be in some way separate from or above the Flow, or to expect it to somehow act in ways that will specifically benefit them. Actually, the occasional problems everyone experiences in life usually originate from a person's failure to anticipate or notice changes that are occurring in the Flow of Tao and to account for them, and then the problems are worsened if the person refuses to acknowledge and accept those occurrences as being natural rather than personal, and then worsened even more if he or she allows themself to experience and react with unpleasant emotions because of them.

Unhappiness comes from that sort of dissatisfaction with

what the Flow sometimes has brought one. It also comes from impatiently waiting for less-than-perfect times to end and hoping for some eventual idyllic future to finally come to be. Life consists of constant interactions with the Flow of Tao as it continuously unfolds. Some such interactions will just naturally be more enjoyable than others. The only eventual future ending that there will ever be—probably not idyllic—will be when each person's life eventually ends. Happiness is a result of continuously accepting and appreciating what those daily realities of the Flow of Tao has brought and one's current place in it, no matter what they might be. And achieving the objectives of one's choice while doing so is life's purpose.

With a diminished ego that is carefully monitored, with a comfortable attitude about oneself, and with acceptance and appreciation of whatever daily events the person experiences within the Flow of Tao, there is little for anyone to ever feel the need to lie about. Taoists pride themselves on their honesty. Lying about mistakes and one's part in them inhibits one's ability to learn how not to repeat them. When Taoists make mistakes, as all people sometimes do, they take responsibility for what they have done and therefore can learn more easily not to make similar mistakes in similar situations in the future.

The damage done to people's lives and to society in general as a result of lies is underappreciated. Lies distort everyone's personal understanding of what has happened in the Flow of Tao— the teller of the lies as well as their intended target or targets. The target or targets might suffer some loss of some sort if they act on the misrepresentation they have received, but usually the worst consequences of any lie fall on the liar. After lying, they find themselves having to hide or discredit any new information that might refute the lie they told or perhaps might even feel the need to manufacture and then present evidence to those involved that might seem to support the lie. Each lie creates a complex of tangled thoughts of different scenarios that must always be carefully processed so that inconsistencies are not revealed and so that strategies can be developed to avoid uncovering the embarrassing truth behind the lie in some other accidental way. And, of course, once others have realized that the person has a tendency to lie, those others are not likely to totally believe anything he or she ever says again in the future. Honest truth all the time makes everything easier for everyone!

With a diminished ego that is carefully monitored and with the absence of embarrassing or reprehensible ego-driven lies and behaviors forever needing to be covered up, there is little for the Taoist to ever fear, to be embarrassed about, or to feel guilt over. Most embarrassing emotions that occur to other people can be traced back to their egos and things done to support their egos, but the dedicated Taoist finds that whatever emotions they usually feel come as a result of feelings they have about other people they care about and not related to themselves and their own personal needs and fears.

Lives lived with honesty, comfortable emotions, and objectives aligned with Tao will be lives lived with openness and inner unity. Every aspect of one's body and mind—upper, lower, conscious, and unconscious—will always be able to unite toward the fulfillment of each objective pursued because there is no reason for it not to. And from unity comes focus. Unity and focus help bring success, and from frequent successes comes self-confidence.

Relationships with Others

The beliefs and perspectives of Taoism will not only affect the adherent's view of himself and of the world he lives in, but also of his relationship with others. First of all, his drive to recognize and minimize his own ego will necessarily cause him to become aware of the behaviors of others that are being driven by the demands of their own egos. But the Taoist, as an aware part of Tao just like the other and knowing how difficult it is to control egos, will avoid judgment.

The Taoist knows that all of us on Earth, whether Taoist or not, supposed "good" guy or "bad" guy, male or female, this skin color or that, upper class or lower class, or even this species or that species, are all similarly just manifestations of a part of Tao—none inherently more or less significant than any other. Being a follower of the Taoist philosophy benefits the individual who is following it, and hopefully it also benefits society and the planet in general but believing in Taoism does not make one any better or worse than any other, or more special to Tao, which is, of course, unaware of us all except through the eyes of ourselves and others.

Competition between people in the earliest days of our species was often, most likely, a serious business. People and groups of people had to find and often fight for limited sources of necessary food and other scarce resources, and for opportunities to breed with desirable partners. Egos were involved and the competition was, no doubt, often a life-or-death struggle. In the modern world competition is still important, but especially within the last century or so, it rarely involves anything more significant than amusement, challenges to the satisfaction of noncritical objectives, or ego boosting or deflating. Except in wartime, serious pain or death is rarely involved. So, for Taoists who deemphasize ego, most competition takes on a whole new less-significant role.

Competition is certainly not necessarily bad. Competition in sports and other games is what makes them fun for the participants and entertaining for the observers. Competition challenges people and stimulates them to exert the greatest possible effort toward what they are doing. But in the modern world, competition rarely ever calls for deep aggressive actions or angry emotions. That type of reaction in today's world is usually just the effect of threats to the egos of non-Taoists and reactions to those threats.

Life today rarely needs to be a battlefield, and there is no reason for anyone to purposely make it into one. Except in rare "life or death" situations like war, competition should usually just be treated as an entertaining challenge. Beyond pursuing their objectives, Taoists feel most strongly about preserving the interests of the Flow of Tao anyway, and when pursuing common interests like that, people do not so much need to compete with each other as to work together. The people that Taoists do compete with most seriously are always themselves—to become better in all that they do—and they do that calmly and with patience.

Taoists often have a natural advantage in competitions anyway because of the realities and effects of their philosophy, and winning, when too easy, becomes an exercise of ego rather than an entertaining challenge. Taoists believe, therefore, in a code of chivalry and compassion that includes consideration of others they are competing with and a desire not to humiliate anyone who is sensitive and has a disadvantage in the competition. Taoist sympathies, in general, often tend to go toward the underdogs—the outcasts and social rejects, and those who are victimized or made fun of by the rich, powerful, and famous. Without chivalry, competition can sometimes turn ugly and emotional for such people, and to the Taoist, with his or her reduced ego, there is rarely a need to reach that extreme.

All people are different, and even though we are all one in Tao, people naturally interact with each other in ways that reflect that reality. And even though Taoists might sometimes tend to find themselves to be most comfortable interacting with other Taoists because of their commonality of beliefs and values, they know that most individuals, whether Taoist or not, are good people who usually mean well and are just trying to get by and enjoy their lives, families, and friends. But some people are more driven by their egos than others. Such people still usually mean well and have functioning moral compasses, but a desire for the trappings of success and victory in competitions may sometimes tip the balance within them when they are setting their objectives and deciding how to achieve them. Such people don't usually mean to hurt anyone or anything, but the lure of what they consider to be wealth and success sometimes allows moral compromises.

There is a very small percentage of people who are so seriously perverted for one reason or another that they might seem to be beyond redemption. Taoists generally avoid such people whenever they can. But if they can't, they deal with them to the extent and in the manner that they must. Minor bruises to egos are insignificant to Taoists, but they do not allow themselves to be victimized in important matters, and the maintenance of Taoism's important objectives, as mentioned above, cannot be allowed to be compromised to any significant extent, no matter what.

Taoists never have any desire to hurt anyone physically, emotionally, or socially. Having minimized egos, they never feel any need to do so on their own behalf. They always seek to avoid conflict and serious forms of competition whenever they can. Usually they are straightforward in their intent and have no secret agendas. Their words can be trusted. They act with honor, and they generally hope for the success of others and are frequently willing to go out of their way to help insure it whenever they can.

That said, true Taoists are not fools. They cannot easily be taken advantage of. They tend to know and accept what is going on in the Flow of Tao around them, who they can trust, who they should help, and who they must watch most carefully. Taoists, because they have gotten to know themselves, are usually good judges of the characters of others.

The basic concepts and values of Taoists and their attitudes toward others are usually reflected back at them in the way other people view them. Most will realize almost immediately that the

Taoist they are interacting with is no threat because most people are naturally good judges of such things and because Taoists truly are not threats. But people's reactions to others also sometimes come from within them as a result of their own inner mental realities and past experiences, and therefore some will first see Taoists' lack of guile and artifice as weakness or gullibility and disrespect them as a result—or even see them as potential victims. Others might feel jealousy or suspicion of Taoists because of their usual happy and comfortable ways.

But whatever their initial reaction, after a few minutes of interaction, most people will come to realize that the Taoist, because of his or her beliefs, is honest, dedicated, straightforward, perceptive, and pleasant to work with, and will, as a result, be receptive to helping him or her in whatever ways they can with whatever it is the Taoist is trying to do. In that way, once again, the perspectives that result from following the Way of Tao help allow achievement with little friction.

8

The Current Moment

"That's all wonderful," you might be thinking to yourself about the last couple of chapters. "I'll try to keep it in mind, but I don't think I could possibly implement all that in my own life." Well, that might be easier than you think. The three ancient Taoist sages did not address the issue, but stoicism, from the ancient Greco-Roman world at the other end of the Silk Road, does provide us with some tools that can help.

We speak of the life of someone who is no longer living as having been between such and such dates and as having taken place here or there. We say that he or she did this thing and then did that thing. We say of someone who is still alive that they are a certain age, live in some location, and have accomplished such and such. And we would most likely describe our own lives in the same way. But that way of looking at a person's life, while convenient, does not describe the reality of how someone actually experiences life. You and I are each in reality only alive in this current moment. Everything else is just memory or imagination.

We get up each day and proceed through our morning rituals. We use the toilet, brush our teeth, shower, dress, drink coffee, eat breakfast, and whatever else follows. Then we go to work, take care of business, converse with others, satisfy objectives, commute home, interact with family and friends, and then eventually go back to bed. Each activity—the tooth brushing, the shower, the commute to work, and every other one—consists of "current moments" that we experience at the time we are doing it. Our daily routine consists of a series of such current moments. And those current moments are the actual reality of our lives. All that happened before each separate current moment is nothing but history and no longer exists, and all that has not yet happened is still nothing but possibilities of what might happen later in what we call the future.

Looking at your current moment now as you read these words, everything that took place in the past is not real anymore. It does not exist except in your memory and in whatever evidence, artifacts, and commitments remain from it—such as documents, consequences, videos, obligations, properties, diaries, and children (ha-ha). But the past can't be changed, you can't control it, and you can no longer experience it with your sensory organs. The only value the past really has for any of us now in this current moment lies in whatever we can learn from it. And if we did something notably foolish or notably clever in that now-gone past, in the current moment (or perhaps some future one), we are likely to either be suffering from it or enjoying its consequences.

Our relationship with the future is very different than that with the past. Instead of remembering things, as we do with the past, we dream, imagine, and fantasize about and plan our possible futures. Like the past, you can't live in the future and you can't experience it because you can always only live in the current moment. And like the past, you can't control it—not totally and for sure, anyway. But unlike the past, you can manipulate some aspects of the future somewhat and sometimes. In fact, many of the current moments of most people today are taken up by either trying to anticipate, prepare for, benefit from, coordinate, or alter the future. In the far distant past, hunters and gatherers probably did not think much about the future at all, other than considering where they might go hunting and foraging the next day. In ancient civilizations, prophecy was big business; farmers had to keep track of the seasons, of course; and food was stored during times of plenty for future lean times. But in modern society, almost every type of business is dedicated in one way or another to trying to anticipate, manipulate, and profit from the future. (The stock market is one obvious example!) Every one of us dedicates many of our own personal current moments each day to think about how to make our own futures better or toward actually doing things that we think will accomplish that, such as going to college, investing money in an IRA, pursuing a prospective lover, or brown-nosing a boss. So, while our bodies and brains are always necessarily in our current moment interacting with the current moment of the Flow of Tao, our minds and imaginations are often busy thinking about and trying to anticipate the future.

Since it's so necessary for each of us in modern society to spend so much mental time in the future, and since it's so important for our happiness and personal success to do it well, the tenets of Modern Taoism, as discussed earlier in this book, teach the concepts of "achievement with little friction." It's important for the modern Taoist to know how to do it most successfully so that he or she will be most likely to be successful and happy, and if he or she has an exceptional system for dealing with the future, they will also be able to spend less mental time there and more in the current moment being in tune with the Flow of Tao.

The problem with spending too much mental time in the future (or in the past) is that our bodies and sensory organs are always actually in the current moment, and if our minds are elsewhere, we miss out on some of the realities going on around us. Our current moments are designed to mesh with the current moments of the Flow of Tao, and therefore our sensory organs constantly tell us what is going on in the here and now. If we do not pay attention because our awareness is elsewhere, we miss out on much of that information. And of course, no matter how good we are at anticipating the future, the Flow of Tao is far too uncertain to always predict everything very successfully—which sometimes leads us to a lack of success and resulting unhappiness. Oddsmakers might usually be right about what will happen in the future on a percentage basis, but in our own personal lives, the unexpected happens all the time, wrecking plans that we have so carefully developed. And if our minds are dreaming of events elsewhere, we are likely to miss real impending disasters that threaten to happen to or around us.

So, we must actually exist in the ever-progressing current moment and use the lessons we have learned from the misty past to help decide now what to do and what to plan for the unpredictable future. With each day that comes and goes, those misty past sources of experience that we use as a basis for learning become a little longer, and that often uncontrollable and unpredictable source of possible fulfillment—the future—becomes a little shorter until ultimately we run out of all future current moments completely.

The here and now is always where the real action is. It's where the current moment of the Flow of Tao is. It's where you actually experience things and where you have at least some aspects of control over what happens. Thinking of a life as something that occurs between one date and another and consisting of achievements in one place or another is misleading because that's not really the way anyone experiences their life. It also prevents you from seeing how to maximize all of your current moments. Real life consists of our personal current moments constantly interacting with a sequence of current moments in the Flow of Tao. If one learns to synchronize their own with Tao's in ways that make him or her most successful, they are most likely to be happy as well. And that is the ultimate challenge and goal for everyone.

Being successful and happy starts by getting all you can out of your current moments. Since all you can control, all you actually experience, and all of your actual sensations of happiness or anything else take place during present current moments; you don't want those precious, ever-evolving current moments to amount to no more than a sequence of mindless spontaneous reactions to the stimuli you experience at each given one. Instead, you want to make the most out of all of them. You want to widen them. You want to craft them. You want to make them as impactful and effective toward achieving your aims and desires as possible, whatever those might be. You want each current moment to be as happy for you as possible, and you want to set up future ones so that they might (hopefully) be even better because, while you can't control the future with any certainty, you can affect it, and it's better to try to affect it in positive ways for yourself than in negative ways, or to just live your life from day to day, reacting reflexively to whatever happens.

Types of Current Moments

To start to learn how to make the most out of our current moments, let's examine different types based on how much focus they require from the person experiencing them. In reality, of course, each current moment is unique, and each must be dealt with in its own way, but for the sake of this discussion, I will talk about four general types of "current moment." It doesn't matter exactly what they entail (whether conversation, learning from a book, physical interactions, exams, interviews, or whatever). All that matters to us here is the extent of the focus that is required of you when experiencing each type.

"Idle time" means a current moment when you are experiencing very little sensory input and when there are no pressing demands for you to immediately satisfy. The purest "idle time" of all is probably when one is lying sleeplessly in bed or is alone with nothing important to do because there are no sensory inputs taking place, no decisions to make, and no one currently making demands on your attention.

This is the best time to consider the past, including achievements you are proud of and actions you took and words you said that you are not proud of, and use each case to learn from them. Remember that you can't change the past though, so don't dwell too much on bad behavior and unhappy outcomes. The point is only to learn from the memories.

It's also the best time to consider the Flow of Tao that you have experienced through the past and into the present so that you might notice patterns to help you detect where the Flow might be going in the future. There is never any certainty that things will work out as you anticipate, of course, but practice makes perfect (or at least better), so the more you try, the more likely it is that you will become ever more adept at it.

It's also a good time to consider your goals for the future, to imagine how you might accomplish them and what actions in future current moments might help to achieve them. And it's a good time to consider specific problems you might be having in your life and how to best solve or neutralize them because in general, during such "idle times," thoughts can be made casually, and the mind can safely wander freely.

And when you have such moments when it's daytime and you are up and about, it's the best time to observe and reflect on the wonders of life and of the world around you!

During **"casually engaged"** moments, you are doing something that only requires minimal attention to sensory input, and any decisions that need to be made can be contemplated casually because of the lack of any other mental demands. You might be engaged in routine tasks, working at a hobby, in the company of a spouse or friend who is also self-engaged, housecleaning, or doing home repairs or any other such semi-mindless activity.

There is plenty of time for introspection, and you can tune out safely from most sensory input at the moment, although the situation could easily change depending on events. This is a good time for the same type of introspection you allow yourself during your "idle time," to engage in thoughts about solving problems or working toward bringing about any goals and objectives you might have created earlier, but you can't lose track entirely of what's going on around you.

There are many different types of **"significant activity"** current moments, but no matter what they entail specifically, such moments all have certain characteristics in common. For instance, they are not stressful or intense and often involve pleasant interactions with family or friends. Examples of "significant activity" moments include conversations with friendly people, doing whatever work you do (if it's not too stressful), shopping, driving in traffic, or playing with children.

Because of the somewhat casual nature of "significant activity" current moments, it's easy to let your mind drift for short periods to thoughts of the past, planning the future, or decision-making not related to the current moment; but that can be dangerous because often during such times if you happen to lose focus on what is going on around you, there could be negative consequences such as losing track of conversations, missing subtle but important hints about events or people that are important to you, making mistakes or even injuring yourself in some more physical activities, or accidentally hurting the feelings of a loved one. You will often also need to make sudden, impactful decisions at such times, and you will not have much time to think about your options. It will be important for you to not make foolish or unvirtuous decisions so that you do not suffer negative future consequences for yourself or create them for others by doing so.

A **"full attention"** current moment is one wherein a drifting mind could have serious consequences for one's career, relationships, or health. At such a time, one must be totally aware of what is going on. Important conversations are taking place. People are counting on you. You are doing potentially dangerous things. Little mistakes could cause big problems. Already accomplished work could end up being wasted. Money could be lost! But, whatever the exact situation, decisions are likely to have to be made quickly, and it's important that they are made right! This is a time when you will need to have firm, virtuous values deeply instilled in your mind so that you can make the right decisions almost automatically and continue to successfully follow the Way.

The important thing to take from this conversation for the Taoist following the Way is that there are current moments best suited for contemplation and there are current moments that call for full focus, and it is important to recognize the differences between the two and learn to use each most advantageously. If current moments well suited for contemplation are used thoughtfully and effectively to plan out how to solve problems and toward the realization of objectives, current moments that require more focus can be more easily focused on. Additionally, it points out the importance of having well-known and even deeply engrained criteria in mind for making important decisions so that during "significant activity" and "full attention" current moments, you will, with more certainty, be prepared to make effective and virtuous ones.

Maximizing Current Moments

You might think that since you can't control either the past or the future with any certainty, you should at least be able to fully control your present current moment, but in truth, much of that is also beyond your control. The places you must be and the things you must do in any given current moment are often required of you by bosses, spouses, or just by past events and obligations. Anything that involves people other than yourself also makes the details of events and outcomes of present moments uncertain. Coincidences of weather, the physical environment, illness and other bodily problems, or a host of other circumstances could cause otherwise expected current moments to change in surprising and perhaps undesirable ways, too. These are all things that you might have expected to have control of, but unexpected circumstances prove that you really do not.

Stoics believe it is foolish to ever trust your happiness to things that you don't have total control over. You can hope that good things will happen, but you should always remember that no matter how clever you are and how hard you try, you can't control everything that happens around you with any certainty at all, and you must just accept the realities of the Flow of Tao that might prevent it stoically (hence the name) and not allow yourself to become upset or emotionally devastated by events that you have no possible way to completely control.

So, you might be thinking, "Wait a minute; if I can't control the past and can't control the future or even the present, what can I control? And if I'm only supposed to allow myself emotional reactions to things I can control completely, and there's nothing I can control completely, doesn't that mean I have to be a zombie for the rest of my life?"

Of course not! There are a few important things that you always have complete control over. For instance, you have complete control over the amount of attention you choose to pay to the sensory input you receive from the Flow of Tao going on in and around you during each current moment. Remember that your only connection throughout your entire life to the Flow of Tao is the input you receive from your five sensory organs during all the current moments of your life. Without that input, you would have absolutely no idea what is going on around you. Paying attention to the information your sensory organs supply you with is important. When you are doing things and interacting with people and events, it is important for your mind to be focused on what is going on. Pay attention. Don't be lost in the past or the future or thinking about your ego. If you miss important subtle information about what is happening, you will not be able to understand or react to things most advantageously. Part of what Modern Taoism is meant to teach you are when and how to focus on that which is really important.

And you do have complete control over interpreting the input you experience accurately from your five senses. Assign and categorize it in your mind, but don't make casual assumptions about its significance. Be careful with value judgments. Never respond spontaneously or emotionally to sensory input, especially if there is any chance you don't understand it correctly. If it's important and you're not sure, try mentally stepping back and examining the situation from a more distant perspective. Take your ego out of the equation. Things are often not what they first seem to be. Seek explanations from others or information from other sources. After all that, if appropriate, consider dispassionately how ongoing and unfolding events affect your understanding, your life, and your plans. React unemotionally but appropriately. React as soon as you are certain of what is happening, if that is what is most appropriate. Otherwise, wait for "idle time" or "casually engaged" moments to think about it. Are there changes that need to be made? Do plans need to be revised? Do decisions need to be considered? Is there anything about it you can learn regarding yourself or your understanding of the Flow of Tao? It's essential that you get these initial things right because if you don't, decisions you base on that information will be faulty, and memories you accumulate about it will be inaccurate.

Then, perhaps most significantly, you do have complete control over the decisions you make as a result of what you experience during your current moments. Those decisions, when made properly, allow Taoists to follow the Way of Tao best so that they can strive to become sages. The most significant requirements for following the Way are making effective and virtuous decisions that allow the Taoist to successfully intertwine his current moments with those of the Flow of Tao as he successfully achieves his personal goals and lives a happy and fulfilling life.

Decisions that need to be made during current moments come in all types as do the different current moments in which they are made, but all important decisions, whether they are momentous or just barely significant, should be made using the same basic considerations.

1. What objectives am I trying to achieve? What am I hoping to accomplish?
2. What would a sage do in this situation, and how would he or she do it? You have read the words of the three ancient sages in earlier pages of this book. Do any of them apply? Imagine how they would decide if the decision were theirs to make.
3. What are my best options?
4. How virtuous or unvirtuous are each of the options I am considering? How do the options hold up to the values discussed in the previous chapter? Remember that being virtuous is not something you do just to be nice to others; it benefits you in a multitude of important ways as well.
5. I should never consider options that are just based on the preservation or inflation of my ego; that are selfish, prurient, or aimed at sensory desires; or that only involve the accumulation of wealth, power, fame, or personal possessions (unless there is some worthwhile purpose for accumulating them).
6. I should never do things that I know will physically or emotionally harm others, especially those I love or those who

love me, or things that will hurt my community, my country, or the planet in general.

7. I should always pick options that encourage healthy positive relationships with and between others.

8. Is the option I'm considering honest? I will not do things that perpetuate lies. Honesty is one of the most important cornerstones of Taoism because without it, understanding the Flow of Tao becomes distorted for everyone who hears and believes the lies, and therefore the lies make it more difficult for everyone to make good decisions.

9. I don't make decisions to do or not do things due to fear. I must never fear anything that I don't have total control over because what is the point? And the only thing I do have total control over is myself, including such things as my own bad choices, miscalculations, and inadequacies.

10. How do options fit in with my understanding of the Flow of Tao? Actions that fit in with it well are easier to accomplish, less likely to meet resistance, and less likely to disrupt society than those that don't.

11. Is the option I am considering worth the trouble of achieving it? I don't want to waste my valuable time on insignificant things. The time allotted to me during the current moments of my life is the most valuable and least renewable thing I have. Is the option worth the time it would take to achieve it? But that does not mean that I must work and accomplish things constantly. Decompression from stress is important. The enjoyment of friends and family is important. Time to consider my past and future is important, too. What I always need to avoid is doing nothing of value for no good reason.

12. And finally, since I have slimmed my choices down considerably by now, I will go back and reconsider step one.

Do the decision choices I am still considering advance my worthwhile objectives? If not, I will start over again from the top.

13. If there are no good options, sometimes the best decision is just not to do anything at all yet. During some future current moment, perhaps the whole problem and the best options to solve it will become clearer, or the problem will just resolve itself.

Try to memorize and internalize these considerations during "idle time" and "casually engaged" moments so that during moments of "significant activity" or "full attention" you will be less likely to make foolish or unvirtuous decisions and find yourself losing the Way.

Then, after the decisions are made and you are in the process of doing things to carry them out, be sure to do as good a job at accomplishing them as possible. Your decision-making processes were well thought out. They were not made casually, and therefore, you must commit to pursuing them with diligence. But don't focus excessively on specific outcomes. The Flow of Tao is always changing and never totally predictable. That means that your targets may be changing, too. Focus on the process of aiming perfectly and then aiming perfectly again and then again and again. You will never have complete control over being able to actually hit any exact target. Success lies in being the best you can possibly be at persistently aiming and then re-aiming as the target evolves, and you get closer and closer to successfully achieving it.

With a Taoist attitude, you never really fail at anything anyway because each and every current moment is a learning experience, and every failure to hit the target is an opportunity to re-aim. And you learn more from missing the target and re-aiming than you ever do by actually hitting it. Constantly struggling for success and happiness is what life is all about. Whatever stands in the way becomes the Way. Emulate the Way of Water. Overcome or erode impediments or wait patiently for the impediments to move themselves. Everything is always changing. Use the changes to go with and use the Flow of Tao to fulfill your objectives.

And be sure to enjoy yourself as you do it all. Never forget that the point of everything is to help you synchronize the interface of your current moments with the current moments of the Flow of Tao so that you can live a smooth and effective life and be as happy and successful as possible now and in your future. Experience it all with humor and joy and have fun with your life.

In chapter 6, we examined the physical and social bases of Tao and its Flow. In chapter 7, we talked about the fundamentals of the Way of Tao and the value of each aspect of it to the Taoist who follows the Way. In this chapter, we have discussed how each person experiences the Flow of Tao and how the Taoist can best interface his or her current moments with the Flow's current moments to follow the Way and try to attain the noble traits of a sage. The "Sage of Tao" is a concept that represents a Taoist who has been able to synthesize and internalize all the concepts of the three chapters flawlessly. In the next chapter, we will explore what the noble traits of such a sage might actually be like.

9

The Sage of Tao

Who and What Is a Sage

The concept of the "Sage of Tao" is meant to portray an imaginary role model that represents the ideal Taoist—a perfect follower of the Way of Tao and a longtime adherent who has absorbed the philosophy to his very core and never falters or errs in practicing it. But, of course, perfect people aren't real, and real people aren't perfect. Therefore, in the real world, there can be no real sages, and while someone might call someone else one, no true Taoist would ever claim the title. But for the sake of this discussion, I will describe what I believe a sage would be like if there actually were any.

With that in mind, almost anyone you might ever meet could conceivably be a sage. A sage could be of either gender or any sexual orientation. He or she could be from any ethnic background or economic social class, could have an outgoing personality or be more introverted, could be tall or short, lean or stout, or wear one style of clothing or any other. It would be impossible to tell a sage from his or her appearance or any short-term or casual contact. Sages feel no need to announce their philosophical alignment to those they don't know well, and they certainly don't have any reason to proselytize. Tao doesn't have any need to gather followers, and since Taoism is just a personal philosophy, there is no "church of Tao" that needs donations or other financial support. When you first meet a sage or interact with him or her casually, you'll find that they are pretty much just like anyone else.

But if you get to know a sage a little more, you might start to notice a few small differences between him or her and most other people you know. Because of their minimized egos and other values of the philosophy, sages are never purposely mean, hateful, or cruel. They are never greedy or power hungry, and they aren't ever braggarts, show-offs, hedonists, or sycophants. The honesty, modesty, confidence, and lack of guile that characterize sages as a result of Taoism might make their personalities seem a bit less complicated perhaps than that of some other people who feel that they must always defend their egos and who must sometimes protect past lies from being exposed.

Because of the philosophy of Taoism, a sage might also seem somewhat naïve to anyone who does not know him well. The sage's steadfast commitment to honesty and acting according to his or her values regardless of consequences might seem somewhat foolish to those unfamiliar with Taoism. The sage says and does what he believes to be true and accurate to the best of his ability and accepts any consequences that result dispassionately. To others, that might seem rather silly, but to the sage, that is just the way things are meant to be.

The different understandings that are part of living in accordance with the Way of Tao might also make the sage seem slightly odd or eccentric. He knows that he and everything else is a part of Tao and accepts the responsibility of being one of its representatives. What is inside him and what is outside are all really the same—just different manifestations of Tao. Borders and boundaries are all somewhat artificial and arbitrary to him. That, when added to his honesty and lack of guile, gives him a little more freedom to do and be anything he wants to do and be;

because there are few limits, there is nothing to hide, nothing to cause embarrassment, and little that is likely to prevent him from doing so.

The sage therefore has the freedom to go his own way. He doesn't feel any obligation to follow convention. Accepting responsibility for his own choices, he follows the path that he finds to be proper and most rewarding and then he accepts the consequences. Never forgetting to enjoy the process, he decides whatever he wants to do and then achieves his objectives step by step, always anticipating the next most likely one.

There is no certainty of anything in the Flow of Tao, and therefore any specific sage might or might not be successful in accomplishing their more difficult objectives, but the beliefs and perspectives they all adhere to increase their odds of success considerably. After all, other people soon realize that they are honest and can be trusted to do the right thing, so few people are likely to resist them; they follow the Flow of Tao and do not fight against it, so the Flow is not likely to resist them; and they achieve their goals with steadfast virtue, so none of the various aspects of their own personality are likely to resist them. Such realities and others tend to bring the sage "good luck."

So, the sage might seem to others to be rather lucky but also kind of naïve and a little eccentric. But every person in the world is unique and unusual in one way or another, and the sage is just another one, like the others, living his life and interacting with the world around him. The sage wouldn't have it any other way. The goal of sages when interacting with acquaintances and casual friends is to be like a clear mountain lake—mirroring the world around them most of the time but being open to a mutual exploration of Tao's fascinating depths for anyone wishing to look past those reflections. If you should ever get to know a sage well and ask about Taoism and what they feel they might have gained from following it, you will find that they are more interesting and complex than you had anticipated.

The Personality of a Sage

The sage knows that the Tao of the ancients is based on what they understood at the time about nature and the science we now call physics. He or she has learned the basic principles of the quantum field, the structure of atoms and molecules, and biochemistry. He knows that he, himself, as well as all the things and people he can experience around him are physically just matter, a form of energy, that happens to be a little denser in some places than it is in others due to the laws of physics, allowing us in those places to be able to see and feel them. Otherwise, the objects are just parts of the interconnected and interacting quantum field like all else. He also knows a little about what is now known of the origin and history of the universe, and he makes a point of seeking out whatever he can understand about the Flow of Tao as it has changed through the past and into the present. And he knows that he has a small but significant role to play in what it is now and what it will be during the remainder of his lifetime.

The sage understands that as temporary manifestations of atoms and molecules in the quantum field, he and the people and all the things he ever experiences will only maintain their present form for a short while, will constantly change as long as they exist, and will all then eventually and inevitably sink back into the undefined quantum field from which they came. He knows that all that happens in the Flow of Tao, except individual acts by individual people and a few more intelligent creatures, occurs as a result of what has happened before as dictated by the laws of physics, and that all such transitions could be predicted if people had the knowledge and mental capacity to see and understand all the interactions that are taking place around them. The complexity of it all is far too great to do that with any certainty, of course, and the individual actions of people in society make it all even more uncertain, but the sage pays attention and makes a point of trying to understand the Flow of Tao taking place around him as much as he can; he also tries to understand that some trends and cycles can sometimes be predicted, and some insights into what can be expected in the future can sometimes be attained. The sage consciously tries to detect all that he can, and because it is important to him, his subconscious mind becomes sensitive to it all as well. That is important because the subconscious mind, working without the limitations of words, can often understand the complexities of the Flow of Tao better than the conscious mind can with words, and sometimes it can even help guide him, without him even being aware of it, toward personal successes.

Because of his understanding of and engagement with the Flow of Tao, the sage almost melds with its Flow. All he does is in harmony with it. Because he sees himself as one with it, his understanding helps him to do what he wants to do, and he, in turn, is careful not to do things that would significantly disturb its natural flow.

However, because of the complexity of it all and the limitations of human sensory organs and mental abilities, much happens that the sage does not expect, and that might be contrary to his interests. Whatever the Flow does bring, the sage accepts dispassionately, learns from, and adjusts his understandings and views of the future to compensate for it. There is no point in reacting emotionally to something that he cannot, with any certainty, control.

So the sage tries to use whatever knowledge he has accumulated to improve his decision-making and actions for the future. One challenge in that regard is the natural human tendency to understand things in relationship to one's own ego. The only aspects of the Flow of Tao that might be personal for or against anyone are the words and actions of individual people; otherwise, it is completely unbiased. The sage understands this and does not see the actions of the Flow as being personal. He also does not see these aspects as just being either beneficial or detrimental to himself personally. He just accepts the events and alters his view of the present world and what might happen in it next and alters his goals and plans to compensate for what he experienced. And, of course, he tries to learn from whatever happens.

Our egos make us seem separate and more important than the rest of Tao to us, when in fact we are each just another part of it just like every other, whether animate or not. Our personal needs are not at all important in the broader picture of the Flow of Tao. The sage understands these realities and monitors his thoughts to recognize any self-centered thoughts, and then he ignores them as much as possible. Other than his continued healthy survival and worthwhile accomplishments, his personal needs are rather insignificant. The sage recognizes himself as just a part of Tao, not inherently any more or less compelling than any other.

The human ego creates many such misimpressions and counterproductive thoughts and behaviors in people, and therefore much of what makes a sage a sage is his ability to recognize the effects of his own ego and control it or redirect it toward more productive ends. Egos often create imaginary personalities within people for public display, and then they cause the people to get embarrassed or upset anytime the masks, hiding the real personalities behind them, somehow slip. But when an ego is closely examined and devalued by the person it is supposed to represent, the mask can slowly be dropped, and the person's unique blend of real personality traits—their inner nature—is revealed and can be examined. That can be a frightening experience at first for the fledgling Taoist, but the fear gradually fades, and once that initial shock is past, marvelous changes can result. The sage, having already accomplished it, gains the ability to really know where and when he is comfortable and where and when he is not, what he really enjoys and what he doesn't, what his real weaknesses and fears are and what he is confident about, what he feels he needs to improve about himself, and what he is satisfied with just as it is. Because of the process, the sage no longer has the burden of trying to maintain the mask, and those he interacts with no longer have the burden of dealing with an imaginary personality.

After the sage's true strengths and weaknesses were first exposed, his natural strengths simply needed to be recognized, encouraged, and developed. The weaknesses—including such things as bad habits, embarrassing truths, fears, insecurities, and deep, dark secrets—all just needed to be recognized, accepted, and then calmly and consciously dealt with one by one in whatever way was most appropriate.

Now, after having minimized his ego in that way, the sage has no false face, and his real person is exposed for all to see. And in a significant way, that makes him free. He no longer has to pretend to be anyone or anything. He has little reason anymore to want to lie and little to fear. He has no ego need to be in the spotlight, to be jealous of anyone else, selfish, or self-conscious. He finds it easy to be respectful and humble toward others and to value their opinions. He cares what others think about other things, but he does not care what they think about him. He just is what he is. He doesn't feel like he needs to express an opinion about every topic that comes up in conversation or even talk at all if he doesn't have something worthwhile to say. And he doesn't have any desire to get involved in everything that happens around him or to always be the center of attention.

But egos, no matter how hard one tries to suppress them, always try to reassert themselves, so the sage always pays attention to whatever emotions suddenly pop up within him, for such emotions will usually be symptoms of his ego trying to make itself important within him once again. One strategy he uses to deal with it when that happens is to consciously transfer his concerns about its image of him to concerns about whatever he is actually doing. He directs his ego concerns toward the satisfaction of his carefully crafted objectives instead of toward maintaining the mask.

Since the sage does not direct his objectives toward the preservation or enhancement of his ego, and since he doesn't direct them toward the accumulation of wealth, power, fame, or material objects (since he sees all those as tools rather than objectives), he can focus them on more significant goals. Those he does decide to pursue are chosen because they align with his interests and talents, because they are in tune with the Flow of Tao as he perceives it, and because they follow Taoist virtues. He does not choose them because they are popular in the media at the moment or because a teacher or friend once suggested them as good fields to follow. The sage knows that what he spends his time doing defines who he is, so his choices of life objectives, and less significant "little" objectives needed to accomplish them along the way, are not things to be casually chosen.

Having objectives be in tune with the Flow of Tao is definitely one important requirement for the sage because those that are in tune with it are easiest to achieve, are more likely to avoid resistance by others and by society in general, and are least disruptive to society as a whole when accomplished. The sage looks for any noticeable cycles, patterns, and trends in the Flow and tries to follow them in his imagination into the future to help him make his more important decisions.

The sage aims himself toward the satisfaction of his long-term goals by imagining or visualizing the steps required to accomplish them frequently during his idle current moments. By not specifically itemizing exact steps in the procedure with words, he can remain more flexible in the accomplishment of goals as the Flow of Tao passes and changes occur, as they inevitably do. That way, the aim toward his target objectives can change as the target objectives themselves change over time. Especially for long-term objectives, effective proper aim toward objectives is more important than worrying about the specific targets being aimed at, since the final target objectives are bound to be at least somewhat different when achieved than they were when originally perceived. With that procedure in mind, the sage pursues his objectives doggedly because they define his life, and because he carefully chose those that matched his interests, they were in line with the Flow of Tao and were virtuous.

The pursuit of virtue is perhaps the most significant goal of the sage. He or she considers himself or herself to be an advocate for Tao, the Flow of Tao, and the natural planet. He or she honors the earth, nature, and society. He or she chooses goals with at least some consideration toward keeping our human species physically, mentally, and spiritually healthy; goals that keep our knowledge and wisdom growing; goals that expand the strength and compassion of our societies; and goals that keep our sciences and technologies developing.

But in addition to those benevolent reasons, the sage knows that being virtuous is the healthy and natural way for him to be and that it will make him a happier and more successful individual to be that way. Being honorable and virtuous is natural. The Tao itself is never cruel or selfish—it just always does what it needs to do next. Creatures of nature are rarely cruel or selfish. Animals usually just do what they need to do to survive and maintain their homes and territories and protect their young. People who are mean or cruel display traits that demonstrate their own internal pain and insecurities, and those traits are just as unhealthy for themselves as they are for their victims. The sage does not need to do any of that, and by treating others with virtue, he or she can remain at peace within themselves.

As an important part of his virtue, the sage values truth greatly because without it, the path of the Flow of Tao becomes unclear to all, including even those who told lies, and then the Way becomes much harder to follow for everyone. Decisions end up being based on inaccurate information, and actions that are taken based on bad information tend to yield unhappy results. Therefore, the sage always tells the truth as he understands it and encourages others to do so, too. He admits to anyone affected when he has made a mistake and seeks out truth about important subjects whenever he is uncertain what the truth might be. And why not? He does not have to worry about protecting his ego.

It is to the advantage of the sage and the accomplishment of his objectives to have a good relationship with others. And without the whims of an out-of-control ego urging him to do undesirable things, there is no reason for him to not have good relationships with them. After all, he does not contend socially with people; he does not try to manipulate, dominate, or show off to them; and he doesn't always find it necessary to try to prove himself right. He follows a personal code of chivalry and compassion that prevents him from putting people down or purposely hurting their feelings. Whenever possible, he gives everyone the benefit of the doubt, and he knows that hurting others physically or mentally hurts himself even more and for a longer time because of the realities of guilt.

In general, the sage tries to be righteous without being self-righteous, honest without being judgmental, straightforward without being harsh, and confident without being arrogant.

And because of the virtues that the sage so steadfastly follows, every decision he makes and every action he takes can be done with total inner unity. His conscience is clear. There have been no lies or deceptions. He can always speak and act with openness without concerns about what others might think. If he is honored for something he has done well, he will be unfazed by the compliments because he knows that he just did what he was supposed to do. And if he is unfairly blamed for something he did or didn't do, even if the whole world tries to punish him, he will feel no shame because he will know that he only did what he believed to be the right thing to do at the time, which is all anyone can ever do. He will just try to learn from it so that he might not upset everyone so much in the future.

The Synthesis

The sage is made whole through his or her integration of all these aspects of Taoism despite any unfortunate trials and tribulations he or she might have experienced earlier in their life. Many people entering adulthood feel they were damaged by the events of their childhood. They might feel that they weren't loved as much as they needed to be; that they were abused in some way; that they missed having a father or a mother in their home; that they never had the money to have the same nice clothes, fancy homes, or cars that others in their schools might have had; that they were bullied; or that they far too often felt lonely. Those, of course, are legitimate complaints and are a source of pain for any youth who suffers through them, but to the sage, all that is nothing but unpleasant memories now. There is no way to change whatever happened in the past. It must just be accepted and learned from, and any problems it caused should be somehow overcome. That is the only solution. As an adult, it is now he who has control over his destiny, not those who controlled him back then. With the knowledge, skills, and tools of the Way of Tao, he or she has the means to control their destiny in the current moments for the rest of their life in their own way to yield the positive results they seek.

The sage has a new understanding of himself, his place in the world, and his purpose in life. He is self-confident and has focus. Now he is the adult and not the child at the mercy of others. Of course, he must submit to legal and social standards and the requirements of survival in the world of business, but otherwise, he is in control of his world and what he does in it. And because he has risen above his ego's insecurities, he no longer feels any need to cater to its demands for attention, selfishness, hedonism, self-pity, or unhealthy and unhelpful emotional outbursts.

In general, the sage is happy with himself and the world around him. All at the current moment is exactly as it should be, given what has happened before. But of course, there is always work to be done. The sage knows that he can always improve himself and work on whatever shortcomings he still perceives within himself, and he will always want to do just that. And he knows that there are many injustices in the world that he might be able to help in some way to vanquish.

As a sage, he is quite aware that he is now defined by what he chooses to do in the current moments remaining in his life. And his tool for best accomplishing those things lies in understanding and maximizing the potency of those remaining current moments. As a sage, he has learned to use them effectively to best accomplish whatever he chooses to accomplish.

He uses his idle moments to ponder and learn from the past; consider his impressions of the Flow of Tao; dream about, imagine, and plan for his future; and make virtuous decisions about what he should do now and in the future. He uses his active current moments to focus intently on carrying out his decisions and accomplishing his objectives. There is no reason for him to waste a single one of his few remaining precious current moments.

Unusual Abilities of the Sage

Because of the synthesis of concepts that are all parts of following the Way of Tao and especially with the minimization of his ego, the sage finds that he has gained the ability to adapt to every situation he ever finds himself in more easily than he ever could before. He now no longer thinks of himself as a more-or-less set entity with more-or-less set characteristics. Instead, he now sees himself as being infinitely changeable, just as the Flow of Tao he lives within and is a part of is also infinitely changeable. He can now easily recognize and enhance his more beneficial personal characteristics in each situation and can more easily recognize, accept, and correct his negative ones. This newfound flexibility brings him confidence that he can handle almost anything he might ever happen to encounter.

The sage experiences each situation knowing that what seems today to be a "bad" thing will often turn out in the long run to be a "good" thing, and what seems today to be a "good" thing will often turn out in the long run to be a "bad" thing. And some might revert at a later time to the original assessment. Therefore, part of becoming a sage is dropping old, preconceived notions and value judgments. Everything in the Flow of Tao is always exactly as it should be, given what took place in the past. From the perspective of Tao, nothing is ever really "good," and nothing is ever really "bad." All is just as it is meant to be. To fully experience the Flow and understand it, the sage sees it in that same way—without the filter of value judgments. Most are just products of egos anyway. The sage first views the Flow without value judgments and only then, if he feels he must, assigns his own according to his moral beliefs and objectives. Without value judgments, all that happens in life can be appreciated for what it actually is.

Without preconceived opinions and old value judgments, the sage can observe, deduce, and apply whatever he sees going on around him much more easily. He sees things almost as if for the very first time—what is rather than what is supposed to be. From that viewpoint, he gains the ability to see the simplicity behind the complexities of life, and that assists him in the achievement of his objectives. It all turns out to be something not to be intimidated by but instead something to enjoy and learn from. The sage realizes that he or she can usually overcome almost any barrier that he or she chooses to overcome, neutralize almost any problem that he or she chooses to neutralize, and accomplish almost anything that he or she chooses to accomplish.

But the Flow of Tao itself does not purposely make any one person's life any easier or any more difficult than anyone else's. The sage, like everyone else, will experience situations and periods that are difficult or sometimes sad, and others that are enjoyable and rewarding. Often the times experienced will, at least in part, be consequences of something or some things he or she did at an earlier time, and sometimes they will have nothing at all to do with them or their past—they are just movements in the Flow of Tao. Especially when they are a consequence of things he did in the past, the sage makes a point of recognizing that and learning from it.

But whatever their origin, good times and difficult times will always come and go because that is part of the nature of life. The sage does not get angry or sad or resentful or bitter over the difficult times. Life would be meaningless and tedious without their occurrence. Without problems, there would be nothing to learn, no challenges to overcome, no personal growth to achieve— nothing ever really to accomplish at all. Life would be nothing more than bland, day-to-day existence. Without battles, there can never be victories! What matters the most about such challenges is how one deals with them.

The most important factor is attitude. No matter the cause of difficult times, it's always easier to endure them and do what is necessary to correct them if one first accepts them cheerfully and does what one does about them with a positive and confident attitude, and on the other hand, it always makes solutions harder to achieve or even impossible if one becomes bitter and resentful and assumes a defeatist attitude about such problems.

With his positive and confident attitude, the sage often just reviews situations that at first seemed negative and realizes that with just a little change of attitude and strategy, those seemingly negative situations can be made beneficial!

And sometimes, instead of just accepting the reality of a negative situation and adapting his attitude and strategy to make it positive, the sage realizes that he can also change the relevant Flow of Tao, subtly and just a little over time, and in that way transform the negative into a positive. Sometimes more assertive changes are necessary, but always the sage uses the direction and the momentum of the Flow of Tao to his advantage to accomplish his objectives. Working with and within the Flow of Tao always makes the achievement of any objective easier!

How does the sage change the Flow of Tao? He does so by knowing history, closely following all that is going on in the relevant present, and maintaining a happy, confident attitude. He notes the movements and interconnections in the Flow of Tao's many relevant aspects, and he learns to anticipate its future movements as best he can. He changes the Flow by studying, learning, coming to understand who and what affects who and what, and then influences those important levers in whichever ways he can with respectful, patient, and honest persistence to achieve his worthwhile objectives.

And the sage also changes the Flow of Tao through the power of his convictions. Once he is sure his convictions are absolutely correct, no matter what the Flow of Tao in general does to him, no matter what other individuals do to him, and no matter what society or government does to him, he stands by them without wavering. The sage knows that for the good of the Flow of Tao and its impact on society and life in general, his convictions are more important than his ego, his comfort, his other less important objectives, or even his life. In this way and others, the reality surrounding the sage gradually evolves into what he and the Flow of Tao together make it!

To best fulfill his convictions in a contentious world, the sage often patterns his strategies after the lessons of water. Water in the high country gathers into rivulets and small streams and then flows happily downward. Anywhere the ground under it is dry, some of it sinks into that ground; and in some very dry and porous ground, it all eventually sinks downward and disappears from the surface altogether. Water that gets collected underground, though unseen and unseeable, nevertheless continues its journey. It is pulled by gravity and pushed by the water behind it to move in the direction it must go—downward and outward. It flows between pebbles and grains of sand and soil and, over time, as a result of its movement, gradually moves those grains along with it and out of its way. When it encounters a layer of rock that it can't go around, it seeks out tiny cracks and crevices to ooze patiently through, dissolving minerals and slowly making the cracks and crevasses wider, thereby allowing water that comes after it to pass through more easily. Eventually, the water breaks free of the rock and soil and into a waterway on the surface and thereafter can flow faster and more freely. That water, along with the water it joins that never soaked into the ground, flows through low places in the contours of the land. It curves around hills and hard rocks, slowly eroding away cliffs and bluffs that happen to impede its progress. It picks up material in some places and drops it off in others. And sometimes, when the circumstances and timing are just right, there is a flood, and the environment is changed dramatically by its torrent. That is the Way of Water, and it illustrates movement in the Way of Tao. Eventually, the water always reaches its destination!

Visit our website at
AWOTao.com
to read our blog about all things Tao
and to shop in our store of Taoist literature
and other interesting Taoist themed merchandise.